MIRACLE AT THE LITZA

Hitler's First Defeat on the Eastern Front

ALF R. JACOBSEN

CASEMATE
Philadelphia & Oxford

To Tommy

Published in the United States of America and Great Britain in 2017 by
CASEMATE PUBLISHERS
1950 Lawrence Road, Havertown, PA 19083, USA
and
The Old Music Hall, 106–108 Cowley Road, Oxford OX4 1JE, UK

Copyright © 2014 Alf R. Jacobsen
Original Norwegian language edition titled *Miraklet ved Litza*, first published by Vega Forlag in 2014.

All efforts have been made to find rights holders for all the photographs and illustrations in this book. If there are errors or omissions in the list of illustrations, please contact the publisher.

Translation by Frank Stewart

Hardcover Edition: ISBN 978-1-61200-5065
Digital Edition: ISBN 978-1-61200-5072

A CIP record for this book is available from the Library of Congress and the British Library

All rights reserved. No part of this book may be reproduced or transmitted in any form or by any means, electronic or mechanical including photocopying, recording or by any information storage and retrieval system, without permission from the publisher in writing.

Printed and bound in the United States of America
Typeset in India by Lapiz Digital Services, Chennai

For a complete list of Casemate titles, please contact:

CASEMATE PUBLISHERS (US)
Telephone (610) 853-9131
Fax (610) 853-9146
Email: casemate@casematepublishers.com
www.casematepublishers.com

CASEMATE PUBLISHERS (UK)
Telephone (01865) 241249
Fax (01865) 794449
Email: casemate-uk@casematepublishers.co.uk
www.casematepublishers.co.uk

Contents

Preface		iv
Prologue	*August 1940, The Northern Front*	vi
Chapter 1	The Jigsaw Puzzle	1
Chapter 2	Bluff or Business?	17
Chapter 3	Into the Finnish Corridor	23
Chapter 4	The Bunker line is Broken	36
Chapter 5	The Battle of Fisher Neck	50
Chapter 6	The First Attack	62
Chapter 7	Bloody High Summer	78
Chapter 8	The Royal Navy Ventures North	88
Chapter 9	Red August	100
Chapter 10	A Very Effective Offensive Along the Coast	112
Chapter 11	Defeat	126
Epilogue	*A Heroic Struggle*	137
Appendix I	*Missed Opportunities – A Futile Campaign*	145
Appendix II	*The Red Army 1941*	167
Endnotes		173
Bibliography		184
Index of People		188

Preface

Despite the significant effect Operation *Barbarossa* had on the Arctic war, we have until now lacked an in-depth work about what happened on the northern sector of the Eastern Front in the summer of 1941 and its relevance to the negotiations about aid to the Soviet Union.

From a military point of view, the closest we have come to a comprehensive account has been *The German Northern Theatre of Operations 1940–1945*, by the American military historian Earl F. Ziemke. However, Ziemke's book was written before 1959 and based on a rather pedantic study of German documents without use of diaries, eyewitness accounts or interviews with the leading officers who were still alive at that time. Soviet sources were excluded, and Norwegian sources were not used. As a result, Ziemke missed out on the conflicts of interest and the important strategic perspectives which resulted from Stalin's requests for a second front in the north and an occupation of Spitsbergen and Bear Island. His work must to a large extent be considered outdated.

Miracle at the Litza is an attempt on my part to fill this gap. My narrative is based on many years of work in archives in Norway, Great Britain, Germany and Russia, and I am particularly grateful for the support I have had from Axel Wittenberg who combed through the German military archives in Freiburg, and Miroslav Morozov who discovered important information in the Russian military archives in Moscow.

We don't yet have answers to all the questions. Nevertheless, I hope that this study will take us a few steps forward in understanding what happened in the northern regions during that dramatic and bloody summer of 1941. I am particularly glad that the opening of the Enigma archives for the first time has made it possible to give an accurate description of the codebreakers' contribution to the Royal Navy's enormously effective offensive against the German convoy traffic along the coast of Finnmark during the decisive weeks in August and September 1941.

Alf R. Jacobsen
2 July 2017

PROLOGUE

August 1940

The Northern Front

Trondheim, Thursday 15 August 1940

Rain was still falling when Colonel General Nicolaus von Falkenhorst's motorcade drew up in front of the monumental façade of the Britannia Hotel. The cathedral bells had just struck nine, and a hundred homeless engineering students were gathering outside the student accommodation agency after a cold night on the park benches. The persistent rain was ruining the strawberry harvest, and in the surrounding countryside many of the cornfields had been flattened by a storm a few days earlier. Out in the fjord, however, the fishing boats were already on the way to Ørland, where the herring bonanza of the century had just taken place. The new freezer in the cold-store at Ravnkloa fish-market had been made ready just in time.

'Now all that fine oily herring that used to go to waste can be frozen and preserved by our new rapid freezing system,' explained manager Bjarne Øwre, who had invited the town's leading citizens to the opening ceremony on Saturday, 'we should never lack fish either in the North or anywhere else.'

The white-painted industrial building with the Birdseye revolutionary patent plate freezers was financed by German capital and represented a vital stage in the process of incorporating occupied Norway in the new European greater economic area (*Grosswirtschaftsraum*) as main supplier of fish to the Wehrmacht and other major customers on the continent.[1] But the Führer's crazy fantasies knew no boundaries, and the freezer installation was just the beginning. In the coming years, Trondheim was to be developed to become the new cultural centre of the North on a scale that would make 'Singapore look like a child's toy.' Albert Speer, Hitler's favourite architect, had already ordered several thousand tonnes of marble, granite and reinforcing iron for a series of monumental new buildings. A suburb with room for 250,000 Aryan immigrants was being planned and a four-lane motorway would link the old cathedral town to the metropolises of the Thousand Year Reich. German artists would give the fantasies of world domination an aesthetic gloss, and at the weekend the gorgeous ballerina Bianca Rogge from Berlin had spellbound soldiers and civilians to the strains of music from concert pianist Emil Debusemann.

Falkenhorst, a stockily built man, hardly had time to think about the many aspects of the occupation before he was met at the main entrance by General Eduard Dietl, who had established the headquarters of the Mountain Corps Norway in the luxurious Britannia Hotel after the victory at Narvik two months earlier. We have no reason to assume that the meeting between the two German commanders was warm and friendly. In the summer of 1940, Falkenhorst was at the apex of the power pyramid of the northern theatre of military operations. In April he had been awarded the Knight's Cross of the Iron Cross, in May he had adorned the front page of *Time* Magazine as the conqueror of Norway, and in July he had been promoted to colonel general.[2]

However, in the aristocratic Prussian officer corps, 55-year-old Falkenhorst was seen as an upstart and intruder. In a condescending evaluation, Lieutenant Colonel Hartwig Pohlman wrote: 'He was not nominated by his superiors to be head of the attack on Norway because of his military achievements; it was Hitler who had found his name in the reports of the landing in Finland in 1918 and spontaneously given him the supreme command.'

Pohlman was from a military family in Berlin and had dreamt of becoming a general, like his father. But his hopes were dashed and his career ruined when Falkenhorst, without warning and without meeting him face to face, dismissed him from his position as operations officer in the invasion army. Pohlman detested Falkenhorst. He reckoned the apparent explanation for what he considered falsehood and double-dealing was to be found in the general's background.

'He was capable and well educated, but he earned no respect among his colleagues and subordinates. People felt that he lacked sincerity,' Pohlman wrote. 'It may have been a hangover from his obviously Slavic ancestry. When he was a young lieutenant in the 7th Grenadier Division he changed his name from Jastreczemski to Falkenhorst; his contemporaries just called him by a Slavic word for a leader – *Starost*.'

Nobody doubted Falkenhorst's talents as a staff officer, but he had been born into an impoverished aristocratic family in the old Slavic regions in the East and that was a fact he could never escape, even by changing his name. In the ultra-snobbish Prussian elite he was always a sparrow, never a falcon.[3] This gave him an inferiority complex, which he sometimes concealed behind an unstoppable flow of words.

> To a certain extent, he lacked coherence and consistency in leadership style and in the giving of orders. This caused a lot of extra work when he repeatedly made complete changes to previous orders. He was also famous for his talkativeness, with a tendency to jump from one topic to another. The other participants in a conversation often failed to get a word in without him appearing to notice.

Dietl's first meeting with him in Berlin in the winter of 1940 during the planning of the invasion of Denmark and Norway (Operation *Weserübung*) was a typical example. The bronzed officer from the elite 3rd Mountain Division came into Pohlman's office, shaking his head. 'Can you tell me what I really should do in Narvik? The chief talked like a waterfall for two hours without me becoming any wiser. I didn't even get a question in. He didn't let me get a word in edgeways.'

Pohlman gave his guest a summary of the plans. As soon as Dietl had left the room, Falkenhorst stuck his head in the doorway and asked: 'Is he gone?' Pohlman confirmed that Dietl had left and was amazed to hear Falkenhorst reply: 'Isn't it dreadful how some people can never express themselves concisely!'

In other situations Falkenhorst came up with inflexible demands for discipline, which didn't enhance his status among the rank and file. During a tour of inspection in the North he had exploded when Dietl's mountain troops assembled on parade in non-uniform attire. They had copied the Sami and were wearing colourful scarves – partly for decoration and partly for protection against the cold.

'He couldn't understand that things could not always be done north of the Polar Circle in the same way as at Tempelhof Airport,' wrote the head of the 2nd Mountain Division, Major General Valentin Feurstein, who felt the full weight of the general's wrath: 'The scarves were to be removed, irrespective of the temperature. They had to be packed away in the rucksacks until Wotan [King of the Gods] had moved on.'

The relationship between the army's supreme commander and his leading field officers had been strained from the start, and it was not helped by the events which took place in Narvik in April and May 1940.[4] Dietl was the complete opposite of Falkenhorst – down to earth, confident and enormously popular among the troops and the junior officers. He was the son of a tax collector in Bavaria and a first-class skier and mountaineer. What he lacked in formal military competence he made up for in personal charisma. Doubtless many of the general staff officers regarded ex-corporal Hitler with disdain, as a political charlatan and scoundrel. But for Dietl, the Führer was much more – a guide through the darkness of the inter-war years. As a young lieutenant in *Freikorps Epp* in Munich in June 1919 he had organised Hitler's very first public event. Dietl was excited by the war veteran's fiery rhetoric. He joined the Brownshirts and supported Hitler's coup attempt in 1923.

As the Führer put it, Dietl was one of the leading midwives of the National Socialist Party. When the takeover of power was complete ten years later, Dietl stood out as one of the officer corps' most convinced Nazis. He was a member of the party's inner circle and he went in and out of the Reich Chancellery and Hitler's private home almost at will. Beneath the popular facade, the Nazi's depraved ideas were firmly rooted: hatred of the Jews, Bolsheviks and other groups whom Hitler wanted to exterminate; belief in the Germanic Thousand Year Reich and the predestined role of the Master Race. In a pep talk to the soldiers of the Mountain Corps he had even advised them against marrying Norwegian women, who were 'inferior representatives of a neighbouring race and racial flotsam'.

In the euphoric days after the Narvik campaign he had received his first recognition for his lifelong loyalty to Nazi ideology and Hitler's leadership: he was presented in the propaganda as a military leader of historic stature, appointed a full general and leader of the Mountain Corps and selected as the first German soldier to be awarded the Knight's Cross of the Iron Cross with Oak-leaves – to Falkenhorst's bitter envy.

'Dietl had never gone through the hard school of training required of a staff officer,' wrote the Austrian military historian Roland Kaltenegger. 'He was a born tactician, but Falkenhorst knew better than most that as a leader of military operations Dietl had advanced far beyond his real level of competence. It should be added that Dietl was honest enough to recognise his limitations. Earlier in his career he had aspired to becoming a major, but nothing more. It was only when his party comrade seized power that rapid advancement followed.

In Germany, Hitler had been restless since the great victories in Scandinavia and on the Continent. He allowed his troops to rest and he commuted apparently aimlessly between Berlin and Berchtesgaden. Militarily, the Wehrmacht appeared invincible. A whole world trembled – except for Great Britain which, under Churchill's fearless leadership, refused to budge an inch.

The non-aggression pact between Germany and Russia was still in force, but in Moscow Stalin had become alarmed by the pace of Hitler's conquests. So he had arranged for Estonia, Latvia, Lithuania and the eastern provinces of Romania to be incorporated into the Soviet Union in quick succession and had put increasing pressure on Finland. In the Eagle's Nest high in the Bavarian Alps, the Führer brooded over a growing number of alarming reports, which at the end of July gradually led him to shift his attention from West to East.

'I am fully aware that Stalin only signed the pact with us in order to set off a war in Europe,' he had surprisingly said to his closest military collaborator, General Alfred Jodl, after a morning meeting on Friday 26 July, 'But he hadn't reckoned on us conquering France so quickly. That's why he moved so fast to occupy the Baltic states and the provinces in Romania.'[5]

Reports from Abwehr, the German military intelligence organisation, confirmed that the Red Army was being built up in border regions that Hitler had stayed away from. With only five eastern divisions in readiness, the Wehrmacht would not be capable of reacting if Stalin pursued further expansion plans.

> Russia's goal has been unchanged since the time of Peter the Great. The country wants to swallow the whole of Poland, Finland and Bulgaria – and then continue to the Dardanelles. So war with Russia is unavoidable. We really should launch an attack this autumn.

During World War I the Allied blockade had slowly choked the German economy. Hitler was very anxious this should not be repeated, and ever since taking power he had worked hard to make the country self-sufficient. The problem was that within its own territory, Germany lacked most of the strategic raw materials that modern, mechanised warfare required in enormous quantities. This applied particularly to crude oil – the basis for production of petrol, diesel and paraffin – and to rubber, copper, iron ore and the metals nickel, manganese and chromium – needed to make alloys required for the production of armour plating and stainless steel.

Fuel was mainly obtained from the oilfields in Ploiești in Romania, and iron ore from Northern Sweden. Nickel was to be sourced from a newly opened mine in the Finnish corridor in Petsamo, only 12 kilometres from the Norwegian border. If Stalin implemented his threats and went on to invade Finland and Romania, the flow of raw materials would be cut off. This would seriously impair the Wehrmacht's capacity to continue the *blitzkrieg*.

Hitler did not want to take this risk. In further meetings with the military elite in late July and early August, he gave orders to begin planning for an attack on the Soviet Union. He also gave instructions to be ready to take counter-measures in case the Russians should begin to stir. If the Red Army moved against Ploieşti and Petsamo, the Wehrmacht would strike back swiftly.

Major General Walter Warlimont, the head of the army section of Hitler's personal staff was awaiting orders on the command train *Atlas*, sat in the suffocating summer heat at a rural railway station in Bavaria. 'I was called to a meeting with General Alfred Jodl on Monday 29 July,' he wrote.[6] The detailed plans for an invasion of England had been ready for a long time. All that was missing was the starting signal, but the Führer had suddenly changed his ideas. 'Jodl told me that Hitler had decided to attack the Soviet Union. Planning was to start immediately, with May 1941 as a provisional D-day.'

The orders struck Warlimont like a lightning bolt. 'The attack on Soviet Russia was to happen without taking into consideration the continuing war in the West. A victory in the East would bring England to its knees – if we had not succeeded by other means.'

On board *Atlas*, the maps of the Soviet Union were rapidly produced. Panzer General Georg Stumme in Vienna was ordered to have the 40th Army ready for a possible advance on the oilfields in Romania, and Falkenhorst was called to an urgent meeting with Hitler in Berlin on 13 August.

There is no accurate surviving report of their conversation, but the following day Hitler summarised his points of view to the Wehrmacht's ten newly appointed field marshals, who were assembled in the Reich Chancellery to be given their batons of office, clad in red velvet and gold.

> There are two regional dangers which can set off a confrontation with the Soviet Union. Number one: The Russians advance into Finland. That would cost us control of the Baltic and make a subsequent attack on the Soviet Union more difficult. Number two: A further penetration into Romania. We cannot allow that, because we need the fuel supplies from the oilfields in Ploieşti.[7]

Face to face with Dietl two days later in Hotel Britannia in Trondheim, Falkenhorst expanded on the Führer's thoughts: 'For Germany at war, Northern Scandinavia is an irreplaceable source of raw materials. Besides the Swedish iron mines in Lapland, which the victory at Narvik has secured, there are several other important mineral sources which Germany cannot forego. That applies particularly to the nickel deposits in Petsamo, which are the most important in Europe.'[8]

After the battles around Narvik, the two main formations of Mountain Corps Norway – the 2nd and 3rd Mountain Divisions – were resting. The main force was in Nordland, with a few scattered security detachments in the northern counties of Troms and Finnmark. All of the vast area between Narvik and the Finnish border in the east was unoccupied. This was an unacceptable situation, in the light of the threatening developments in the relationship with the Soviet Union. The Northern Front would need to be secured to protect lines of communication between the Baltic, the iron mines in Kiruna and the nickel mines in Petsamo, which were too valuable to be allowed to fall into Stalin's hands.

The new smelter in the Finnish corridor would be able to satisfy Germany's needs for nickel for many decades to come and had to be defended at any cost. In the remaining months of 1940 alone, the engineers reckoned on processing 8,000 tonnes of ore and 400 tonnes of pure nickel, rising to 70,000 tonnes of ore and 3,600 tonnes of nickel in 1941. Hitler had therefore ordered Falkenhorst to send fresh troops northward on a forced march. At the first sign of a Soviet attack on Finland they would advance over the border and occupy the mining district round Kolosjoki and the Jäniskoski power station at the outlet of Lake Inari.

'In wartime all unoccupied areas exert a particular attractive force, not only on immediate neighbours but on all parties to the conflict,' Falkenhorst explained. 'It's a question of a new form of warfare, about being in the right place at the right time. By being on location at the right time one can avoid armed confrontation, as the risk to the enemy is too great for him to try to occupy the position later. Whoever gets there first has won. So we need to be the first into Finnmark. *That* is what it all depends on.'

At 12.30 p.m. the same day the supreme commander and his retinue travelled back to Oslo by train. Ten minutes later the Mountain Corps received their first orders to begin moving north. An armoured company was sent from Trondheim on patrol vessels 101 and 102 on Friday 16 August. On the same day, the steamships *Alstertor* and *Trondenes* were directed to Alta to embark Machine Gun (MG) Battalion 13 for transport onwards to Kirkenes.

The commander of 2nd Mountain Division, Major General Valentin Feurstein, had to break off his leave and fly directly to Northern Norway from Innsbruck. He arrived at Kirkenes a week later as the first plans for Operation *Renntier* were being drawn up. A pioneer battalion and parts of 136th Mountain Regiment were posted in Svanvik with a direct view of the nickel mine on the other side of the border. The rest of the division was stationed between the Varanger and Porsanger fjords.

It would be many weeks before all the troops were in place. From the end of August, however, the plan was clear: The nickel mines would remain under German control, whatever the Red Army did.

In London, Churchill and his war cabinet were unaware of the change in German strategy. The Secret Service had no agents with access to the discussions in Hitler's inner circle, and the codebreakers in Bletchley Park had, at this point, only partly managed to crack the secrets of the German Enigma machine.

'This contribution [the flow of accurate information from reading of deciphered German telegrams] did not begin till the spring of 1941 – eighteen months after the outbreak of the war,' wrote the intelligence service historian, Professor Harry Hinsley. 'Although decrypts from the German Enigma were obtained regularly from the spring of 1940, they were confined for the next twelve months to an Enigma key used only in the Norwegian campaign and to two keys used by the German Air Force.'[9]

For the codebreakers who toiled day and night to crack the German naval radio traffic, the situation was very frustrating. The ether was full of Morse signals which the listening station at Scarborough Head in Yorkshire picked up – between land stations and swarms of U-boats, military vessels and merchant ships at sea. The fleet that brought the 2nd Mountain Division from Nordland to Finnmark in August and September 1940 consisted of dozens of vessels, and the German Navy had found it necessary to set up the position of Admiral of the Polar Coast in Tromsø to handle the logistics.

The long distances meant that orders had to be delivered by radio. Traffic volume increased sharply, but that didn't help very much. Despite intense effort over many months, the mathematical genius Alan Turing and his co-workers had not managed to break the German naval code. The telegrams remained an incomprehensible assemblage of random characters, their content unknown.

In the manor house at Bletchley Park, which had become the headquarters of Secret Service codebreaking, the mood was gloomy.

'I am worried about our work on the naval Enigma,' wrote the veteran Frank Birch in a report to his superiors on 21 August.[10] Birch was a man of many talents who had left a professorial chair at Cambridge University to become an actor. He had worked in the intelligence service in World War I and had been called in as section leader of the highly gifted but eccentric codebreakers who inhabited the temporary huts in Bletchley Park. As the days went by without result, he became steadily more disheartened and depressed. 'I have been worried for a long time, but I haven't wanted to say anything. Turing and Twinn are like people waiting for a miracle – without believing in miracles. They are brilliant, but like many brilliant people they are not practical. They are untidy, they lose things, they can't copy out right and they dither between theory and cribbing. Nor have they the determination of practical men.'

Circumstances were no clearer on Kola, the 100,000-square-kilometre peninsula which was Russia's northern outpost to the ice-free part of the Barents Sea.[11]

From time immemorial, the harsh landscape had been reserved to Sami and Pomors, who lived on reindeer and fishing. Geologically, the area was part of the Baltic Shield with deposits of iron, copper, apatite, nickel, cobalt and many other minerals and metals. The hunt for rich ores had started with the development of industrialisation, and the mining industry had sent geologists north at the end of the nineteenth century.

The Kola Peninsula was strategically important because of a climatic phenomenon. The Gulf Stream sent a warm current into the eastern part of the Barents Sea, which kept the coast ice-free all year round and enabled direct contact between Soviet Russia and the West. In World War I the central harbour town of Murmansk on the east bank of the Kola Fjord had been developed as a receiving port for supplies from the West, which were then taken south to Central Russia on a new railway line.[12]

When they seized power, the Bolsheviks carried on what the tsar had begun. The resources of the North were to be utilised, and heavy-handed methods were used. Mines were opened, smelters built and waterfalls tamed to generate electricity. In just twenty years the population of the peninsula increased tenfold, from 23,000 during World War I to 318,000 in 1940. Of these, about 250,000 were kulak peasants and political prisoners whom Stalin deported north and placed in forced labour camps.

About half the population lived in the rough, newly built town of Murmansk, which was the region's military centre and headquarters of the 14th Army. The army commander was the Bolshevik Valerian Aleksandrovitsj Frolov, who had been a delegate and had seen Lenin rise to power at the hugely historically significant Second Soviet Congress in the revolutionary year of 1917.

With his barrel-like body and dark beard, Frolov looked like a wrestler. But the energetic and efficient 46-year-old from St. Petersburg was first and foremost a master of infantry tactics. He was the son of a shop assistant and had been a junior officer in the tsar's army during World War I, before he joined the Red Guards and distinguished himself as a company and battalion commander in the civil war in Western Russia.

He had risen through the ranks in the Red Army until he completed his higher military training at the Frunze Academy in Moscow in 1932. Five years later he was sent as military adviser to Spain, where he took part on the republican side in the bloody battles at the River Ebro. In the Winter War, as a newly appointed general, he had led the 14th Army in the struggle against the Finns, which meant that he was familiar with the terrain and the tactical situation in Petsamo.

Frolov had two land-based military formations available for the immediate defence of the border: the 14th Rifle Division under Major General Alexander Zhurba and a battalion of border guards under the NKVD General Kuzmas Sinilin, who would become famous a few months later as the city commandant in Moscow.

The problem was that the current Soviet military doctrine took little heed of the possibility of a direct attack across the border at Petsamo. The army's theorists had not forgotten that in 1918 the West had intervened in the civil war on the side of the 'white' Russians and had landed by ship in Murmansk and Archangel. They had also studied Hitler's combined attack on Denmark and Norway in 1940 and had concluded that the main threat came from the sea, not from the trackless tundra west of Titovka.

To defend the Fisher Peninsula and the Kola Peninsula from a threatened invasion, Frolov had spread the 14th Division with supporting troops and associated mobile and stationary batteries along a coastline of several hundred kilometres, mainly without supporting infrastructure. The 325th Regiment was in Teriberka, north-east of Murmansk, while 135th Infantry Regiment was split between the fishing stations of Eina Guba, Novy Oserko and Kutuvaja on the Rybachy or Fisher Peninsula.

Along the border at Petsamo there were a mere 350 border guards from Sinilin's battalion, armed only with small arms and police dogs, with 95th Infantry Regiment as back-up. The regiment would normally have had a war-time complement of 3,200 men, but the ranks had not been replenished after the Winter War. With the exigencies of warfare and arctic training the complement in 1941 had probably fallen to around 1,600 men. Including artillery units, auxiliary troops and administrative units, Frolov had available a force of 5,000–6,000 men to defend a border that stretched from the coast to the dense and mainly uninhabited Finnish forests 200 kilometres further south.

This was far too few, and Frolov had started a series of measures to improve the situation. As soon as the ground began to thaw in the spring of 1941, 600 reservists were sent to the range of hills a couple of kilometres behind the border. A bunker line would need to be created as quickly as possible if the border guards were to be able to withstand a sudden attack.

In the Northern Fleet's headquarters in Polarnoje on the other side of the Kola Fjord, Rear Admiral Arsenij Golovko was also a worried man.

During Stalin's terror, 300–400 officers had been purged from the defence forces in the North. About a quarter of these were released and reinstated in the service, some ended up in prison and others were executed. Among others, this had been the fate of the head of the fleet, Konstantin Dusjenev, who had been arrested and shot in 1938. His successor, Valentin Drosd, was a veteran of the Spanish Civil War, but he had fallen out of grace in the summer of 1940 and been transferred to the Baltic Fleet.

That had opened the way for Golovko, the 34-year-old son of a vet, who had also fought in Spain and who had been born about as far from the Arctic Sea as it was possible to be – in the Cossack town of Prochladnaja in the Caucasus Mountains in Southern Russia.

'Up there in the North there is neither order nor discipline,' Stalin had growled when Golovko was summoned to the Kremlin at the end of July. 'Your predecessors preferred to quarrel with the fishermen, and that sort of thing gives no results.'

The tyrant knew the history of the world war and gave the newly appointed rear admiral a vague strategic warning.

> You are operating in an important maritime theatre that is much more complicated than the Baltic or the Black Sea. In the North we are dealing with a real ocean – with openings both west and east. You mustn't forget that in the First World War, communication between the western powers and Russia through the northern seas was more secure than the links through the Baltic ports.

The dark and sinewy young Communist was a man of the steppes and mountains who as a child had never dreamt of a life as a sailor. He had been educated at a workers' school in Rostov early in the 1920s and had financed his studies working as a labourer on the barges that plied the Don. He went on to Moscow and was admitted to the prestigious Timirjasev Academy for agricultural research. But when the Communist Party's Youth League, Komsomol, asked for volunteers for the new Soviet Navy some time later, Golovko was ready.

'My apprenticeship as a seaman lasted fifteen years,' he wrote in his memoirs, *Zwischen Spitzbergen und Tiksibucht*. 'I was in the lowest grade of the crew on board ship and in nautical colleges. I sailed different seas and oceans – the Baltic, the Black Sea, the Caspian Sea, the Pacific Ocean, the Arctic Ocean and the Amur River which forms the border with China. I was navigation and mine officer, first officer of the watch on a destroyer, head of a flotilla of fast vessels, head of staff for a brigade, squadron leader and chief of staff for a fleet – until the party gave me responsibility for the Northern Fleet. The meeting with Stalin and the Politburo was the highlight of all my years in service.'[13]

Stalin had cut the interview short: 'So, what does Comrade Golovko say? Will he accept the job?'

He had replied: 'I shall do my utmost. But I cannot guarantee that I will succeed.'

That was a wise response. When Golovko came to Murmansk and Polarnoje in August 1940 – about the same time that Hitler gave orders to start planning the invasion of the Soviet Union and the 2nd Mountain Division advanced towards the border – he faced a depressing sight.

> The situation was dreadful. The eight destroyers in the fleet had been used as transport ships during the Winter War against the Finns and were badly run down.
> There had been peace for five months, but little had been done. All the ships – even the newest – were in urgent need of repairs and maintenance. The problem was that the Northern Fleet did not have a workshop which could do the job.

Frolov and Golovko had been given command over a land area the size of Belorussia and a coast several thousand kilometres long. They knew that the defences had been neglected and neither the 14th Army nor the Northern Fleet were battle ready. But in Berlin, Hitler was set on war and the troops were on their way north. For Frolov and the officers in the Red Army, the urgency was greater than ever.

CHAPTER I

The Jigsaw Puzzle

England, the Soviet Union and Germany, spring 1941

The mood among the codebreakers in Hut Number 8 changed as if by magic in the spring of 1941. After months of fruitless toil Alan Turing and his brains trust had realised that they needed access to manuals, tables, instruction sheets and other secret material to enable them to understand and master the complicated Enigma machine used by the German Navy.

'It was a very frustrating period for Hut 8,' wrote Jack Copeland in his biography of Turing. 'Just a few yards away, Hut 6 was successfully reading generous quantities of the much easier to break Air Force Enigma – and was producing intelligence that helped Fighter Command in its life-and-death struggle with the Luftwaffe… While *Seelöwe* [the invasion of Britain] had been averted, the Battle of the Atlantic was still raging… Hut 8 looked on helplessly during the winter of 1940–41 as the U-boats sank appalling numbers of merchant vessels in the freezing Atlantic waters. Hut 8 with its hi-tech machinery was producing no significant intelligence'.[1]

The breakthrough came at the beginning of March as a result of the British-Norwegian raid on the Lofoten Islands. The destroyer HMS *Somali* intercepted the German armed trawler *Krebs* at Svolvær harbour mouth and put a salvo of high-explosive shells into the wheelhouse. The skipper and several crew members were killed instantly. When the boarding party clambered aboard the burning wreck, the vessel's Enigma machine had gone. But in the chart room they found spare coding wheels and a bundle of vital documents with up-to-date instructions for the synchronisation and use of the machine.

Copeland wrote that 'the Royal Navy pulled off a pinch that came to be seen as a major landmark in Hut 8's history.'

As soon as the destroyer was back at the quayside, the bags of captured material were brought by courier from Scotland to Bletchley Park and the contents carefully studied. Turing came into his own. Helped by other seizures from weather-reporting trawlers and U-boats in May and June, the previously insoluble machine code was cracked. Throughout the spring and summer of 1941 increasing numbers of telegrams were deciphered, translated and sent on from Bletchley Park to the Admiralty Operational Intelligence Centre in London, where the officers could follow the orders and reports flowing between German Naval Headquarters, U-boats and surface ships and organise counter-measures. Results followed quickly: The convoys were directed away from the prowling packs of German U-boats. Aircraft and naval vessels were sent to suitable positions to counter-attack. Disruptions and delays still happened due to lack of trained staff and the huge electro-mechanical computers needed to crack the codes, but the fundamental problems were solved.

'The capture of the February 1941 keys during the Lofoten raid changed the whole position', wrote the British chess grand master, Hugh Alexander, who was on Turing's staff. 'In April we all settled down to an attempt to break the traffic as nearly currently as possible.'

The war against the U-boats was priority number one, but time was sometimes found to study the radio signals that were being sent in increasing numbers between stations in the far North of Norway. One of the first to be read was a telegram addressed to General Dietl's transport officer from the new admiral in Tromsø, intercepted at about 6 a.m. on 27 February. The coded text had withstood all attempts at decryption until the material from the Lofoten Raid reached Bletchley Park. On 14 March it was ready to be sent on to the Admiralty Operations Centre:

> Important. Station Report 06.00 27 February 1941:
> Tromsø harbour: *Thorland, Walter Kölln, Schiff 18.*
> Kirkenes harbour: *Stuttgart, Anita Russ, Schillinghörn.*
> Hammerfest harbour: *Stamsund*
> Alta harbour: *Netal²*

Superficially, this report could appear prosaic: A German command post was informing another command post which ship was in which harbour at a given time. But the text gave the intelligence analysts new pieces to add

```
TO  I.D.8.G.                             ZTP 47
FROM GERMAN NAVAL SECTION G.C AND C.S.

    5030 KCS                 T.O.I.0604/27/2/41
       T.O.O.0602/70

FROM:  FLAG OFFICER, TROMSOE
TO  :  CENTRAL COMMUNICATIONS OFFICE, NORWAY,
       NAVAL COMMUNICATIONS OFFICER, NARVIK
       FOR TRANSPORT OFFICER, MOUNTAIN CORPS.

IMPORTANT.
       STATION REPORT 0600/27/2/41:
PORT OF TROMSOE:   THORLAND, WALTER KOELLN, SHIP 18.
PORT OF KIRKENES:  STUTTGART, ANITA RUSS, SCHILLIGHOERN.
PORT OF HAMMERFEST: STAMSUND.
PORT OF ALTA  :    NETAL.

1302/14/3/41/8TC/LLB
```

The British seized vital coding information during the raid on Lofoten in early March 1941. A few days later, on 14 March 1941 (the date bottom left) a telegram from Tromsø that had been intercepted at 6.04 a.m. on 27 February (T.O.I: time of intercept) was interpreted and read. (National Archives London)

to the jigsaw puzzle which would eventually reveal Hitler's intentions. The steamships *Thorland*, *Schilinghörn* and *Stamsund* had been commandeered by the Wehrmacht and were being used to transport troops and equipment along the Norwegian coast. The most interesting piece, however, was the presence in the border town of Kirkenes of *Stuttgart*, a 15,000-tonne transatlantic passenger ship belonging to the national shipping company Norddeutscher Lloyd. She had been converted in 1939 into a hospital ship with 485 beds. The fact that *Stuttgart* had been moved to Varanger could indicate that the Germans reckoned on needing the ship's 140 doctors and nurses to take care of the sick and wounded following a possible armed conflict with the Soviet Union.

The codebreakers had lifted a little corner of the veil concealing the change of strategic priorities that had taken place in Berlin. The invasion of England was cancelled. Despite the non-aggression pact and the assurances of everlasting friendship, Hitler had since the autumn of 1940 gradually been moving new divisions eastward – from Finnmark in the north to Poland, Czechoslovakia and Austria in the south.

The final step had been taken on Wednesday 18 December when Hitler signed the infamous *Barbarossa* directive, which ordered a total ideological war against the Soviet Union.[3] As soon as winter ended in May or June 1941, three army groups totalling three million men, supported by 5,000 aircraft and 3,000 tanks, would deliver a crushing attack on the Red Army, overthrow Stalin's regime and occupy the territory west of a line stretching in an arc from Archangel on the White Sea to Rostov on the Black Sea. Russia would become a slave state from the western border to the Ural Mountains, under the domination of the German master race. The intelligentsia would be murdered and the land would be plundered for valuable items and raw materials.

In the far north, Dietl and his mountain corps would break through the Soviet defences and secure the Arctic coast between Kirkenes and the Kola Fjord. This was to be done in a combined operation with the Finns, whom Hitler for historic reasons considered to be natural allies. Further south, German and Finnish forces would drive a wedge towards the White Sea, cut the railway line to Murmansk and turn south towards Lake Ladoga and Leningrad.

In Oslo, the head of Army Command Norway, Colonel General Nicolaus von Falkenhorst was far removed from the discussions which were taking place in the planning offices in Berlin. He knew nothing about *Barbarossa* until his Chief of Staff, Colonel Erich Buschenhagen, returned from a visit to Germany in early December 1940 with remarkable news.

'He told me that I had been chosen to lead an operation against Murmansk from Finnish territory,' he wrote in a personal account as he sat in prison in Hamburg after the war. 'That came as a complete surprise to me.'[4]

The suave and diplomatic Buschenhagen, who would later be awarded the Knight's Cross of the Iron Cross with Oak Leaves and survive ten years in a Soviet prison camp, was in his homeland to celebrate his 45th birthday when he was summoned to Army High Command in Zossen outside Berlin on Saturday 7 December. In the 1930s, Buschenhagen had served as operations officer under the commander-in-chief of the army, Field Marshal Walther von Brauchitsch, and knew many of the Wehrmacht's leading figures. He was probably present when the *Barbarossa* plan was tested in a war game that weekend under the chief of planning, General Paulus.

'According to what he said, the plan was to strike out towards the Murmansk railway line with three corps operating along independent axes of advance,' wrote Falkenhorst. He was called to Berlin along with General Dietl a week later and given his first briefing by the Chief of the General Staff Franz Halder.

> The planning had progressed a good bit further, and the outline had been set: One corps would attack Murmansk in the High North, another would attack Kandalaksja on the White Sea and a third would attack Kemi in Karelia.

It would be Dietl's job to lead the northern thrust. His soldiers in the 2nd Mountain Division had been in position on the border in Pasvik, weapons at the ready, since the end of August, prepared to advance and secure the nickel mines in Petsamo. But the Finns had very skilfully balanced on a knife edge and it had not been necessary to put Operation *Renntier* into action. Soviet Foreign Minister Molotov had received a clear message in Berlin in November that Hitler would not tolerate any new armed intervention in Finland, and the despot in the Kremlin had chosen to back down.

Construction works were continuing at Kolosjoki, and the first cargoes of nickel ore had already been shipped from Kirkenes. If the Jäniskoski power station came on line in the autumn of 1941, the first shipments of refined nickel would reach Germany a few months later. The German engineers were confident. They estimated that annual production could rapidly be stepped up to more than 10,000 tonnes, which would immediately solve the German arms industry's supply problem.

Falkenhorst and Dietl did not consider their new mission with the same equanimity. The more the staff officers thought about Directive No. 21, the more impossible the operation appeared.

Hitler wanted the Mountain Corps to take Petsamo with a lightning-fast advance, annihilate the Soviet 14th Army on the Kola Peninsula and capture the port of Murmansk. It was only 120 kilometres from Kirkenes to the Kola Fjord. The operation looked easy on the map, and Hitler believed that Finnish troops would join the attack.

The problems were that the Finns still knew nothing about the plans, and that the map didn't match the terrain. The officers sitting behind desks in Berlin interpreted vague lines on the maps as passable roads. In reality, they represented old reindeer tracks, telegraph lines and former boundaries. The hill ranges between Petsamo and Murmansk stood only 300–400 metres above sea level, but the vegetation resembled what could be found at 2,000–3,000 metres in the Alps. The landscape was tundra scored with ravines, ice-cold rivers and lakes. The contrasts were fierce. The temperature could rise above 30°C in summer and fall below -40°C in winter. In the two Soviet divisions which had advanced from Petsamo towards Lappland in the Winter War, 22,000 Red Guards had sustained frostbite. The remaining combat-worthy troops had been held in check by a small but hardy Finnish battalion.

From a military point of view, the landscape consisted of an endless series of natural obstacles which gave the defenders great advantages. A single battery with four 7.5 cm field guns in a mountain division consisted of 324 soldiers and 160 horses and mules. In a land without roads and grazing, logistics would be a nightmare. All provisions, hay and ammunition would have to be transported over the bogs and crags. When the animals gave up, the men would have to step in. Equipment would need to be carried to the soldiers in the front line under constant enemy fire. The wounded would need to be transported back by the same means. Those with experience of living and operating in the mountains immediately realised the consequences: The march on Murmansk would be a trial of strength, especially for those tasked with the logistics.

The wildness of nature was not the only challenge the mountain troops faced. Relationships between the Nazi bigwigs in the Reich Chancellery in central Berlin and the Prussian aristocrats in the headquarters of the Army's High Command in the suburb of Zossen were frigid. Army Commander-in-Chief von Brauchitsch and the Chief of the General Staff Franz Halder had both advised against the Führer's military aggression and had come close to supporting the opposition's plans for a coup in 1939. Both had crumbled in the face of Hitler's rage and ruthlessness and had withdrawn at the last minute. The big victories in Scandinavia and France had made the Führer's position almost unassailable, and Brauchitsch and Halder had been neutralised. They probably lived in chronic fear that the Gestapo would discover what they had been up to, and they appeared more and more to be cowed opportunists. This did not elevate them in Hitler's eyes, who in private referred to the two army chiefs as Cowards no. 1 and 2.

The *Barbarossa* plan was Hitler's work, and the Army High Command had loyally developed it. The same applied to the idea of including the surrounding states in the war of extermination, with Finland, Romania and Hungary first in line, and that caused more trouble.

'Brauchitsch and Halder were strongly opposed to involving Finland in the war,' wrote Falkenhorst. 'They were also opponents of the operation I was to lead in the North.'[5]

According to information he received from the then head of the army's operations department, Colonel Adolf Heusinger, *Barbarossa* would stretch the Wehrmacht's resources to the limit. The army would have only 12 divisions in reserve, as compared with 60 divisions during the campaign in France.

> The decisive battle will be on the central front in Europe. If we succeed in defeating the Soviet army there, the rest will be irrelevant. Seen in that light, the operation in Lapland was an insignificant extra side-show the main effect of which was to weaken the main force. All the forces – to the last division – should instead have been put into the central front and the military presence in outlying theatres reduced to the bare minimum needed for defence. So I declared my agreement with Brauchitsch and Halder, but Hitler and his staff forced their will through.

The underlying disagreement was expressed as soon as Falkenhorst's staff presented the first study of the plans for Operation *Silberfuchs* (*Silver Fox*) at the end of January 1941.

'The task requires Army Command Norway to carry out an operation starting from Finland, breaking through the Soviet front line and advancing to the White Sea to eliminate all the forces around Murmansk,' Falkenhorst wrote in the preamble to the study. 'Then there will be an advance south along the Murmansk railway line to Lake Ladoga, without the occupation of Norway being weakened.'[6]

What he was describing was a gigantic pincer movement through the Arctic wastes: One corps attacking from Petsamo in the north would surround and smash the Soviet 14th Army in a joint operation with another corps, attacking from Salla, 400 kilometres to the south. The combined force would then turn and follow the railway line into the Karelian forests east of Leningrad, which at the same time would come under pressure from the main German forces from the west.

The plan was wildly overambitious. Supply lines through the mostly uninhabited and trackless northern regions would be several hundred kilometres long. The plans anticipated Finnish troops playing a major role in the attack, Swedish cooperation, domination in the air, control over sea routes between the Norwegian Sea, the Barents Sea and the Baltic Sea, and support troops on a scale beyond what was available.

The planners in Zossen grew pale, and Falkenhorst was immediately ordered to put a damper on his ambitions.

'The request for reinforcements in the form of infantry and support detachments can only be met to a limited degree,' stated a telegram on 11 February from the Army High Command to Falkenhorst's staff in Oslo. 'Army Command Norway is therefore requested to re-assess the matter on the basis of actual conditions.'

The telegram represented a cautious reprimand, but Falkenhorst stood his ground, as if he wanted to demonstrate the hopelessness of the undertaking.

'Even in a limited form the operation presents significant risk, especially in relation to supplies,' he replied the next day. 'Nevertheless, Army Command Norway is willing to take on the risk provided a minimum of requirements is met.'

A limited Operation Renntier as part of Operation Barbarossa presented little problem, to advance into the Finnish corridor and secure the nickel mines in Kolosjoki with the help of 2nd Mountain Division and with one regiment of 3rd Mountain Division as reserve along the road to the Arctic Ocean.

But the next phase could only be carried out if Sweden made its territory fully available for the troop movements with roads, railway lines, airspace, telephone connections and accommodation. All civilian traffic would need to give way for a time, and the Swedish railway authorities would have to be persuaded to make locomotives, train drivers and 5,000 wagons available – conditions which for a while would make Falkenhorst military overlord in the northern parts of neutral Sweden. If in addition he got 700 lorries, 1,750 horse-drawn carts and modern German weapons he *would* attack with the available forces – one and a half divisions in the north and two and a half divisions in the south. The two groups would together destroy the Soviet forces on the Kola Peninsula and capture Murmansk, but Leningrad would have to wait.

'The negative reply to the request for reinforcements means that a continuation southwards will no longer be possible,' wrote Falkenhorst. 'A new supply base will first have to be built up in Kandalaksja on the White Sea.'

In his personal post-war account he added:

> For understandable reasons, Von Brauchitsch and Halder made me promise that I would not appeal to the Führer for extra divisions. That could quite plainly not be done. I complied and obeyed orders. With the modest resources allocated to us, I obviously realised that it was not at all certain that our goal would be achieved, however brave the troops were.

The intrigues between the Nazi bosses and the army leaders had left Operation *Silberfuchs* like an abandoned child, and the situation appeared deadlocked till the Lofoten Raid in March 1941 again changed perceptions. Hitler was furious when he learned that the occupying army had been caught 'napping', and the Nazi Commissar of Norway, Josef Terboven, accused Falkenhorst, Admiral Hermann Boehm and Air Marshal Hans Jürgen Stumpff of gross neglect of duty.

'If the British are to still have hope of winning, they must go onto the offensive as soon as we attack the Soviet Union,' declared Hitler, who took the raid as new evidence of the superiority of his instincts. 'Norway with its long coastline will be the most tempting target. The Mountain Corps' main duty must therefore be to secure the Norwegian coast against a British landing.'[7]

The authority of the top officers was weakened. Nobody protested in mid-March when Hitler removed responsibility for the Arctic theatre of war from the Army. The operations known as *Renntier* (Reindeer), *Silberfuchs* (Silver Fox), and *Platinumfuchs* (Platinum Fox) would from now on be directed by the Supreme Command of the Wehrmacht, which again was under his own personal control.[8]

A few days later, on 26 March, he issued a new directive on the defence of Norway.

'After the raid on Lofoten we must in future anticipate new British raids on the Norwegian coast,' wrote Field Marshal Wilhelm Keitel, on behalf of the Führer. 'Tying up strong German forces in other theatres of war could encourage the British to attempt a bigger landing, supported by the superior British fleet.'

Falkenhorst's army in Norway was therefore put on alert and ordered to intensify the surveillance of the Norwegian and Barents Seas and turn the long and rugged coastline into a fortified part of the Atlantic Wall.

> The army will as soon as possible transfer to Norway 160 batteries suitable for defence of the coast and protection against attack from the air. Forces for early warning and manning of the batteries, engineer battalions and units from the National Labour Service will be made available in necessary numbers.

Keitel added a threat which led Falkenhorst to put four exclamation marks in the margin: 'Any reduction of these forces requires the Führer's personal approval.'

There was no longer any talk of reducing the defence of Norway to 'the bare minimum', as von Brauchitsch, Halder and Falkenhorst had wanted. On the contrary, the forces and fortifications were to be significantly strengthened. This raised a tricky further question: Where should the extra forces to attack Murmansk be taken from?

'I don't have enough people,' said one of those who was most worried, General Eduard Dietl, 'but if I am told to attack, then I will attack.'[9]

Falkenhorst's rival had been selected to lead the operation, and he was losing patience. His loyalty to Hitler and the Nazi party was greater than his loyalty to the leadership of the army. Moreover, he was a personal friend of the Führer's and had not made any promise to keep his distance. Sometime at the beginning of April 1941 he took a plane to Berlin to find out what was going on.

On Sunday 20 April Dietl participated in Hitler's 52nd birthday celebrations in the Alpine village of Mönichkirchen in Austria. In a new unrestrained outburst of rage after the coup in Yugoslavia at the end of March, the tyrant had turned his overwhelming military power against the Balkans and Greece and ordered that Belgrade be flattened to the ground.

Field Marshal Wilhelm List's 12th Army and Göring's Luftwaffe struck mercilessly in a campaign which was the prelude to several years of terror and bloody conflict between the occupying forces and various factions. The instigators of the Yugoslavian coup surrendered on 13 April, the Greek Metaxas Line was broken a few days later, and the British expeditionary force of 53,000 men put to flight.

Churchill considered the Balkan debacle one of the darkest moments of the war, but Hitler was euphoric when he received the reports of victory on board his armoured train *Amerika* at the railway station in Mönichkirchen. Complications did arise on Monday 21 April when the Greeks surrendered to Field Marshal List and not to the Italian High Command, an act considered a gross insult by Mussolini. There was a hectic round of meetings, and it took several days to pacify *Il Duce*. However, Hitler was still in a very good mood when Dietl entered *Amerika*'s luxurious conference carriage.

According to SS Obersturmbannführer Karl Schmidt, a map of the northern flank was rolled out by one of the adjutants, Lieutenant Colonel Gerhard

Engel. Hitler put on his glasses, bent forward and pointed his index finger at Murmansk: 'It's only a hundred kilometres from the nickel mines!'

He put another finger on Kirkenes: 'And only a further fifty kilometres to Kirkenes. If the Russians come there, it will be a catastrophe! We will not only lose the nickel mines, whose importance for our steel industry cannot be over-stated. No, it will be a strategic setback to the whole campaign in the East. Stalin will threaten the Finns from behind, have an open road to Sweden and put our ports in Northern Norway at risk.'

The Führer straightened up and took off his glasses. 'It all stands or falls with your Mountain Corps, Dietl. You must neutralise this danger as soon as the campaign begins. Not by waiting, but by attacking! You must capture these ludicrous hundred kilometres to Murmansk and put an end to this ghost once and for all!'

After such a tirade, many generals would have snapped their heels together and lifted their right arm: *Heil Hitler!* But Dietl was the Führer's favourite soldier and could afford to take certain liberties. He didn't think the tundra was ludicrously easy, and he promptly produced the analyses the staff officers had prepared.

'*Mein Führer*, up there the landscape looks as it did when the World was created. It is a wilderness without woods, roads or people – just stone and gravel. Round Murmansk there is an uninhabitable zone of a hundred kilometres which protects the town as effectively as an armoured shield.'

To be able to push through the wilderness and conquer Murmansk the Mountain Corps would need to be provided with considerable numbers of soldiers, heavy weapons, building machinery, haulage vehicles and trek animals.

Hitler was busy and gave no immediate promises. He just replied briefly: 'I'll see what I can do.'

The massive preparations for *Barbarossa* could not be kept hidden for long, and during the spring of 1941 rumours about a forthcoming attack circulated worldwide.[10]

The NKVD and the Soviet Military Intelligence Service had built up a network of agents throughout Germany and Eastern Europe, who sent a stream of warnings to Stalin and his red court in the Kremlin.

As early as 29 December 1940 a source in Berlin had reported that Hitler had given orders to prepare for an offensive against the Soviet Union, and that war would be declared in the spring of 1941. A few weeks later, a deciphered telegram sent to Tokyo from the Japanese ambassador in Bucharest reported – with reference to the German ambassador – that the situation had entered a decisive phase. 'Germany has completed its full deployment from Finland to the Black Sea, and is convinced of an easy victory.'

A senior SS officer who visited a doctor in the same city had boasted that the German army would advance along a line between Ukraine and the Baltic. 'The entire continent will fall under our influence. The Bolsheviks will be chased beyond the Urals.'

The two courageous key agents in Berlin – the economist Arvid Harnack, codename *Corsicanets*, and the Luftwaffe officer Harro Schulze-Boysen, codename *Starshina* – supported the oral reports with information from top-secret documents to which they had access as trusted workers in the Business Ministry and the Air Ministry.

> Hitler's intention is to seize the Soviet Union's economic base in Ukraine. As soon as Ukraine collapses, the Wehrmacht will continue towards the Caucasus in an operation that is expected to last twenty-five days. According to the Chief of the General Staff Halder the capture of the agricultural areas and ore deposits in Ukraine and the oil fields in Baku will be straightforward.

Observers along the border and in the central troop marshalling areas in what had been Poland further confirmed the reports with a long series of visual observations: New troop transports were constantly arriving from the west; barracks, depots and ammunition dumps were being built; roads, bridges and railway lines were being strengthened. At the same time, the Luftwaffe was becoming increasingly bold and active in mapping the Soviet defensive positions from the air. Illegal incursions into Soviet air space were reported almost daily.

In the middle of the month the British Ambassador to Russia, Sir Stafford Cripps, joined the messengers when on the basis of sources in Swedish and American intelligence, he asserted that Hitler would attack Russia before the end of June.

Finally, Churchill received a decrypt of an Enigma telegram that said that the Germans had moved three armoured and two mechanised divisions from Romania to Poland. That led him to send the following personal message to Moscow on 4 April:

> I have reliable information from a trusted agent that when the Germans thought they had got Yugoslavia in the net, that is to say, after March 20, they began to move three out of the five Panzer divisions from Romania to Southern Poland. The moment

they heard about the Serbian revolution this movement was countermanded. Your Excellency will readily appreciate the significance of these facts.[11]

This cryptic report was the British war leader's first direct warning to Stalin about the coming danger, and Churchill claimed that it was of historic significance.

In fact, the effect was the opposite. The notoriously suspicious Soviet leader interpreted the flow of warnings and intelligence reports with great scepticism and regarded them mostly as western disinformation. He had built the Soviet Union's security policy on the basis of the Non-aggression Pact and friendship with the Nazi regime, and refused to realise that he had made a political mistake of tragic dimensions. The build-up of forces in the border areas was indeed an unmistakable fact, but Stalin chose to shut his eyes to the acute threat and accept the reassurances from Berlin that they were a preparatory manoeuvre for an invasion of the British Isles. Nor could he or would he accept that the war he had wanted to avoid was suddenly at his door.

As a master of *realpolitik* he could not believe that Hitler would be so reckless as to start a new war before England had been defeated. Stalin reckoned that if the ambitions of the despot in the Reich Chancellery were still unsatisfied, he would receive any territorial or economic demand from him *before* a possible military action was set in motion, and that this would lead to negotiations. In that case the concentration of troops was a move in the war of nerves prior to putting demands on the table. Above all, Stalin thought that he still had time. Now what mattered first and foremost was avoiding provocation and keeping the door open for negotiations.

'Look at that,' he had said to the Red Army Chief of Staff, General Georgij Zjukov, when he received the warning from Churchill, 'We are being threatened with the Germans and the Germans with the Soviet Union. They're playing us off against one another. It's a subtle political game.'

Hitler yielded to party comrade Dietl's arguments – to a certain extent. The *whole* of 3rd Mountain Division and the 10,000-strong, motorised SS Kampfgruppe Nord were released for the invasion of the Soviet Union, together with several special units: two machine-gun battalions; engineer battalions with special equipment for building bridges; 12 units with almost 15,000 men from the National Labour Service; a police battalion; communications units and other groups who would help to secure the northern sector of the coming Eastern Front.

The next few weeks were a nightmare for the transport officers. An invasion army with supporting units amounting to about 60,000 men together with thousands of horses and vehicles would need to be transported north in record time – in addition to the 58 new coastal batteries which were earmarked for Northern Norway.

In Operation *Fischzug*, the SS group, the machine-gun battalions and the youth sections from the National Labour Service were taken to Finnmark by train and ship. In Operation *Wallfahrt*, the 199th Infantry Division, which was to take over from the 3rd Mountain Division, was sent from Oslo to Narvik. As soon as these troops were disembarked, the ships proceeded to Varanger with 3rd Mountain Division in Operation *Herkules*. Finally, 137th Mountain Regiment and the rest of 2nd Mountain Division moved to Kirkenes in Operation *Siegfried*.[12]

'Operation *Wallfahrt* began in Oslo on 25 April and was completed on 3 June,' wrote Captain Vilhelm Hess, who had recently been appointed as Senior Quartermaster in the Mountain Corps. '*Herkules* took over and was completed as planned on 21 June, as if it had been run by stopwatch. It was altogether a remarkable achievement.'

Frequent storms raged over the Finnmark coast throughout the spring of 1941, and many of the German and Austrian soldiers were encountering the sea and Arctic conditions for the first time.

'We reached Varanger after several days on board and were set ashore with vehicles and equipment on a temporary quay,' wrote Toni Wiesbauer, a junior officer in 137th Mountain Regiment. The landscape appeared to be a cold, empty tundra. Our time was filled with hard tasks in a harsh terrain.'[13]

Thousands of soldiers were gathered in the border area, which buzzed with feverish activity. The twisting roads were full of marching units and long columns of vehicles. Every available empty house was commandeered, but that was far from enough.

'Barracks, store buildings, ammunition depots and pyramids of hay and straw shot up like toadstools,' wrote local historian Finn Fløtten, who grew up on a farm near Høybuktmoen where the Germans laid out a new airstrip, just 15 kilometres from Kirkenes. 'The work was managed by Organisation Todt, which had 12 companies in its service in addition to many Norwegian workers.'

In Murmansk, General Frolov and his officers watched the build-up of forces with increasing unease.

The local unit of the NKVD was under the command of Major General Aleksej Rutsjkin and had a network of agents in Northern Finland and Finnmark. Some of them belonged to a group of about fifty Norwegians who had fled from Varanger to the Soviet Union with their families after the German occupation. Stalin feared *agents provocateurs* more than ever, and the refugees had been imprisoned even though most of them were convinced communists.

In late autumn 1940, a handful of them had been faced with a choice between five years of hard labour for illegal border crossing, and service as spies for the Soviet Union.

'In late November I was called up to an office on the first floor where there were a NKVD lieutenant and the interpreter who had followed us to prison,' wrote Otto Larsen in his book, *Jeg var Sovjet-spion* (*I was a Soviet Spy*). 'The lieutenant came straight to the point: Would I consider joining the intelligence network in Norway? I asked what the work consisted of, and what it was about. He explained that the Germans were currently bringing a lot of war materials to Northern Norway and into Finland. This could only be interpreted as preparation for an attack. I didn't think about it for long before agreeing, and he explained what the job consisted of. I was to transport intelligence agents over to Norway.'[14]

The 28-year-old fisherman from Kiberg was fearless. Together with his brother Olaf and shoemaker Åge Halvari he set up a permanent route with the cutter *Storskjær* between the harbours on the Kola Peninsula and occupied Varanger. The main contact was one of the great heroes of the resistance movement in Finnmark, fisherman Alfred Mathisen, who had two brothers among the refugees in the Soviet Union.

'We had a regular arrangement with Alfred. He would pass on the information from Norway and we would have regular meetings with him at sea,' Larsen explained. 'We worked together without a hitch. Alfred had contacts across the whole of Finnmark who gathered information about fortifications and troop movements, refugees and war materials and anything else of interest, including drawings of German construction works. He did a good job. In fact, the Russians got to know about every single German soldier who came to Finland from Northern Norway. When we met, it was usually I who went on board to get his written reports. We usually sat and chatted a little over a reunion dram down in his cabin while I made a lot of notes.'

The picture being built up during the spring of 1941 in the reports from Mathisen and his network of contacts was very disturbing.

> The Germans have 50 planes on the airstrip in Kirkenes and more than 32 in Lakselv. Troops, tanks, guns, and horses are being unloaded from ships in Tana and Varanger. Soldiers are building defence works along the coast. The number of soldiers in the area around Kirkenes is estimated at around 20,000.[15]

For the time being it was impossible to establish accurately from where and when a possible attack would come, and Stalin's paranoia precluded more offensive counter-measures.

The overall picture was becoming more and more gloomy. 'There was no doubt that the Fascist beast was getting ready to spring in our direction,' wrote Rear Admiral Golovko, 'But what were we to do? There was silence from Moscow. We were given no orders on how to tackle the situation.'[16]

CHAPTER 2

Bluff or Business?

England, Germany and the Soviet Union, May to early June 1941

Stalin was not alone in misinterpreting Hitler's intentions. In Britain, neither the Foreign Office nor the military intelligence service found any special reason in early April 1941 to trust 'the numerous reports that Germany intends to attack Russia in the near future.'[1]

In widely accepted evaluations, the Joint Intelligence Committee maintained till the beginning of June that Hitler's 'main objective was the defeat of England, by blockade and air attack if possible, by invasion if necessary.' The rumours and the troop movements could altogether be part of the continuing war of nerves to prevent Soviet intervention in the German operations in the Balkans and soften up Stalin prior to forthcoming negotiations.

> Germany undoubtedly has its eyes on the Ukraine and the Caucasus, and Russia is fully aware of this. But Russia will do all it can to avoid the clash, and so will Germany. The many rumours to the contrary are probably designed to frighten the Russians. The concentration and movements of troops may have been undertaken for the same purpose. Such preparations will enable Germany to move against Russia if it is decided at a later stage that its chances of eliminating Great Britain during 1941 are receding.

Throughout May the codebreakers in Bletchley Park delivered a growing flow of decoded German messages confirming the massive movement of troops and materials to the East. The Wehrmacht's central communication systems were still impenetrable, but the communications of the Luftwaffe, some naval units, the German railways and various diplomatic stations were being read with less and less delay. The officers and academics at the Government Code and Cipher

School who translated and coordinated the numerous texts, were in little doubt about their significance.

'From rail movements towards Moldavia in the south to ship movements towards the Varanger Fiord in the far north there is everywhere the same steady eastward trend,' said an Enigma analysis on 31 May. 'Either the purpose is blackmail or it is war. No doubt Hitler would prefer a bloodless surrender. But the quiet move, for instance, of a prisoner-of-war cage to Tarnow looks more like business than bluff.'[2]

The analysts agreed with the diplomats in the Foreign Office that it would be foolhardy of Hitler to start a war on two fronts. 'But the answer may well be that the Germans do not expect the struggle with Russia to be long. An overwhelming eastward concentration, a lightning victory, an unassailable supremacy in Europe and Asia – such may be the plan behind the procession of troop trains from the Balkans to the eastern frontier.'

The analysis exposed Hitler's arrogance and over-confidence with surgical precision, but he was not alone. Most people believed that the Red Army would disintegrate in a short time, and in the High North the invitations to the victory banquet were already printed. It was to be held in Hotel Arktika in Murmansk on 20 July, less than a month after the start of the campaign.

At the beginning of May, Hitler had for the first time given Oberkommando der Wehrmacht permission to enter into real discussions at staff officer level with the Finns, who until now had been kept in the dark about the details of the *Barbarossa* plan. It soon became clear that he had not mistaken the willingness of the Finnish elite to cooperate.

With guarantees from Berlin protecting Finland's exposed position, agreement was reached between 20 May and 5 June on all the basic questions.[3]

Finland would march as a brother-in-arms beside Nazi Germany along three lines of attack on the Soviet Union: one in the far north, one in mid-Finland and one in the south, directed towards Leningrad and the lost territories of Karelia. Colonel General von Falkenhorst would have command over the northern theatre of war with his headquarters in Lapland's capital city, Rovaniemi. Finland's grand old man, Marshal Mannerheim, would have the corresponding role in the southern half of the country.

In the meantime Dietl's Mountain Corps and the support units were moving into the area between Tana and Varanger in steadily increasing numbers. The weather was still unsettled. Thaw and frost were alternating, and heavy snowfall could reduce visibility to zero in minutes.

'On arrival in the new area the troops had to start building barracks straight away, because of the lack of available houses.,' stated a report from 2nd Mountain Division. 'Because of the melting snow, others had to be set to improving the road to Pasvik and the Finnish border, while Pioneer Battalion 82 built a bridge 300 metres long and 1.5 metres wide over the River Pasvik south of Svanvik, as a reserve route in case the bridge at Boris Gleb was damaged.'[4]

There was chaos on the roads, and the port of Kirkenes was totally congested. 'We arrived at the town at 12 noon on 28 May, but the harbour was packed with other steamships,' wrote 112th Mountain Artillery Regiment in their movement report. 'We had to wait until 6 o'clock next morning before debarkation could begin.'[5]

To avoid attracting attention, General Dietl remained on board the confiscated passenger ship *Black Watch* in the remote Kå Fjord in the western part of the county, where he spent the time fishing from another commandeered vessel, the luxury 90-foot motor yacht *Kvitørn 2*, which had belonged to the owner of the Steen & Strøm department store in Oslo.

'The general's passion was fishing, which he did with the Norwegian skipper, the first mate, the chief surgeon and the chief vet,' wrote his personal adjutant, Colonel Kurt Hermann. 'They usually went out about 2 in the afternoon and came back a few hours later with so much cod that there was enough for both the officers' mess and the crew's mess.'[6]

But time was becoming short, and Hitler had already set Sunday 22 June as D-day for *Barbarossa*. The Finns had stated that they would need nine days for full mobilisation as soon as the result of the negotiations had been confirmed by the government. Despite the snow and the chaos, Dietl demanded that the German preparations be completed in good time beforehand, and that the corps must be ready to march towards the Finnish border within 72 hours from Monday 9 June, the day the Finns had given notice of full, final acceptance of the cooperation with Nazi Germany. On receiving the code word *Renntier*, the troops would move into the Finnish corridor and establish a strong defensive position round the nickel mines in Kolosjoki. As soon as the next code word – *Platinumfuchs* – was distributed, the corps would cross the border into the Soviet Union, destroy the Red Army units in the area and capture Murmansk.

On 6 June Dietl sent *Kvitørn 2* eastward along the coast. Two days later, he followed by plane.

The listening station on Scarborough Head picked up the radio signal about the motor yacht's departure almost immediately. The telegram was interpreted

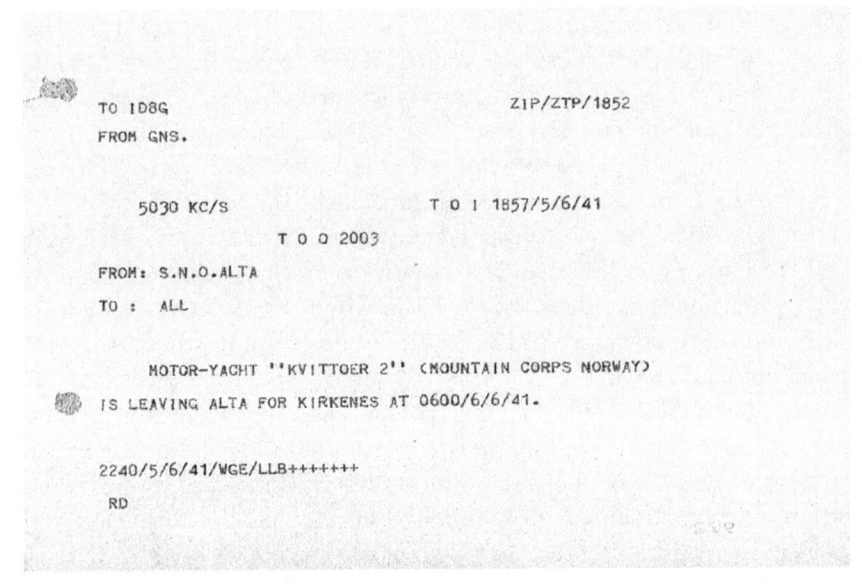

```
TO ID8G                          ZIP/ZTP/1852
FROM GNS.

    5030 KC/S              T O I 1857/5/6/41
                T O O 2003
FROM: S.N.O.ALTA
TO :   ALL

      MOTOR-YACHT ''KVITTOER 2'' (MOUNTAIN CORPS NORWAY)
      IS LEAVING ALTA FOR KIRKENES AT 0600/6/6/41.

     2240/5/6/41/WGE/LLB++++++++
     RD
```

Dietl's yacht Kvitørn 2 *had been commandeered from the owner of the Steen and Strøm department store. It left Alta early on the morning of 6 June 1941. De-coding and translation from German to English took three hours and 43 minutes; TOI 18.57, sent by telex 22.40. (National Archives, London)*

by the codebreakers at Bletchley Park and reached the Admiralty Operations Room in a telex just three hours later: 'Motor yacht *Kvitørn 2* (Mountain Corps Norway) is leaving Alta for Kirkenes 0600/6/6/1941.'[7]

The telegram was only one in a cacophony of signals which was emanating from Kirkenes and other military base towns in Northern Norway and contributed a few days later to the British changing their view of Hitler's intentions.

The Luftwaffe were busy establishing themselves on the airstrip at Høybuktmoen, where the 40-year-old veteran from the Condor Legion in Spain, Colonel Andreas Nilsen, was appointed Fliegerführer Kirkenes, in command of about a hundred Messerschmitt fighters, Stuka bombers and reconnaissance planes. The hectic radio traffic between the airfield, Oslo and Berlin gradually slotting into the emerging pattern, and the picture built up by the intelligence services became more and more clear as other sources were added. Among these was the Swedish Secret Service in Stockholm, which was tapping the telephone and telex cables between Oslo, Helsinki and Berlin, and which had come to the conclusion that the attack would take place sometime around the middle of June.[8]

On Monday 9 June, the same day that Dietl called his divisional and regimental commanders to the first briefing conference in Kirkenes, the Foreign Office in London finally changed its opinion. Foreign Minister Anthony Eden and his civil servants had insisted until the last moment that the war rumours were disinformation, disseminated to camouflage continuing negotiations between Berlin and Moscow. On the basis of the daily flow of steadily more alarming messages, the Foreign Office had now come to recognise that 'all the evidence points to an attack … the most astonishing development on the grand scale since the war began.'[9]

Three days later the stubborn Joint Intelligence Committee was forced to admit that it had got things wrong. A decoded telegram to Tokyo from the Japanese Ambassador in Berlin revealed that Hitler had declared in a confidential meeting that 'Communist Russia must be eliminated. Romania and Finland will join Germany against Russia, and the campaign will soon be over.'

The altered view was expressed laconically in a short note on Wednesday 12 June: 'Fresh evidence is now to hand that Hitler has made up his mind to have done with Soviet obstruction and intends to attack her. Hostilities therefore appear highly probable, though it is premature to fix a date for their outbreak.'

The situation was considered so acute that in meetings on 10 and 13 June, Soviet Ambassador Ivan Maisky was given a full briefing and strongly advised to send all the available information to Stalin immediately.

'Foreign Office Permanent Secretary Cadogan was speaking in a monotonous voice, naming more and more places and ever new military units,' wrote Maisky in his book, *Memoirs of a Soviet Ambassador*. 'I was writing down under his dictation almost mechanically. In my imagination there arose the image of the Nazi troops, vast masses of Nazi troops – infantry, artillery, tanks, armoured cars, aeroplanes – which were irresistibly streaming to the east, ever further to the east. And all of this avalanche, breathing fire and death, was at any moment to descend upon our country.'[10]

With his dark goatee beard and hard look, Maisky vaguely resembled the American film star, Edward Robinson. He was one of the brutal Soviet regime's experts in self-preservation, but even he did not have the guts to challenge Stalin's biased opinions.

> I obviously didn't accept Cadogan's word as 100% truthful. The British had their own interest in stirring up a war in the East, and in the telegram I criticised quite a lot of what he had said. But altogether the information was so serious and so detailed that it ought to give Stalin something to think about and in any event cause him to give the border posts strong orders to be on the lookout.

Cadogan had also passed on a request from the British government to send a military mission to the Soviet Union to discuss possible cooperation against what appeared to be a common enemy. This initiative would in due time become the foundation stone for the great wartime anti-Nazi alliance, but in early June Stalin's attitude was still unshakeable.[11] His attempts to placate Berlin had become increasingly desperate throughout the spring. He openly invited the Germans to negotiate, refused to put the Red Army in a state of alert and forbade any actions which might provoke Hitler. Even small gestures were used to demonstrate good will and accommodation. He insisted on using Nazi German diplomats in the negotiations to free the Russians who had been in Franco's prisons since the days of the Spanish Civil War. Moreover, in May the Norwegian, Belgian and Czech ambassadors were expelled without warning as the nations they represented allegedly no longer existed.

The answer to the warning from the British came in a communiqué issued by the Kremlin on Thursday 14 June and published by the press bureau, Tass:

> Rumours about the imminence of war between the Soviet Union and Germany have recently appeared in the British and foreign press ... In spite of the evident senselessness of the rumours, responsible circles in Moscow have nevertheless thought it necessary to authorise Tass to state that such rumours are clumsily cooked-up propaganda by forces hostile to the USSR and to Germany ... Germany is as unswervingly observing the conditions of the Soviet-German pact of Non-Aggression as is the Soviet Union, in view of which, in the opinion of Soviet circles, the rumours about Germany's intention to tear up the pact and undertake an attack on the Soviet Union are devoid of any foundation.

This grovelling statement was studied with head-shaking bewilderment throughout the world. In Berlin it was met outwardly with ominous silence and inwardly with contempt and derision. The Finns, however, were alarmed and asked for an immediate confirmation that the *Barbarossa* plan was still valid. Hitler replied reassuringly. The brother-in-arms had not been deceived. The attack would go ahead as planned.

Stalin had played his last card – and lost.

CHAPTER 3

Into the Finnish Corridor

Petsamo, 2.30 a.m., Sunday 22 June 1941

Heavy rain had swollen the River Pasvik, and muddy brown water swirled around the stone pillars supporting the lonely bridge. The midnight hour should have been the year's lightest: bright, mild and filled with laughter, happiness and midsummer celebrations. Instead it was as if nature itself felt sorrow and anxiety. There was a biting, frosty wind from the Bøk Fjord, and rain clouds lay like a widow's veil over the ridges separating Norway from Finland. Only fourteen days before, the last snowstorm of spring had howled through the birch woods as a reminder of who really ruled in the Arctic. The new snow had thawed, but the earth was raw, cold and lifeless. For the many thousands of German and Austrian mountain troops waiting in trenches and boggy hollows, there was little comfort and no peace of mind.

'The night was miserable and wet,' wrote 44-year-old teacher, author and SS officer Karl Springenschmid, who had made his talents available to the Nazis and in 1938 earned lasting infamy as organiser of the first mass burning of books in Salzburg, Austria. 'It was dark, with the midnight sun hiding behind a low layer of cloud. The horses and mules had been unhitched from the wagons and were foraging among the scrub. On both sides of the gravel road, groups of soldiers in full battle gear discussed the coming mission in low, murmuring tones.'[1]

Rumours had been circulating for a long time, but the objective of the attack had only become widely known a couple of days earlier: Murmansk.

> People were already making bets on when the town would be captured. Everybody had been told about the *mere* hundred kilometres they had to travel. For troops who had marched ten times that distance under fire, the prospect didn't sound too scary.

24 • MIRACLE AT THE LITZA

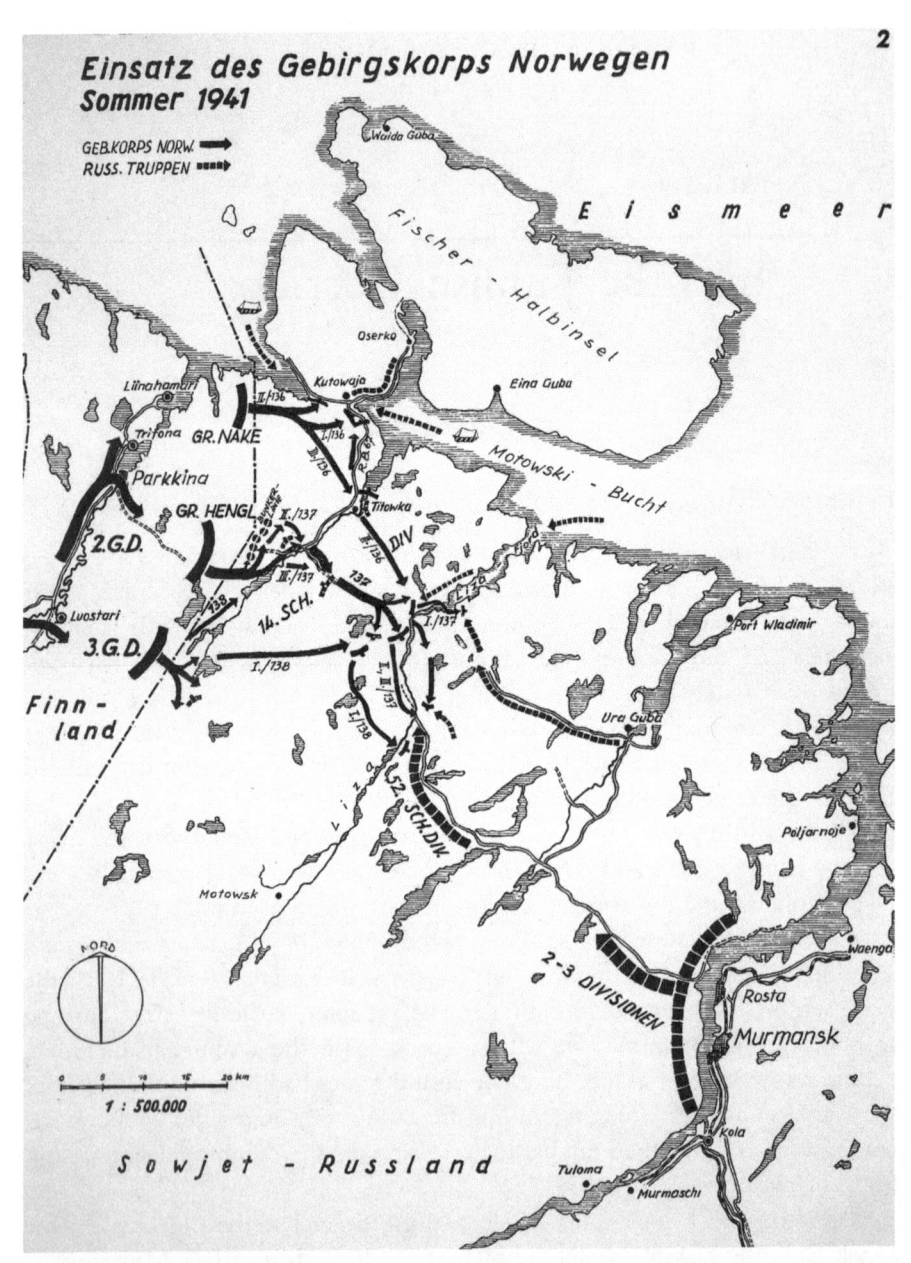

This German map shows Kola with the Fisher Peninsula and the important Motovskij Fjord with the three German troop concentrations west of the then border between Finland and Russia: Group Nake in the north, Group Hengl in the middle and 3rd Mountain Division in the south. The Germans managed to cross the River Titovka, which was the first line of defence, but were stopped at the River Litza, which runs into the Litza Fjord, a branch of the Motovskij Fjord. (Rüf: Gebirgsjäger vor Murmansk)

The unknown factor was the Russians. Would they let themselves be defeated as easily as the others? That was the big question.

Most of the soldiers were accustomed to winning and kept any doubts to themselves. The transport column stood drawn up in an endless line on the muddy gravel road nearby: lorries with food and ammunition, field-guns, anti-aircraft guns, armoured vehicles, staff cars, ambulances and horse carts with everything required for an invasion force of 60,000 men and 6,000 draught animals. Every so often, despatch riders hurried past on motorcycles. Orders were whispered, timetables consulted. 'There is something awe-inspiring about a deployment like this, a display of power which gives each soldier confidence.'

One of the last people to pass along the lines was the corps' chief quartermaster, Captain Vilhelm Hess, who personally inspected the column from the first to the last vehicle.

'I felt proud and grateful for what we had achieved,' he wrote in a private note a few weeks later. But at the same time I was too tense and too aware of the importance of the moment to be able to relax. I kept wondering how things would turn out. Russia lay before us like endless tundra. In comparison with the new mission, the Norwegian campaign seemed like an insignificant training exercise.'[2]

For Hess, the decision to attack the Soviet Union had come as 'a quite extraordinary surprise, viewed in the light of the war's and the politicians' many unsolved problems.' The shortage of shipping capacity had turned the massive troop movements in April and May into an endurance test, and the staff officers had had to work day and night to prevent the operation from collapsing. It had succeeded with no time to spare. The corps that now stood marshalled in correct order had discipline and fighting skills that had been tested, from Lemberg in Poland to Narvik in Norway.

Hess was however in some doubt about the wisdom of the whole enterprise and was not scared to commit his thoughts to paper. 'No question should be suppressed. Dietl has always been clear about that.'

The otherwise educated and well-informed logistics manager did acknowledge Hitler's motives – with the help of the same hateful and anti-Semitic lies as filled the columns of *Völkischer Beobachter* and other Nazi publications. 'The Russians appear to believe that they can stand on the side-lines while Germany and the Western nations bleed to death. Then they can deceitfully overpower the weakened peoples and realise their old Bolshevik dreams without difficulty. The Jews who are behind this war have a lot of influence over there. They are undoubtedly in contact with their cousins in the democracies who have stirred up this global conflagration.'

The Soviet Union must therefore be destroyed, and this was a task that filled Hess with dark forebodings. 'The colossus in the East is a major power. To bring it to its knees in the middle of a war with England is an enterprise whose scale and significance we little people cannot comprehend.'

There was only one person he and all the others could trust: Adolf Hitler. 'We bow in awe before the Führer's broad vision, daring and decisiveness. That's the only thing we can do. He alone sees the necessity and the possibilities in it all.'

His Nazi ruminations stopped soon after 2 a.m. on Sunday morning. The horses were hitched to the carts, the Maybach engines coughed into life and the companies were drawn up in marching order. Cycle Battalion 68 headed the column. Their mission would be to occupy the nickel smelter. Next came the partly motorised 7. Battalion of the 139th Mountain Regiment and 2. Company of Pioneer Battalion 83 with bridging equipment.

The 2nd Mountain Division alone consisted of 18,500 men and 2,800 horses, and the 3rd Mountain Division had similar numbers. There were also several thousand gunners from the 111th and 112th Mountain Artillery Regiments and pioneers and specialists from many other support units. The main column stretched from Bjørnevatn to Elvenes, and all the adjoining side-roads were chock-full.

At 2.30 a.m. precisely, the corps commander, General Eduard Dietl, and his climbing companion from the Alps, Major General Ernst Schlemmer, marched to the border post. Amid the flash of cameras from the propaganda company's photographers, the boom was raised and the column set in motion. Operation *Barbarossa* was underway at the northern end of the Eastern Front.

Half an hour later the guns opened fire along the European Central Front. More than three million men with the support of planes, tanks and artillery attacked the Soviet Union along a front that stretched 3,000 kilometres from the Baltic to the Black Sea – without war having been declared. This invasion initiated a bloodbath and material destruction the horror and extent of which would be unparalleled in world history, costing almost 50 million lives over the next four years.

Since 14 June, Stalin had been waiting in increasing desperation for a message from Hitler to come to the conference table. However, the fateful statement published by Tass had not elicited a reply. Instead, the reports of German war preparations had grown into a flood of warnings, with little effect. Apparently encapsulated and blinded by his own prejudices and arrogance, the Soviet leader dismissed all other opinions with growing wrath and irrationality.

On 17 June he received from Harro Schulze-Boysen in Berlin a very detailed report warning that an attack could be expected at any time. Stalin's responded by writing on the report: 'Tell the so-called source in Luftwaffe Headquarters to go and fuck his own mother. He's no source, he's a disinformant.'

When Zjukov and Timoshenko tried the next day to persuade Stalin to authorise full mobilisation, the tyrant exploded with rage: 'Timoshenko is preparing everyone for war. He's a fine man with a big head but a small brain. Germany will never fight Russia on her own. He should have been shot.'

Stalin stormed from the meeting. A moment later he poked his head round the door again before it was finally slammed shut: 'If you are going to provoke the Germans by moving troops to the border without our permission, then heads will roll. *Mark my words!*'

On 21 June, a warm summer Saturday, Stalin came slowly to the realisation that he had been tricked. The content of the reports had become steadily more urgent. German merchant ships were leaving Russian ports before they had completed unloading. All superfluous diplomatic personnel had been called home. In the garden of the German Embassy, smoke was rising from a bonfire of hastily burned papers.

When Stalin called his closest political and military minions to the Kremlin at 7 p.m. on Saturday evening, the mood was tense. All questions to Ambassador Werner von Schulenberg had been met with evasive answers. In Berlin, the Soviet envoy Vladimir Dekanozov had been knocking persistently on Ribbentrop's door without answer.

Soon after that, the first German deserters were reporting that the attack would start early on Sunday morning. With only a few hours remaining, Stalin at last had to act. The first mobilisation order, however, was unclear and did not reach the front-line generals until 2 a.m. 'During 22–23 June a sudden attack by the Germans is possible … All units to combat readiness … The task of our forces is *not* to be drawn into any provocative action which could cause serious complications.'

It was hopelessly too late. Less than an hour later the Soviet fortresses, airfields, defence installations and naval bases were engulfed in a firestorm. The surprise was almost total and caught the Red Army off guard. Chaos and death reigned along the border. Stalin's blindness cost tens of thousands of lives in a few hours, and further hundreds of thousands would be added to the list of dead, wounded and missing in the coming weeks.

The battle for the western boundary was lost even before Stalin was awakened at 4 a.m. on Sunday 22 June by a telephone call from Georgij Zjukov, Chief of the Soviet General Staff.

'He reported that the Germans were attacking, and asked permission to counter-attack,' wrote Chris Bellamy in his book, *Absolute War*. 'There was silence. Just the heavy breathing of the 63-year-old autocrat, who was no doubt somewhat the worse for vodka and Georgian wine and very little sleep. Finally, he told Zjukov to bring Timoshenko to the Kremlin and have the Politburo summoned.'

Not everybody had been taken by surprise to the same extent. At the People's Commissariat for the Navy, situated near the Kremlin, the Supreme Commander, Nikolai Kuznetsov, had long been anticipating the outbreak of war. The 36-year-old admiral was a faithful Stalinist but was not afraid to act on his own initiative. The Soviet Navy had observation posts and agents in ports throughout the world, and the reports left little doubt about what was likely to happen. As early as Thursday 19 June, the admiral had ordered all naval units to go to *Readiness State 2*. All leave was cancelled, and ships were to be fuelled and made ready for sea.

'Normally we tried to finish work in good time before the week-end, so that people could have time off,' he wrote in his memoirs, 'but the reports from the fleet were becoming more and more serious and I felt very worried. So I rang my wife and said "Don't wait for me. I'm going to be delayed."'[3]

Saturday 21 June had been sultry and hot, and the streets and parks of Moscow were full of people celebrating midsummer evening with song and dance. A thunderstorm had just passed over the city when Kuznetsov's phone rang. It was Marshal Timoshenko calling him to a crisis meeting.

> When we came out into the street, the rain shower was over. The pavements were thronged with festive crowds. We heard soulful gramophone music from an open window. A few minutes later we climbed up the stairs to the old mansion house where the defence minister had a temporary office.

Stalin's mobilisation orders were being implemented when Kuznetsov entered the room. He immediately understood the seriousness of the situation and asked 'Do we have permission to use weapons if the Germans attack?'

'Permission granted!' replied Timoshenko.

A staff officer was sent across the street at the double to telegraph the order to the four regional commands: the Pacific Fleet, the Black Sea Fleet, the Baltic Fleet and the Northern Fleet. 'All units to go to *Readiness State 1* and be made battle-ready immediately.' Kuznetsov himself picked up the telephone. He wanted to brief the fleet commanders personally.

In the far north, Arsenij Golovko had spent the day with his closest advisers in the Northern Fleet's headquarters in the naval town of Polarnoje on the west coast of the Kola Fjord.

From Polarnoje to Kirkenes is only 120 kilometres as the crow flies, and there had been a worrying increase in naval traffic since April. Reconnaissance flights had been observed over Kola more and more frequently in recent weeks, and on Tuesday 17 June a Heinkel had flown so low over Polarnoje that the pilot's face could be seen from the windows of the naval administration building.

'Our guns didn't fire a single shot, and our ageing fighters were quite incapable of intercepting the intruder,' he wrote in his diary with increasing frustration.[4]

Stalin's reluctance to provoke Hitler had been a dead hand on the border defences. The anti-aircraft artillery was strictly forbidden to open fire, and the Northern Fleet's reconnaissance units were not allowed to infringe Finnish or Norwegian air space.

'Despite many appeals, I got nowhere. We had to grit our teeth and sit with our arms crossed while the enemy became more and more provocative and mobile.'

Kuznetsov's order to go to *Readiness States 2* had come as a relief, but when the Chief of Leningrad Military District came on a visit the next day, he had nothing to add. Lieutenant General Markian Popov had, like Golovko, been born in a Cossack village on the Steppes between the Don and the Volga. Aged 38, he was a member of the generation of young Red Guards who filled the top slots in the Red Army. He was considered to be a very talented staff officer, and had been selected by Stalin to plan a rapid expansion of the northern defences.

'We made trips into the terrain and discussed the building of barracks, depots, air bases and fortifications,' wrote Golovko, 'but when it came to the question of the relationship between the Soviet Union and Fascist Germany Popov said not a word. Perhaps he really knew nothing more than we did.'

A destroyer had been made ready to take the general and his entourage on a tour of inspection along the coast of the Fisher Peninsula, but the trip was cancelled by a surprise telephone call from the Kremlin. Popov was ordered back to Leningrad, and he departed in haste.

'He stood us a farewell drink in the railway carriage. But no further news came from Moscow. Everything was as uncertain as before.'

Popov took only one initiative before he left Murmansk. In response to a request from General Frolov, the 52nd Rifle Division was given orders to move quickly from the inland mining towns of Kirovsk and Montsjegorsk to the coast. The defences behind the immediate frontier were to be strengthened, as discreetly as possible.

On the morning of Saturday 21 June the sun had broken through the clouds over the Kola Fjord. 'Outside our offices an idyllic peace prevailed. The weather was splendid. Anyone who had not been briefed on the tense international situation would have found it impossible to foresee that war was close.'

Golovko himself and his military advisers had spent the evening watching a comic operetta in Polarnoje's new culture house. An ensemble from the world-famous Stanislavskij and Nemirovitsj-Dantsjenko musical theatre in Moscow had come on tour with Offenbach's *La Périchole* and been received with thunderous applause. 'The theatre was crammed full. Many people took our presence as a sign that the tension was easing. I had really wished that were the case.'

When the officers made their way back to Northern Fleet HQ, the telex machines were still silent. 'I poured tea and sat chatting with my Chief of Staff Stefan Kutsjerov, Military Council member Aleksander Nikolajev and our Political Commissar, Nikolai Torik. Somehow or other we got to talking about our ages, and I realised that none of us was over 35.'

Almost unintentionally, Golovko had given a description of the situation in the armed forces. In the years before the outbreak of war, about 34,000 officers had been purged from the services. Many had been murdered or deported to the Gulag labour camps. The replacements were youngsters with military skills and a spirit of self-sacrifice, but without experience.

> We looked at each other. Our expressions revealed deep concern for the men under us. We understood instinctively that from now on we would bear a colossal responsibility every hour, in fact every minute, under extreme conditions.

The night was clear and bright over Polarnoje, and the fiord shimmered in the pastel colours of the early Arctic summer. Clouds were gathering in the west, but the midnight sun glistened on the snow-clad mountain-tops along the inlet. The officers were still chatting over their teacups when the phone started ringing. It was Admiral Kuznetsov calling to pass on Stalin's decision.

'How am I to relate to the Finns?' Golovko asked. There was every reason to fear that Finland would join in the German attack, but Stalin was still living in hope and would not authorise a preventive counter-attack. Kuznetsov had no firm advice to offer.

'What about the German planes that have flown over Polarnoje from Finnish airfields?'

'Open fire on all aircraft that come into our airspace.'

'Can I issue that as an order?'

'Yes you can.'

A few minutes after the phone conversation, the telex machines began to clatter. The time in Russia was 00.56 a.m. precisely, corresponding to 11.56 p.m. in Norway and Germany. The written orders were coming in.

'The telegram reported that 200 German divisions were amassed along the border, and that an attack could be expected within hours,' wrote Golovko. 'Orders were given for the fleet to be made fully ready. With us, that had in effect already happened. Our arms, men and means were insufficient, but in all essentials we were prepared.'

Three hours later, at 4.25 a.m., the reply was sent: *The Northern Fleet is battle-ready!*

The first bombs began falling over Polarnoje at about the same time, without doing significant damage. The war on the Northern Front had begun.

At Chequers, the Prime Minister's country residence outside London, Churchill was woken at 8 a.m. on Sunday morning by his secretary, John Colville, and given news of the attack.

The Prime Minister showed no sign of emotion, but said briefly: 'Tell the BBC I will broadcast at 9 tonight.'

Throughout the previous week a growing flood of decrypted Enigma messages had revealed the German invasion plans in ever more convincing detail.

'From every source at my disposal, including some most trustworthy, it looks as if a vast German onslaught on Russia is imminent,' he had telegraphed President Roosevelt in Washington on 15 June. 'Not only are the main German armies deployed from Finland to Romania, but the final arrivals of air and armoured forces are being completed. Should this new war break out, we shall of course give all encouragement and any help we can spare to the Russians following the principle that Hitler is the foe we have to beat.'

Churchill's telegram didn't imply that he thought the Red Army could win against the Wehrmacht. 'The PM says Russia assuredly will be defeated. He thinks that Hitler is counting on enlisting capitalists and right-wing sympathies in this country and the US. PM says he is wrong: he will go all out to help Russia,' wrote Colville, who teased him for going soft on the communists. 'He replied that he had only one single purpose – the destruction of Hitler – and his life would be much simplified by that. If Hitler invaded Hell he would at least make a favourable reference to the Devil!'[5]

When Churchill sat in front of the BBC's microphone that evening, he again appeared as a war leader of historic stature.

> At 4 o'clock this morning Hitler attacked and invaded Russia. All his usual formalities of perfidy were observed with scrupulous technique. ...
>
> Hitler is a monster of wickedness, insatiable in his lust for blood and plunder. Not content with having all Europe under his heel or else terrorised into various forms of abject submission, he must now carry his work of butchery and desolation among the vast multitudes of Russia and of Asia. ...
>
> We have but one aim and one single irrevocable purpose. We are resolved to destroy Hitler and every vestige of the Nazi regime. From this nothing will turn us. Nothing. We will never parley; we will never negotiate with Hitler or any of his gang. We shall fight him by land; we shall fight him by sea; we shall fight him in the air, until, with God's help, we have rid the earth of his shadow and liberated its people from his yoke.
>
> Any man or State who fights against Nazism will have our aid. ... It follows, therefore, that we shall give whatever help we can to Russia and to the Russian people. We shall appeal to all our friends and Allies in every part of the world to take the same course and pursue it as we shall, faithfully and steadfastly to the end.

Twenty-four hours later, the train of events set in motion by Churchill reached Lieutenant General Noel Mason-Macfarlane, who had recently been appointed commander of the 44th Infantry Division. 'I was halfway through a divisional conference at my headquarters at Canterbury at about 8 p.m. on Monday 23 June when an orderly came in to say that I was wanted on the telephone. I told him to say that I was busy and to take a message. He replied that the Chief of the Imperial General Staff, Sir John Dill, had telephoned and that it was urgent.'[6]

Dill summoned Mason-Mac to London immediately, and in a meeting at 1 a.m. he asked: 'Will you lead the new military mission we are sending to Moscow tomorrow?'

Mason-Mac was given a deadline of 10 a.m. to make a decision, and he spent the rest of the night in discussions with friends and family.

'The more I heard what they had to say, the more convinced was I that my background would let me in for an exceptionally difficult time. The only thing that influenced me in favour of the plan was the vital importance of the work. I got one hour's sleep and woke up to make up my mind that it was wartime, that the CIGS wanted me to take a job – and a good job – and that it was up to me to take it. Having settled in two minutes what I had been debating for six hours I breakfasted and went to the War Office, where Dill and our Ambassador to Moscow, Sir Stafford Cripps were clustered around the plan of a Catalina flying-boat, deciding how many they could fit in and who.'

At 9.15 a.m. on Wednesday 25 June, Mason-Mac and his team started their journey from London to Scotland, where the group of 11 people boarded two flying boats. To allow space for a large short-wave radio transmitter, personal baggage was restricted to one small bag of 12 kg per person. It was cold and cramped in the aircraft, which after a refuelling stop in Shetland took off at 1 a.m. the following night with roaring motors and set course for Archangel.

In the meantime the German invaders had continued their march into the Finnish Corridor. One branch with 2nd Mountain Division proceeded north along the Arctic Highway towards the administration centre at Parkkina and the port of Liinahamari. Another branch with 3rd Mountain Division continued east towards the principal village of Luostari, which had Petsamo's only airstrip.

'The rain was pouring down from low clouds,' wrote Hess. 'The streams and rivers were swollen from the melting snow lying in ditches and on the higher ridges.'[7]

The vanguard reached Parkkina and Luostari at 6.30 a.m. and immediately took up defensive positions around these settlements. Liinahamari was occupied an hour later. The Russian Consulate had been stormed earlier in the night and the 35 staff taken into custody. Immediately east of the abbey church, a pioneer battalion was already busy building a new 8-ton bridge over the rushing 80-metre-wide Petsamojoki River, using Finnish timber and enlisting the local engineering department and 800 Finnish workers.

'The operation is going according to plan,' Dietl reported to Falkenhorst at noon. 'According to reports from our observers in the field, all is quiet at the border. It is our distinct impression that the Russian troops on the other side are still unaware of our presence.'

This observation was correct. Border defence was the responsibility of the 43-year-old Major General Alexander Zhurba, commander of the Soviet 14th Rifle Division and another veteran of the Winter War. 'I knew him well,' wrote Golovko. 'He was an experienced soldier and a brave man.'[8]

The divisional headquarters was located in a hutted camp near the mouth of the Titovka River and had at immediate disposition the 95th Infantry Regiment, two detachments of the 241st Artillery Regiment, parts of the 149th Anti-tank

Battalion and the 35th Independent Reconnaissance Battalion, which together with support units probably amounted to around 6,000 men.

From April onwards, many of the soldiers and a big group of reservists had been working feverishly to extend the road network and create trenches and bunkers on the range of hills between the border and the Titovka Valley. But the bunkers were incomplete and the battalion in the front line had a force of only 577 officers and men to operate machine guns, mortars and six 7.6 cm field guns. Neither Zhurba nor any of his officers yet knew of the danger approaching from the west.

'We did realise from Sunday 22 June that we were likely to be involved in fighting,' said Zhurba's adjutant, Lieutenant Paul Abramoff, 'but we thought that the soldiers on the other side of the border were Finns. We knew nothing about the German advance into the Finnish Corridor, and certainly not that we were facing the Mountain Corps under their celebrated General Dietl who had conquered Narvik.'

The fear of a German attack from the sea – possibly supported by the British – was deep-rooted. The senior commander on the Fisher Peninsula, Colonel Daniel Krasilnikov, sent one of the battalions of the 135th Regiment on a forced march north, *away* from the isthmus known as the Fisher Neck. That further weakened the border defences.

Rumours of the outbreak of war spread rapidly, but the first full report the Russian people got of it was when Foreign Minister Vjatjeslav Molotov's voice came over Moscow radio at 12.15 p.m on Sunday:

> Today at 4 am, without any claims having been presented to the Soviet Union, without a declaration of war, German troops attacked our country … a perfidy unparalleled in the history of civilised nations.
>
> This war has been forced upon us, not by the German people, but by the clique of bloodthirsty Fascist rulers of Germany.
>
> It is not the first time our nation has had to deal with an attack of an arrogant foe. At the time of Napoleon's invasion of Russia our people's reply was war for the Fatherland, and Napoleon suffered defeat and met his doom. It will be same with Hitler, who in his arrogance has proclaimed a new crusade against our country. The Red Army and our entire nation will once again wage victorious war for the Fatherland, for our country, for honour and liberty. The whole country must now be joined and united as ever before. Our cause is just. The enemy shall be defeated. Victory will be ours.

Molotov's words were rousing, but among most listeners they ignited more sorrow and fear than enthusiasm.

'We heard the speech on the radio receiver, which was working very well,' wrote Lieutenant Alexander Gorjatsjik in his diary. The lieutenant was a company commander in the 135th Infantry Regiment, stationed in Novo Oserko, a fishing hamlet on the Fisher Peninsula. He was only 20 years old, newly married with a baby daughter.

> I had a wonderful dream last night and slept perfectly. It was warm and comfortable in the room, and in my fantasy things were just as I wanted them to be with my wife Vera for many, many years. Suddenly, I was wakened by loud knocking on the door. I sat up, startled. What did the staff want so early in the morning? It was sad news. Hitler had gone to war! Hell, I thought, so I probably won't live so long and happily with Vera after all. And I've only just started living! So far I've just been learning, in need and self-sacrifice. First at school, then at high school, then the Finnish campaign and now the very worst – a fight for the fatherland. No, this is really terrible news, which will bring death and destruction to millions of people. It's all dreadfully sad. I don't even know where Mum and Vera are at the moment.[9]

CHAPTER 4

The Bunker Line is Broken

The Petsamo Front, Saturday 28 to Monday 30 June 1941

The first shells landed in the hollows behind the Kuosmoaivi ridge shortly after 9 p.m on Saturday. The explosions threw up earth and stones around the tents and ramshackle huts which for the past couple of days had sheltered the main German attack force, called Gruppe Hengl after the officer hand-picked to destroy the bunker line, Lieutenant Colonel Georg Ritter von Hengl, commander of 137th Regiment of the 2nd Mountain Division.

'Since 9.05 p.m. the Red Artillery has been firing regularly at our base camp,' he wrote in a short note in his war diary.[1] The 43-year-old Bavarian was a cold and calculating officer who would later reach the top ranks of the Wehrmacht as a full general and chief of the army's ideological office,[2] and he had already set the troops moving. The 2. Battalion under Major Johann Vielwerth was given the most difficult mission and wheeled to the left across the ridge and into the scrubland on the other side of the border, with a clear view of the bunker line on Heights 189 and 255.[3]

'Horses, vehicles, backpacks and all unnecessary encumbrances were left behind,' wrote Captain Hans Rüf, who became the corps' chronicler after the war. 'The tension was almost unbearable. We were facing a new and unknown enemy, and everything seemed to be happening slowly, far too slowly for soldiers with their nerves at breaking point. *See you in Murmansk*, someone called to passing comrades, who cursed and replied *See you in the mass grave!* Overall though, morale was high and the mood boisterous. The mountain troops were eager to enter battle.'[4]

The 1,200 soldiers in Vielwerth's strengthened battalion were to attract the Russians' attention and carry out a frontal attack on the bunker line. In the meantime the 1. Battalion under Major Wolfgang Fuschlberger and the 3. Battalion under Major Mathias Kräutler were to cross the border 3 kilometres further south, make their way stealthily across the marshlands in the bottom of the valley and advance north on both sides of the River Titovka. As soon as the machine guns on Height 204 were eliminated, the base area behind the bunker line would be within easy reach. The whole new Russian border defence system would be surrounded and destroyed from two directions.

> The attack was to be initiated by an intense bombardment from 111th Mountain Artillery Regiment and a squadron of Stuka bombers, which had already softened the enemy perimeter that morning.

At 9.50 p.m. the artillery commander, Colonel Friedrich Kammel, was given permission to return fire against the Soviet batteries, and the estimated coordinates were sent to 36 bombers on standby at Høybuktmoen airfield. An hour later, Colonel General Nicolaus von Falkenhorst and General Eduard Dietl arrived at a forward observation post at the Kuosmaivi ridge which was still under intermittent fire. The two senior commanders wanted a ringside view of the attack on the bunker line but did not have much success at first. 'Every time the Soviet salvos came uncomfortably close, they had to throw themselves to the ground.'

The sun had broken through the clouds the previous day, after several days of ice-cold rain. By mid-day the temperature had risen above 20°C. This rapid change had a dramatic effect. 'The mist suddenly came whirling in from the coast, and the ridges and hollows became shrouded in white. The whole attack zone was covered by an impenetrable veil.'

When the code word *Narvik* was whispered from soldier to soldier at midnight, the fog was so thick that the troops could no longer see one another. Kammel's artillery was shooting blindly, and the Stuka bombers had to turn back to base.

However, postponing the attack was not an option. At precisely 3 am the nerve-shattering signals penetrated the whiteness. The mountain troops rose among the barren cliffs and stormed shouting towards the concrete bunkers which could just be made out on the ridges to the north-east.

Three days earlier, the flying boats carrying the British military mission had passed at low level over the sea a mere 100 kilometres to the north of the Petsamo attack zone.

'The Catalinas were cramped and noisy,' Michael Fullover wrote in his account of the non-stop 3,000-km flight of about 20 hours. 'There were no

38 • MIRACLE AT THE LITZA

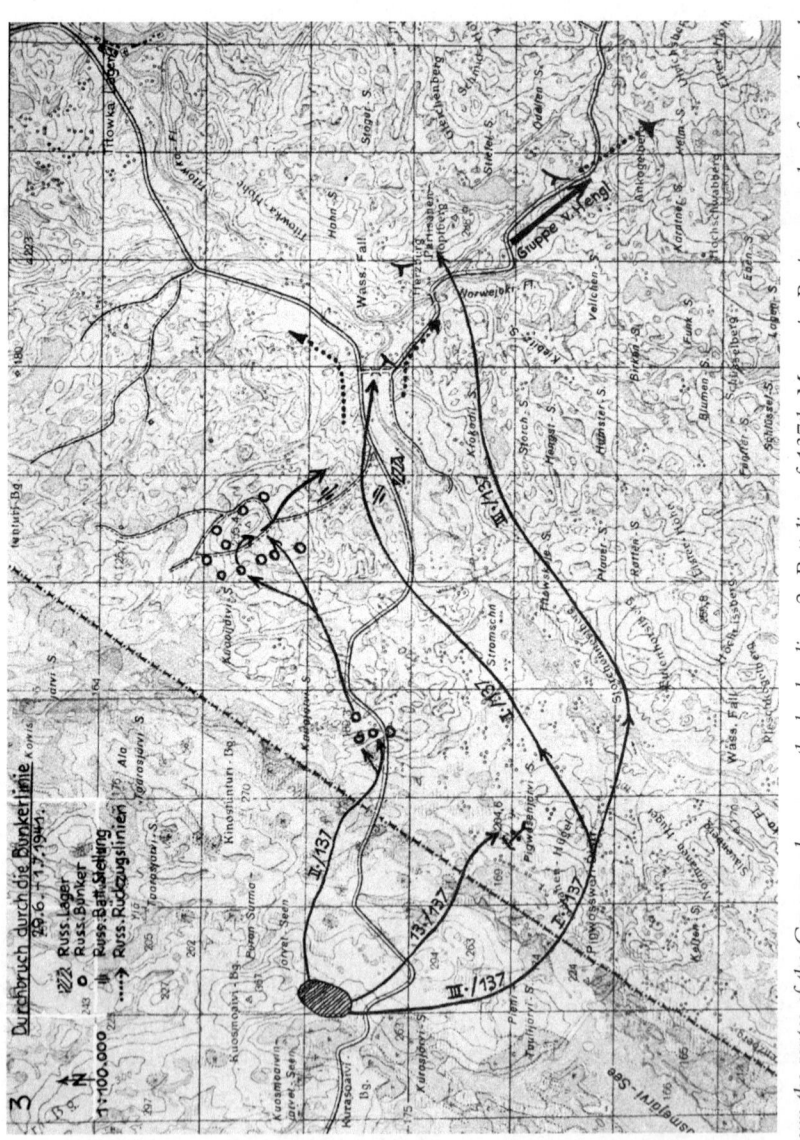

The map shows the routes of the German advance on the bunker line. 2. Battalion of 137th Mountain Regiment made a frontal attack, while 13th Company eliminated a machine-gun post on Height 204 and 1. and 3. Battalions carried out a pincer movement from the south to attack the defenders in the rear. (Rüf: *Gebirgsjäger vor Murmansk*)

amenities on board, and the RAF rations consisted of biscuits, coffee and soup. It became icy cold as soon as we reached the Polar regions.'

Physical and mental hardships were not a new experience for 51-year-old Lieutenant General Noel Mason-Macfarlane. As an officer in the service of the British Empire he had spent large parts of his adult life under primitive conditions in foreign fields – from the trenches in Flanders through the deserts of Iraq to the high plains of India. He was a robust man who had been among the army's leading sportsmen in polo, cricket and golf. But he was also accident-prone and had sustained a long list of injuries from reckless behaviour behind the steering wheel and on horseback. His spine had been injured. A fall during the bizarre British sport of pig-sticking had rendered him sexually impotent, which could partly explain his short temper and eccentric behaviour, especially towards senior officers who came under his mercilessly critical gaze. He loved amateur theatre and was a feared writer of satirical verse, which did not increase his popularity among those who became targets for his scorn. Others lauded him as an exceptionally talented officer, and during four years in Europe as military attaché in Vienna, Budapest and Berne he had become distinguished as a keen and clear-eyed observer of politics, military trends and the rise of Hitler.

'He combines a first-class brain with a remarkable flair for intelligence work,' said a War Office summary. 'He is full of mental and physical energy and with great initiative. He should go far.'[5]

It was precisely Mason-Mac's many years of contact with the secret services as a military attaché and as an intelligence officer during the 1940 campaign in France which made him feel unsuited for this new task. Stalin would probably consider a person with his background to be a spy rather than a real working partner.

'Mason-Mac was very pessimistic and didn't want to go,' wrote Hugh Dalton, Minister of Economic Warfare, in his diary. 'He doesn't like the Russians. He went out thinking that the Russians could not last three weeks.'

Mason-Mac's negative view of the Red Army was shared by Churchill, the Chief of the Imperial General Staff, Sir John Dill and most other members of the British elite.

'Your primary task is the *prolongation* of Russian resistance as this is obviously of very great importance to British interests,' said the instructions, which he had plenty of time to contemplate during the long and uncomfortable flight. 'You are not to enter into any political commitments nor make any promises of aid by men or materials.'

With brilliant political acumen, Churchill had in his radio speech promised the Soviet Union all possible forms of help, but that was more a symbolic gesture than an offer of immediate military assistance. So long as all the analyses indicated that Stalin's regime would fall apart like a house of cards under the pressure of the Wehrmacht, nobody was interested in initiating a large-scale aid programme. Any weapons sent to the East would be captured and turned against Great Britain as soon as the Soviets had been defeated. That was a risk few wanted to take – for the time being.

As history professor Gabriel Gorodetsky wrote in his essay *An Alliance of Sorts*: 'A firm collaboration was viewed only as an unlikely remote possibility, while the instructions concentrated on the more likely event of a serious defeat. The mission was stripped of any authority to embark on negotiations concerning concrete assistance and strategy.'[6]

General Dill was among the most pessimistic and had advised Mason-Mac to encourage a guerrilla war as soon as the Soviet Union fell apart. If resistance seemed hopeless, he should try to make his way over the wild Pamir Mountains to India. 'But this,' Dill admitted wryly, 'would be a very long walk, I'm afraid.'

The flying boat landed in the mouth of the great River Dvina at Archangel at 7 p.m. on Thursday 26 June and was met by a Soviet military delegation. 'The flight was uneventful and, until Cape Kanin was reached no land was seen except for a short glimpse of the Lofoten Islands,' wrote Mason-Mac in his report. 'The excellence of the navigation was outstanding, a landfall being made within five minutes of the predicted time. In the later stages of the flight the weather was cold and there were head winds, low cloud and some rain.'

Mason-Mac was tired and stiff after almost twenty-four hours perched on a hard aeroplane seat. During the arrival dinner on the river-boat *The Red Star*, which lay at anchor in the Dvina, he kept obediently to his instructions.

'Great Britain and Russia are now fighting side by side against a common enemy,' he said to the Red Army officers. 'The arrival of our mission is proof of the desire of the three British services to bring every possible assistance to the fighting forces of the Soviet Union.'

Inspiring words, indeed. Mason-Mac and his officers now had to somehow match that with substance, whilst sticking to their instructions.

In the village of Titovka about 20 km north of the bunker line, Major General Alexander Zhurba had been working day and night to prepare the border defences since the outbreak of war a week earlier. He maintained close contact with his superior, General Valerian Frolov, commander of the 14th Army, who suddenly found himself in an awkward situation.

'The movement of enemy troops into the immediate border area had been discovered very late,' wrote Major General Georgij A. Vesjeserskij in his memoirs. 'Frolov immediately asked Leningrad Military District for permission to move our own formations closer to the border, but he was met with refusal. He was forbidden to take measures which might make the Finns suspicious and provoke them into war.'[7]

Rear Admiral Arsenij Golovko said the same thing slightly differently:

> The order went out that no hostilities were to be started against Finland. It seems clear that Stalin kept hoping to the very last that Finland would stay out of the war. But wasn't it a little too late? We knew that they had completed mobilisation and could join the Wehrmacht's attack at any time.

Completely fresh intelligence reports gave Frolov insight into the danger facing him.

On the night of Saturday 21/Sunday 22 June, Otto Larsen had met Alfred Mathisen on board *Storskjær* out at sea half-way between Norway and the fishing grounds to the northeast of the Fisher Peninsula.

'He had disturbing news: the Germans intended to attack the Soviet Union the very next day. We rapidly said goodbye and went our separate ways.'[8]

The Larsen brothers pushed the old cutter's engine to its limits and reached Murmansk about noon on Sunday. 'Everything was in confusion. Nobody knew anything definite about anything. The only thing that was certain was that Kiev had been bombed and the country was at war. I went up to the NKVD secret service office and wrote up the latest report. We were given no new orders.'

Larsen's report was placed before Frolov at 10 a.m. on Monday 23 June. 'NKVD's agent reports that the force in Varanger now exceeds 80,000 men. Troops are being moved through Northern Finland to Murmansk.'

His NKVD controller shared Stalin's distrustful nature and wrote on the report: *Needs to be checked!*

If an attack really did materialise, the Finns and Germans would have an overwhelming advantage in numbers. In a desperate last-minute effort to save the situation, Frolov set in motion a series of new measures to prop up the neglected front. The crack 52nd Rifle Division was spread out along the single passable dirt road between Murmansk and the River Litza and was ordered to push on. Thousands of volunteers and recruits from the general call-up in north-west Russia were processed and assigned to new battalions being formed. Civilian and military vessels from the Northern Fleet shuttled between Murmansk and the single quay in Titovka, carrying fresh troops one way and evacuating women, children and non-combatants the other.

From Sunday 22 June the air force had permission to operate against targets in Norway. The Kirkenes area was bombed, but the weather was atrocious and the results were insignificant.

'Soviet bombers have been observed in small numbers over Kirkenes for the first time,' said an entry in the German Mountain Corps diary for Tuesday 24 June. 'Bombs dropped near the air base failed to hit their target. One aircraft was shot down by our fighters.'

The area of operations was extended the next day. Stalin gave up hope of Finnish neutrality and ordered a preventive attack against a number of air bases, from Helsinki in the south to Luostari in the north. The Finns responded by declaring war and starting preparations for the main attack on Karelia in the south.

Zhurba himself and his adjutant, Lieutenant Paul Abramoff, were constantly moving among the various units, to build up morale and encourage the soldiers in the bunkers and trenches who watched the mist come rolling in from the sea around midnight on Saturday 28 June.

The major-general was a family man and a sound character. Before finishing his work that evening, he took time to write a letter to his daughter Ludmilla, whose eighteenth birthday was the next day.

> 28th June 41. Greetings and best wishes to Leningrad! I'm in the best of health. Life is good, but remember that I – the old warrior – must also sleep a little. Do write to me again! The situation is altogether not bad. So don't worry. Look after yourself! A. Zhurba.[9]

Just a few hours later the horn signals were heard through the sea of mist. Dietl's corps was starting its attack.

Vielwerth's mountain troops reached the bunker line first, but it was the pioneers in Major Walter Drück's battalion who made the breakthrough, using flame-throwers. The mist and the concentrated fire from well-camouflaged machine guns made the advance over a mainly open landscape very hazardous, and it was almost 9 a.m. before the storming of the defensive positions could begin.

'The Russians fought with desperate courage and defended each and every position with bitter determination,' wrote Hans Rüf. 'Even the knowledge that they were being surrounded didn't seem to crack their morale.'[10]

In the absence of the Stuka bombers, Kammel's 88 mm guns were brought forward to the edge of Kuosmoaivi. But the range was 3,000 metres, and the swirling fog made it almost impossible to identify and hit the firing slits. Instead, the battle turned into bloody close-quarter fighting between the defenders and the German infantrymen who dashed from crater to crater under cover of smoke grenades. The soldiers in the bunkers were held down with the help of machine guns and hand grenades until the flamethrowers were close enough to have a deadly effect.

'From the start of the campaign, the Russian soldiers of whatever unit or race have fought with great courage and defended themselves to the utmost,' wrote operations officer Eduard Zorn in a report on 1 July 1941. The 39-year-old major from Munich was one of the Mountain Corps' fanatical Nazis and wore the Nazi party's exclusive *Blutorden* (Blood Order)[11] as a sign of lifelong loyalty to the Führer. Later, as a divisional commander, he would be awarded the Knight's Cross of the Iron Cross with Oak Leaf for outstanding bravery, and he undoubtedly knew what he was talking about. 'The Red Guards had to be either killed or bodily dragged out before the bunkers were given up. They even continued fighting after the flamethrowers were used.'[12]

Zorn found a clear difference between the reservists who had been hurriedly brought to the front since 22 June and the soldiers who had been serving since the summer of 1940. The raw recruits had a tendency to take to flight as soon as they came under fire. The seasoned soldiers fought on to the bitter end. Even long after the battle was over, the German soldiers who were sorting through the ruins found themselves being shot at. One Russian, his face burnt from a flamethrower, hid himself among his dead comrades for three days before he allowed himself to be disarmed.

'The snipers often lay in well-camouflaged positions until our men had passed, and then opened fire from behind. They were experts in utilising the terrain and very difficult to flush out.'

The thirteen bunkers in the front line each had space for six to eight men with two heavy machine guns, rifles and hand grenades. The rest of the battalion consisted of about 450 men hidden in trenches and caverns in the ravines behind and on both sides of the bunker line. Despite the sparse numbers of the Russians, it took Vielwerth's battalion more than ten hours to clear and secure the position.

'At 1900 on Sunday 29 June Height 235 was finally captured,' wrote Captain Vilhelm Hess in the history of the 137th Mountain Regiment. 'The bunker line had fallen. The border crossing and the western side of the Titovka were in German hands.'

About 300 bodies were found among the ruins, many riddled with bullets and burnt beyond recognition. Between 50 and 60 prisoners were led away. There were no officers among the prisoners, only private soldiers.

'The survivors were a really revolting sight,' wrote the corps' intelligence officer, Major Werner Müller, when the prisoners arrived at the POW camp in Parkkina two days later. Müller's view was darkened by racial hatred, and he showed no compassion. The guards had not failed to obey their orders to handle the prisoners as deceitful and malignant *Untermenschen*.

'They are tough,' wrote the 38-year-old from Innsbruck in a cynical commentary. 'Some of them were wounded and had suffered significant blood loss, but they survived a three-day march of 35 km without food or water.'[13]

The decisive breakthrough against the Titovka bridge was achieved by the southern arm of the regiment's pincer movement. As soon as the machine-gun positions on Height 204 had fallen, the 1. and 3. Battalions under Ritter von Hengl's personal leadership forced their way into the marshy Titovka Valley.

'The weak pockets of resistance were swiftly crushed,' wrote Rüf in his chronicle. 'The wild terrain with stone scree, rushing streams and almost impenetrable scrub of dwarf birch and juniper presented a bigger problem than the enemy.'

But the athletic von Hengl was one of the Wehrmacht's best skiers and mountaineers and had been head of the famous Mountain School in the Bavarian Alps in the 1930s. He led the 1. Battalion north along the west bank of the River Titovka at a murderous pace and reached the cliffs behind the bunker line by 9 a.m. on Sunday. The sun was already warming up the Arctic landscape and dispersing the mist. A stunning scene lay before them. On a plain by the river the Russians had built a temporary camp with tents and barracks for more than 1,000 men, plus storage sheds and stalls for hundreds of horses. 'The camp was in full activity. Soldiers were running around in confusion. Lorries stood in a line along the escape route to the north.'

A high tower with a red star stood above the camp gate. The mountain troops' intermediate objective could be seen only 2 km north-east of the tower: the bridge over the Titovka, connecting with the road which led to their main objective, Murmansk.

The mountain troops stormed down the slope with wild yells. Within a few minutes, the camp was in German hands. The booty was rich: depots of food and ammunition, lorries, armoured vehicles, field guns and about a hundred horses which were now running around freely.

Vodka, black bread and cans of ham from Lithuania were among the mountain soldiers' favourite foods, but von Hengl immediately forbade plundering. The Soviet defences were about to fall apart, the weather was good for flying and explosions boomed like rolling thunder along the bunker line in the west.

By 10.15 a.m. Von Hengl had reported over the radio to Dietl: '1. Battalion proceeding from the camp towards the bridge over the Titovka.'

The first principle of *blitzkrieg* was to maintain the rapid pace, but the mountain troops were beginning to tire. The closer the battalion came towards the bridge, the stiffer the resistance became. The intact companies of 95th Regiment dominated the approaches with machine-gun fire. The roaming 35th Reconnaissance Unit still had some armoured vehicles, and field guns and heavy howitzers from 214th Artillery Regiment were positioned on the ridges east of the river.

'Von Hengl quickly understood that the outcome of a frontal attack on the bridge would not be a foregone conclusion,' relates the regimental history. 'So he ordered 3. Battalion to cross the Titovka and fall on the defenders from behind.'

Drück's pioneers came to the rescue again when they succeeded in setting up a pontoon bridge over the river that afternoon. By 7.30 pm the leading platoon was able to cross to the east side. All the animals had to swim, and heavy gear had to be taken over in rubber boats.

'Group after group followed,' wrote the battalion commander, Major Mathias Kräutler. 'Our objective was the range of hills due east of the bridge, about 10–12 kilometres away. But the terrain consisted of marshes and scrub, and everything had to be carried. The advance was heavy going and exhausting.'

In the meantime Major General Alexander Zhurba's life had become a nightmare. When he wrote the letter to his daughter on Saturday night, he had been calm and optimistic. The anticipated attack had come a few hours later – with much greater force than he had expected. Moreover, German saboteurs had penetrated deep into the rear and systematically cut the telephone lines. Connection between HQ and the many scattered units was lost. The reports which did come in were few and contradictory.

About 11 a.m. on Sunday morning Zhurba left his headquarters in Titovka in a black Emka staff car with Lieutenant Abramoff, the division's artillery commander Captain Gleb Krylov and the operations officer, Major Pietr Popov.

'He arrived at the bridge at 1 o'clock and gave the regimental commander, Sergei Chernov, orders to take command of the right flank. He wanted to lead the fight on the left flank himself, as that was where the most serious threat was developing,' say the Russian sources.[14]

However, away in Kirkenes the skies had cleared and the Luftwaffe's Stuka bombers had again taken to the air. Wave after wave of planes dived with wailing sirens on the positions around the bridge, spreading death and terror among the defenders. The first Russian reinforcements had reached Titovka on the Saturday evening, when two battalions of the well-trained and experienced 112th Regiment under Major Fedor Korotkov had force marched through the mountain pass between Litza and Titovka and dug in east of the bridge.

But the Stuka bombers continued to dominate the airspace and create hell for the defenders.

'The road to the east twisted along a steep, narrow gorge,' wrote Hans Rüf. 'The Luftwaffe had completed gruesome work here. On the left there was a sheer mountainside, on the right a foaming stream. The bombs had blasted big blocks out of the mountain, leaving craters a metre deep. Every moving thing was smashed and blown down into the torrent: guns, vehicles and humans. Tattered horse carcasses, mutilated corpses and ruined equipment piled up in the water as frightful evidence of the brutality of war.'[15]

In the headquarters of the 14th Army there was increasing desperation. The Chief of Staff, Colonel Lev Skvirsky, tried repeatedly throughout the day to get in touch with Zhurba. 'Where's Zhurba? Tell the divisional commander to report immediately!'

But the calls for help got no answer. The major general had disappeared.

The final German attack went in about 3 a.m. on Monday 30 June. An armoured company under Captain Alfred von Burstin had managed using tractors and horses to tow a few light armoured vehicles from Kuosoamavi to the gravel road along the river. At the same time, parts of Kräutler's battalion had reached the valley of death and were threatening to block the retreat for the Soviet forces holding the bridge.

'Korotkov had only two options: either to continue the fight and lose the whole battalion, or to retreat,' wrote General Khariton Khudalov in his book

*Am Rande des Kontinents.*¹⁶ An intense half-hour of bitter radio negotiations followed before approval was given by the 14th Army HQ in Murmansk. Shortly before 4 a.m. the defenders abandoned their positions – some in good order and others in full panic.

> One of the armoured vehicles was sent towards the bridge. To the crew's amazement, they were not shot at. A pioneer jumped out and ran forward to check the bridge supports. He returned equally amazed, to report that there were no explosive charges to be seen. The bridge had not been mined.¹⁷

1. Battalion now advanced across the river without opposition and soon after made contact with von Hengl and his 3. Battalion, who had secured the dominating Height 228.

> From early in the morning all was calm in Gruppe Hengl's camp. Only occasional rifle shots and short salvos from automatic weapons could be heard. The corps' first objective had been reached.

At about the same time as the mountain troops were crossing the Titovka, Lieutenant-General Noel Mason-Macfarlane and the rest of the British Military Mission were climbing the stairs to Foreign Minister Vjateslav Molotov's office in the Kremlin. Stalin's inner circle were night owls, and this squat and stubborn party bureaucrat was no exception. He had called them without warning to a meeting at 3 a.m., and Mason-Mac had no option other than to come. So far, the military mission's stay in Moscow had been an almost complete fiasco, characterised by fear and underlying suspicion on both sides. NKVD agents were following the members day and night. Oral and written questions were seldom or never answered. No conversation took place beyond the purely formal.

'From the earliest days of our arrival in Moscow it became clear that the Russians were prepared to cooperate only when they thought that cooperation would be of direct assistance to themselves,' wrote Mason-MacFarlane. 'They never ceased to disparage the efforts which we were making.'¹⁸

One of his Soviet counterparts in the negotiations, Admiral Nikolai Kharlamov, gave a different explanation for the icy reception.

'They never had a free hand in what they did,' he wrote in his memoirs. 'McFarlane adhered to the position generally accepted by the British government. It stemmed from the British ruling circle's disbelief in the Soviet Union's ability to withstand the onslaught of the German military machine. They thought that the Russians would most probably be defeated, so it would be wise – for the time being – to refrain from any decisive steps towards providing them with help.'[19]

The mission had now been called hastily to the Kremlin, and Mason-Mac was anxious. Developments since the outbreak of war had been catastrophic. There were rumours that the city of Minsk in Belorussia had fallen, which would mean that the German tanks had reached halfway to Moscow. If a real collaboration were to happen, it would need to start soon.

Molotov's opening words were disturbing: 'The situation along the whole Russian Front is extremely serious. It is therefore very important that Great Britain takes immediate action to ease the pressure on the Red Army.'

The question of *where* the priority action should take place surprised both Mason-Mac and the other members of his retinue. 'He emphasised especially the Russian desire for naval and air action in the Petsamo area where some three or four German divisions have been located.'

The lieutenant general had no authority to reply. Instead, he made a new attempt to get access to real information about the military situation, as he had been instructed by Chief of Staff Dill.

> I pressed urgently for more new information regarding the situation on the battle front and pointed out that His Majesty's government would be far more likely to come to a rapid decision if fully informed than if confronted with vague statements. I also pointed out that it would be impossible to come to a decision regarding Petsamo without full local information and asked for joint naval and air discussions on the subject.

Molotov gave a blunt reply: 'Until His Majesty's government undertakes to carry out an operation in Petsamo, no details in connection with such an action can be jointly discussed.'

Mason-Mac didn't give up: 'I am acting in the best interests of Russia.'

'We're wasting time,' replied Molotov. 'If you are not willing to put our request to the government, we shall take up the matter through other channels in London.'

The discussion continued for half an hour without Molotov allowing himself to be persuaded. 'To avoid deadlock I undertook to communicate [his request] to the Chiefs of Staff,' wrote Mason-Mac.

In the telegram, which reached London at 2.30 p.m. on Monday 30 June, he added: 'I think the Russians are genuinely anxious about the Murmansk area. I think they genuinely feel that we now have an opportunity to take advantage of the relative German weakness in the West, in the common cause.

They are determined to find out what we intend to do about this in the immediate future.'

Nobody had heard from division commander Alexander Zhurba since Sunday morning. But the major general was not dead. He had gathered a group of 30–40 stragglers and set up a defensive position on a height on the tundra between the Titovka and Litza rivers.

On Monday the position was over-run by superior German forces. Under intense fire, Zhurba and the survivors retreated north, hoping to escape over the isthmus to the Fisher Peninsula and join up with the 135th Regiment. The major general didn't make it. His 21-year-old adjutant, Lieutenant Paul Abramoff, was taken prisoner and told his German interrogators what had happened:

> Major General Zhurba was killed by a rifle-shot. The army's operations officer, Major Popov, tried to escape by swimming over a mountain river but was hit by a bullet and went under. The artillery chief, Captain Krylov, killed himself to avoid being taken prisoner.[20]

To Dietl and the German mountain troops, the initial attack appeared to be a total victory. The border defences were defeated. The Russian 14th Division had been torn apart and driven to flight, leaving much of its equipment behind.

A victory communiqué stated: 'Austrian mountain troops have in an overwhelming advance broken through the Soviet bunker line along the border east of Petsamo and occupied an important bridge. Among the participants in this campaign, Lieutenant-Colonel Ritter von Hengl, Major Walter Drück and Major Johann Vielwerth have particularly distinguished themselves.'

Dietl was careful not to say too much. Since the breakthrough, Gruppe Hengl had rushed on towards the next river, the Litza. They had been met by a nasty surprise: the only existing dirt road ended 6 kilometres east of the bridge. The mountain pass was barren and wild, and the armoured vehicles had come to a standstill with broken tracks. Some units had been on the move for 48 hours without rest, and stocks of ammunition and food were dangerously low. At the same time, a reconnaissance plane had observed a 15-km-long column of soldiers and vehicles on the far side of the River Litza. A completely new and unknown division was approaching from the east.

Everything indicated that a Soviet counter-attack was developing. Gruppe Hengl was ordered to halt the advance and take up defensive positions.

Kirkenes was the main arrival port for supplies from Germany, Denmark and Southern Norway for the Mountain Corps, which together with its support units had a strength of 60,000–70,000 men. *(Rüf: Gebirgsjäger vor Murmansk)*

The famous signpost in Kirkenes with the distances to the soldiers' home towns in Bavaria and Austria. *(Rüf: Gebirgsjäger vor Murmansk)*

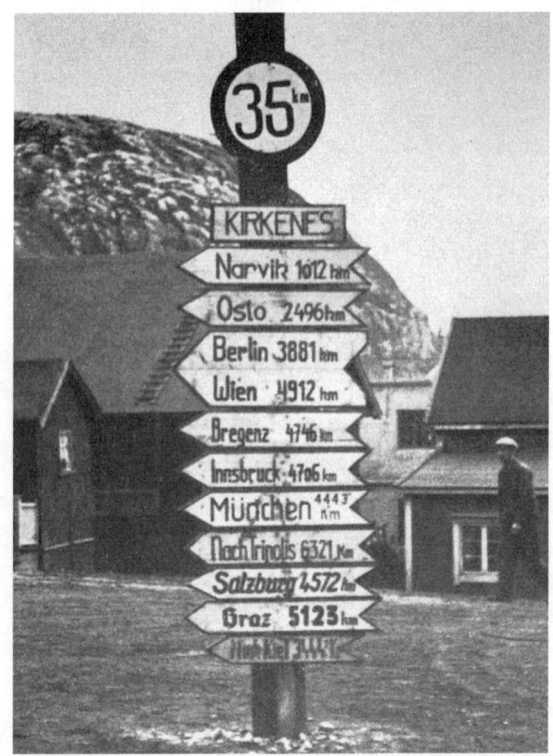

Soldiers resting in mist and rain at the edge of the road in Boris Gleb in the evening of Saturday 21 June, waiting for the order to march into the Finnish Corridor. *(Dag Skogheim's Collection, Arkiv i Nordland)*

The army commander, Colonel General Nicolaus von Falkenhorst (on left), and the corps commander, General Eduard Dietl (with walking pole, on right), met on the mountain ridge at Kuosmoaivi on the evening of Saturday 28 June 1941 ready to observe the launch of the attack. Despite appearances, the two generals were bitter rivals. *(Rüf: Gebirgsjäger vor Murmansk)*

Mountain Corps Norway was considered to be a nest of Nazis, and Dietl had gathered many of the Führer's supporters in his command. Both his chief of staff, Colonel Karl von Le Suire (bareheaded), and his operations officer, Major Eduard Zorn (front right) had been awarded the Nazi party's *Blutorden* ('Blood Order') for their support during Hitler's ill-fated Beer Hall Putsch in 1923. *(Rüf: Gebirgsjäger vor Murmansk)*

Senior German commanders on a tour of inspection in Finnmark in the spring of 1941. From the left: Lieutenant General Valentin Feurstein (who was transferred from his position in charge of the 2nd Mountain Division to take command in Southern Norway); Major General Hans Kreysing (head of the 3rd Mountain Division); SS-Obersturmbannführer Ernst Deutsch (head of 9th SS Regiment), Colonel General Nicolaus von Falkenhorst and SS-Sturmbannführer Paul Herms (commander of the SS battalion in Kirkenes). *(Arkiv Rune Rautio)*

Vehicles were useless in the terrain and had to be towed by men across the heather-covered hills. *(Rüf: Gebirgsjäger vor Murmansk)*

Thousands of reservists in their fifties and 17-year-olds in the semi-military Reich Labour Service were sent north from Germany to build a new road between Petsamo and Litza. *(Dag Skogheim's Collection, Arkiv i Nordland)*

The main road from Parkkina to the front was in terrible condition. Most of the daily requirement of 300 tonnes of ammunition and supplies had to be carried east with the help of horses and mules. Infantrymen and bearers had to walk. *(Rüf: Gebirgsjäger vor Murmansk)*

Beyond the road's end, 6 km east of the Titovka river, motorised transport faced great difficulty crossing the stony plateau known to the Germans as 'Herzberg'. A unit armed with 3.7 cm anti-tank guns is waiting to proceed. *(Arkiv Rune Rautio)*

A Panzerkampfwagen II (light tank) unit under Captain von Burstin took part in the fighting in the Titovka Valley, but got stuck on the mountain crossing to the Litza. *(Arkiv Rune Rautio)*

There was still snow on the valley floors when the 2nd Mountain Division assembled behind Kuosmoaivi Ridge on Saturday 28 June 1941 to launch their attack on the bunker line at the border. *(Rüf: Gebirgsjäger vor Murmansk)*

Each division on the Litza Front was allocated about 3,000 horses, but hundreds of them were killed by enemy fire or perished in the bogs on the way to the front. *(Rüf: Gebirgsjäger vor Murmansk)*

The Germans carried rubber boats for crossing rivers, but had to abandon the biggest ones on the way. Soldiers from the 3rd Mountain Division are crossing the Titovka river with a light anti-tank gun. The heavy artillery was generally left on the west bank. *(Rüf: Gebirgsjäger vor Murmansk)*

Rear Admiral Arsenij Golovko (centre) commanded the Northern Fleet. Chief of Staff Kutsjerov is on the left of the picture and Political Commissar Nikolajev is on the right.

General Valentin Frolov was a Bolshevik from the Russian Revolution and led the defence of Murmansk as commander of the 14th Army.

Fedor Korotkov was head of the 112th Regiment, which fought at the Litza throughout the whole summer of 1941. He finished the war as a general and as Allied Supreme Commander in Denmark, but was arrested during the Second Terror in 1948 and not released until 1955.

The mountain lakes were covered in melting ice until the beginning of July 1941. *(Dag Skogheim's Collection, Arkiv i Nordland)*

Major Johann Vielwerth played an important role as commander of the 2. Battalion of the 137th Mountain Regiment, until he fell at the Litza in early September. *(Dag Skogheim's Collection, Arkiv i Nordland)*

Major Mathias Kräutler, a battalion commander in the 137th Mountain Regiment, at his command post on the Herzberg plateau. *(Rüf: Gebirgsjäger vor Murmansk)*

The mountain troops have surrounded one of the 13 bunkers at the frontier and are now using flamethrowers. Some reports claim that the defenders in the last bunker held out for four whole days before surrendering. *(Dag Skogheim's Collection, Arkiv i Nordland)*

Left: The Germans dominated the airspace over the Titovka Valley on Sunday 29 June, and their Stuka bombers inflicted severe losses on the Russians. The 14th Division disintegrated and abandoned most of their equipment when they fled over the hill to the Litza Valley. *(Top: Dag Skogheim's Collection, Arkiv i Nordland; bottom: Arkiv Rune Rautio)*

Below: About 80 Russians, many of them wounded, were taken prisoner in the first two days. They were forced to march to the prison camp in Parkkina. Many of them were reservists who had only recently come to the front. A further 400–500 men from the 14th Division were killed. Later in the war, prisoners and the wounded were shot without mercy. *(Dag Skogheim's Collection, Arkiv i Nordland)*

Gruppe von Hengl reached the Herzberg mountain plateau on Thursday 1 July. From the top they could see the Litza Valley and the barren landscape they had to cross on the way to Murmansk. However, the Red Guards from the Russian 52nd Rifle Division were busy taking up positions down in the valley. Hengl (with map, facing the camera) established a defensive position to await reinforcements. *(Rüf: Gebirgsjäger vor Murmansk)*

Ritter von Hengl was awarded the Knight's Cross of the Iron Cross in August 1941 for the capture of the bunker line. In the picture he is flanked on his left by Dietl and on his right by the leader of the 2nd Mountain Division, Major-General Ernst Schlemmer. Later, as a full general and top Nazi, he held a key post as head of the army's main ideological office. *(Rüf: Gebirgsjäger vor Murmansk)*

The Soviet Ambassador to London, Ivan Maisky (on left), with the leaders of the first military mission, General Filipp Golikov and Admiral Nicolai Kharlamov. The NKVD representative is standing slightly behind on the left of the photograph. *(Getty Images)*

Lieutenant General Noel Mason-MacFarlane (standing, centre) led the British Military Mission to Moscow in the summer of 1941. His supporter, Ambassador Stafford Cripps, is sitting on the sofa with the dog on his lap. *(Margaret Bourke-White/The LIFE picture Collection/Getty Images)*

A German platoon marching through the snow in a valley between bare hill ridges on their way towards the Fisher Neck, the narrow isthmus connecting the Fisher Peninsula to the mainland. *(Rüf: Gebirgsjäger vor Murmansk)*

Dietl visiting Colonel Albin Nake (on right, with map) during the battle of Fisher Neck in early July 1941. Shortly afterwards, Nake was replaced by Colonel Georg Hofmeister and sent home. *(Rüf: Gebirgsjäger vor Murmansk)*

Soviet infantry attacking an unidentified height on Fisher Neck. The 135th Regiment carried on a heroic struggle against the invading German army and posed a permanent threat to its northern flank. The peninsula was never taken. *(Arkiv Rune Rautio)*

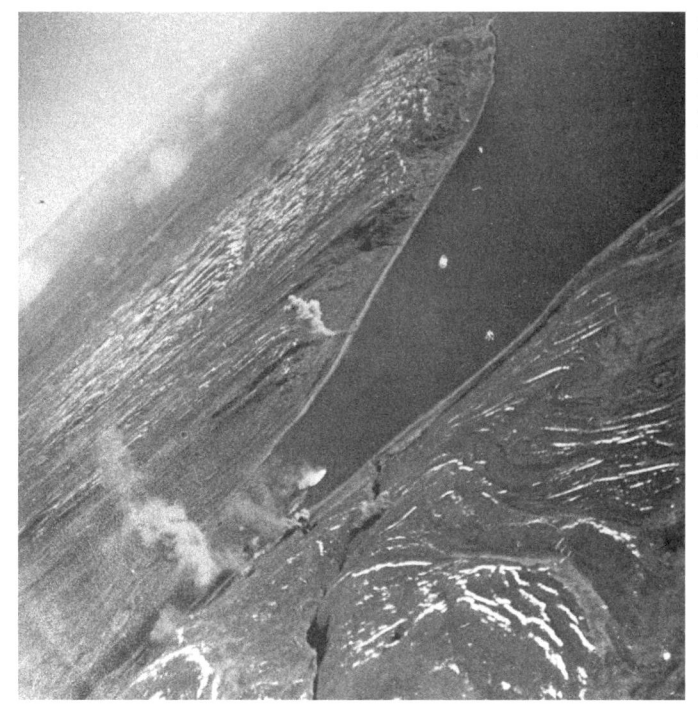

Stuka bombers attacking targets on the Fisher Peninsula, probably at the head of Motovskij Fjord, east of the Fisher Neck. *(Arkiv Rune Rautio)*

About 10 a.m. on Sunday 6 July the mountain troops of the 138th Regiment crossed the River Litza about 5 km south of the bridge, without being fired on. But on their way towards the hills seen in the distance they met increasing resistance, and the hollow between the Brandl and Pranckh heights came to be known as 'The Devil's Gorge.' *(Rüf: Gebirgsjäger vor Murmansk)*

An improvised bridge built over the Litza in the trackless area in the south. *(Rüf: Gebirgsjäger vor Murmansk)*

Left: In the absence of heavier weapons, machine guns were among the most effective weapons on both sides of the front line in the Litza Valley. The standard MG 34 machine gun was deadly effective. *(Rüf: Gebirgsjäger vor Murmansk)*

Below: Alongside the machine guns, mortars were the most feared weapons on the Litza front line. *(Rüf: Gebirgsjäger vor Murmansk)*

CHAPTER 5

The Battle of Fisher Neck

The Litza Front, Monday 30 June to Sunday 6 July 1941

Out at the coast 3 miles north, Lieutenant Hans-Wolf Rohde was in a bad mood. 'The 2. Battalion captured the Mustatunturi mountain, and the 3. Battalion rushed past it, towards the glories of the East,' he wrote in his account of the battle, *Kampf um den Hals der Fischerhalbinsel*. 'The 1. Battalion, to which we belonged, tagged along behind. We were used as mules. It was shameful, and my men were disappointed and furious. They swore like dockers as they stumbled under their burdens.'[1]

Rohde was a company commander in the 136th Mountain Regiment, which was fighting as the northern spearhead of the Mountain Corps. In order to secure its left flank, about 5,000 men under Colonel Albin Nake were to take and isolate the 6-kilometre-wide isthmus that separated the mainland from the Rybachy or Fisher Peninsula, called the Fisher Neck. It was a tough job in extremely difficult terrain, and Nake was short of time.

'The Fisher Peninsula stuck out into the Arctic Ocean like a clenched fist and was a strategic position of the utmost importance for the Soviet defenders,' wrote Hans Rüf in *Gebirgsjäger vor Murmansk*. 'Dietl had considered occupying the whole peninsula, but the campaign planners had calculated that this would require an extra mountain division, which we did not have. Till Murmansk had fallen, in the near future as we believed, we had to be satisfied with closing the Fisher Neck. Later, the rest would fall like ripe fruit into our hands.'[2]

Nake had fought in the imperial Austro-Hungarian army during World War I and transferred to the Wehrmacht after the *Anschluss* in 1938. Promotion had come slowly for him, and at the age of 53 he was among the oldest of Dietl's field officers. His age showed in his wrinkled countenance, and many years of close exposure to the thunder of guns and mortars had rendered him almost completely deaf. But it was not his physical impairments that had held him back in his career. As a senior German officer later put it: 'Nake just didn't have the toughness and determination to lead a division through difficulties of an extreme nature.'

Nake had been weighed and found wanting, but he had not lost his ambitions. 'There were rumours that whoever captured Titovka could be sure of a Knight's Cross,' wrote Rüf. 'Like most other officers, Nake was arrogantly ambitious and *suffered from a sore throat*.[3] He had therefore left the Neck and the Mustatunturi range and force-marched his third battalion towards the east.'

For Rohde and his men, the colonel's ambitions were just an added burden as they heaved and sweated to drag ammunition and supplies from the bottom of the Mattovuoni Valley up the slopes to the plateau.

'We were hungry for a fight, but were being used as pack animals. It was 14 kilometres as the crow flies from the floor of the valley to the new dumps, but the tundra was rough and broken and we had to force our way over rivers, bogs and steep crevices. The journey took us two full days.'

From the hilltop, they had a dizzy view towards Mustatunturi and the steep, shimmering blue headlands of the Fisher Peninsula. The isthmus between the Mattivuoni Fjord and the Kutovaja Bay at the head of the Motovskij Fjord appeared as a narrow plain, enclosed north and south by ridges 200–300 metres high. There was still snow on the screes and in the shaded ravines and crevices, but spring had arrived and the dwarf birch was budding with the tender, almost luminescent green colours typical of Arctic vegetation. It was a peaceful scene, but for one disturbing element: On the coast road between the settlements of Kutovaja and Titovka, soldiers and vehicles were moving. The Soviet 135th Infantry Regiment was on the march. Company Commander Rohde saw his opportunity for a fight.

'A serious threat was developing on our flank,' he wrote. 'The Russians had got there first and were setting up positions on Height 122. We informed the battalion commander of the danger to his left flank and were released from our duty as bearers, with orders to prepare for battle.'

The Red Army had suffered disastrous losses in the first week of Operation *Barbarossa*. Thousands of planes and tanks were destroyed. The number of dead, wounded and missing men was almost half a million. Minsk had fallen on 29 June, and the German armoured brigades were 300–400 kilometres inside Soviet territory.

It looked as though the tragedy was about to be repeated in the north, despite General Frolov and his commanders having had an extra week to prepare. The border defence had crumbled in just 24 hours. Titovka was in flames, and Dietl's

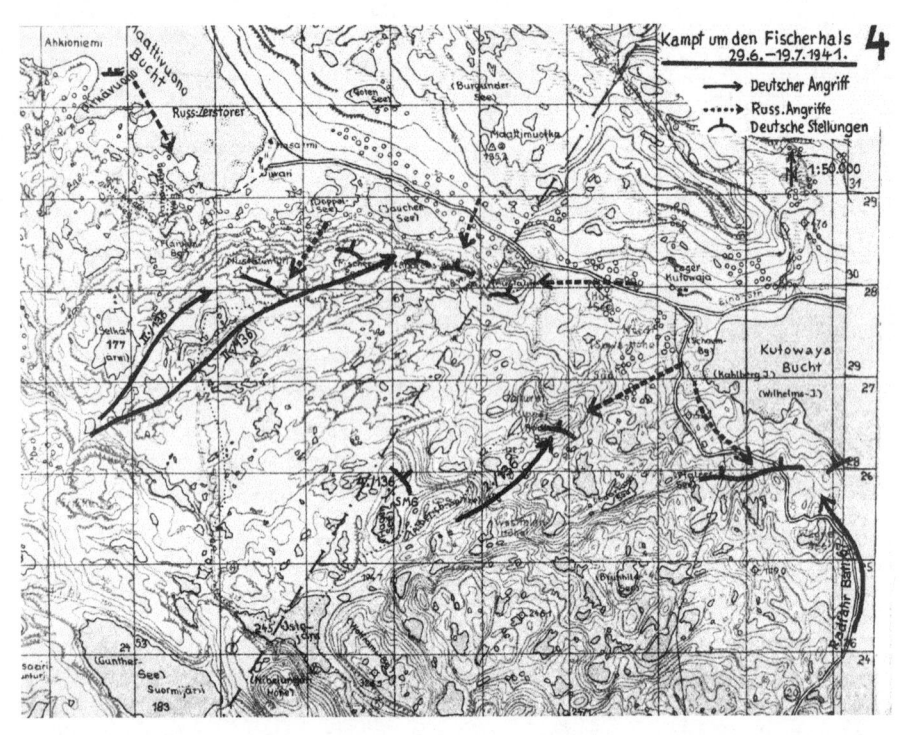

The 136th Regiment attacked the isthmus of the Fisher Peninsula – the 'Fisher Neck' – but were stopped on the ridges to the south. Mustatunturi is to the west (on the left), followed by Height 122 and Height 40 at the east end of the line, near the Kutovaja Bay (Kutowaya Bucht on the map), where Cycle Battalion 67 (Radfahr Batt 67) advanced northward along the coast road leading to Kutovaja (arrow on the right.) (Rüf: Gebirgsjäger vor Murmansk)

vanguard was approaching the River Litza. Communication lines had been cut, and there seemed to be total confusion.

'We received a very worrying message from Frolov,' Rear Admiral Golovko wrote in his diary. 'The situation on land was much more critical than I had realised. The infantry had suffered heavy losses, especially among the officers. The enemy was unstoppably driving us back. Scattered groups of Red Guards were fighting for every single crag. But they lacked artillery and mortars, and the stock of ammunition was about to run out.'[4]

The set-backs seem to have caused the army commander to waver, and he had given the zone commissar, Colonel Krasilnikov, and the commander of the 135th Regiment, Colonel Mikhail Pashkovskij, orders to evacuate the whole of the Fisher Peninsula. They had protested and had pointed out that ships with thousands of people on board would be easy prey for the Luftwaffe. Frolov had rescinded his calamitous instructions and instead given them orders to attack the German flank. The Russians now suffered the effects of earlier blunders. The main part of Pashkovskij's regiment had been moved to the coast a few days earlier, and the return march would take time. In the meantime, Mustatunturi and the hills to the south were defended only by border guards and Lieutenant Barbolin's reconnaissance unit.

'We were covering a front line 6 or 7 kilometres long between Mustatunturi and Height 122,' Barbolin wrote. 'I only had 110 men, which was not nearly enough.'

The shortage of troops on the Fisher Neck was behind Frolov's desperate phone call to Golovko. He was asking the rear admiral for artillery support from naval vessels in the Motovskij Fjord.

Whether to comply was not an easy decision for the young commander of the Northern Fleet. There was little room for evasive manoeuvres in the head of the fjord, and the forward Finnish air base at Luostari was only ten minutes' flying time away.

> There was continuous daylight, and it was clear to me that the Luftwaffe would strike as soon as the ships' guns opened fire. I could provide four fighter planes to help defend the ships, but the enemy was undoubtedly ten times stronger. The crews on the destroyers *Kuibysjev* and *Uritzki* were busy preparing for sea when Naval Commissar Kuznetsov telegraphed orders to us from Moscow to support the army to the very end. I can't say that the phrase *to the very end* was very encouraging.

About 7.30 a.m. on Monday 30 June, Lieutenant Alexander Gorjatsjik saw flames and smoke from the gun turrets of *Kuibysjev*. The shells screamed over the ridges south of Fisher Neck and exploded on the tundra. The young lieutenant's company had been on the march all night and was approaching the starting point for Frolov's counter-attack.

'It was still 30 km from our bivouac site to the isthmus, and the men were exhausted,' he wrote in his diary. 'We had nothing to eat, and vodka was forbidden. I had to order rest stops every ten minutes.'

In a bombardment lasting two hours, *Kuibyshev* fired almost 230 4-inch shells. The observers who had been posted on land earlier in the night reported good results. Just before 10 a.m., *Uritzki* and two patrol boats joined in the bombardment. They were preparing to open fire when the alarm went up. A squadron of 18 Ju-88 bombers was approaching from the west.

'When the planes attacked the destroyer, I thought the battle was lost. My people opened fire at them with rifles and machine guns, but it was useless. At a height of 2,000 metres the Germans were way out of range.'[5]

Inland on the tundra, Nake's regiment experienced the bombardment as unpleasant but not problematic.

'The destroyers were firing wildly,' Rüf reported. 'The shells landed on the ground and seemed to cause more difficulty for the Soviet defenders than for us.'

The colonel's dream of a Knight's Cross was fading rapidly. When the 3. Battalion reached Titovka late in the morning, the village had already been captured by Cycle Battalion 67, who had followed the road north from the intact bridge without meeting any organised resistance.

> 14th Rifle Division's headquarters camp had been abandoned, and the connection to the nearby airstrip blown up. The buildings were in flames, and the centre of the village was being destroyed.

The road continued northwards along the coast, and Nake sent his troops along it towards Kutovaja. 'The closer the troops came to Fisher Neck, the stronger the resistance they faced. Their field rations and the stocks of ammunition were running out. At the same time, the Russians appeared to be sending more and more forces into the gap between the coast road and Mustatunturi, the hill on the other side of the isthmus. It was a complex and awkward situation.'

In the meantime, Lieutenant Rohde's company was working its way steadily towards the ridge marked as 'Height 122' on the map, several kilometres west of the coast road.

> I sent a patrol forward while the rest of the company took cover about a thousand metres from the objective. We could see movement among the stones, and we had to find out whether they were friend or foe.

They were Russians, from Lieutenant Barbolin's reconnaissance unit. Barbolin, a young man about the same age as Rohde, later wrote about the encounter: 'We suddenly saw a group of ten or twelve Germans coming up over the scree. The sergeant asked for permission to open fire, but I told him to wait until the enemy was closer. Soon we could see the faces of the scouts, who were carefully stalking towards us with weapons at the ready. I shouted 'Fire,' and the rifles began to crackle. Five of the enemy fell, four dead and one severely wounded. I sent a corporal to fetch any identity cards and bandage the casualty. When he returned, he reported that his help had not been needed. The last man had also died.'

The ground in front of Rohde fell steeply towards a valley bottom about 700 metres across, with Height 122 looming as a sheer, dark wall in the background.

> We suddenly heard shots and explosions and saw little plumes of smoke spurting up. They were using hand grenades against our patrol! So the enemy has occupied the height. I gave the order: 'Ready to attack in four minutes!

Under cover of machine-gun fire, the company stormed down the scree and across the bogs in the valley bottom. 'We faced sporadic fire, which suddenly intensified. The enemy had at least four machine-gun posts and they hammered at us. The leading men fell, but we struggled on.'

Rohde's mountain soldiers took cover among the boulders at the foot of Height 122 and lay hidden for several hours, awaiting their chance. When the mist rolled in from the sea on the night of 30 June/1 July, they resumed their attack.

> I looked at my wristwatch shortly before we began the climb towards the top. It was 04.50, and I knew that my men were following me. Muffled explosions echoed through the mist. That was the mortars joining in. We worked our way onwards, stooping and looking ahead as in Egger-Lienz's painting, *Der Sturm*. Suspended between life and death and in the grip of our basic instincts, we barely realised that the Russians were firing too high.

During the next two hours, Rohde's and Barbolin's men fought an intense battle among the bare rocks and boulders scattered over the ridge.

'The enemy came uncomfortably close, and Junior Lieutenant Drygin's troop was eliminated to the last man,' Barbolin wrote. 'Soon, grenades were landing in our own position. Our machine gunners were running out of ammunition, and I reluctantly gave the order to retreat.'

Lieutenant Rohde had difficulty distinguishing friend from foe in the poor visibility. 'From time to time there was a gap in the mist, and we could glimpse the Russians creeping from cover to cover with bayonets drawn. We started throwing hand grenades and shooting from the hip with light machine-guns. Among the noise of the salvoes, I suddenly heard yodelling. That was a call the Russians didn't use! The dissonance between the cries of pain from the wounded and the yodelling of the victors was striking, but that was the nature of our first real battle in the hills: a constant contrast between suffering and celebration.'

Finally defeated by this violent attack, the Russians pulled back. At 6.15 a.m. the German lieutenant, still caught up in the excitement of battle, was able to report: 'Height south of Kutovaja captured by 2./135!'

It was a small and very temporary victory, bought at great cost. In the course of a few hours that morning, Rohde's company had lost 27 men: 16 dead and 11 wounded. The Russian losses were at least as great. When the shooting stopped, only two of the defenders were found alive. The vengeance was brutal – the first warning of what was to come. The bodies of the lost German patrol found on the battlefield showed signs of mutilation. 'It was a misdeed the prisoners had to pay for. On my orders, the Soviet survivors were executed by my furious men.'[6]

On the other side of the ridge, the attack came as a shock to Lieutenant Gorjatsjik and his company.

> I was busy reconnoitring the position when firing suddenly broke out from an area which should have been secure. The Germans had forced their way through a gap and were driving our people to flight. I saw several of them fall, and I had to crawl into cover in the scrub where I vainly tried to regroup them. The company was in panic, and many were throwing away their weapons. In a short time we had four dead, twenty wounded and six missing.

Out in the fjord, the destroyers *Kuibysjev* and *Uritzki* had miraculously survived the Luftwaffe bombing and returned to the naval base at Polarnoje. One of the trawlers had been hit and had sought refuge in a nearby bay. A few German planes were still flying over the Fisher Neck when Gorjatsjik came to the edge of a lake, with a bullet wound in his left foot.

> I had to swim twenty metres past an overhang to get to safety. I was soaked through and my foot was very painful. But rest was out of the question. A fresh counter-attack on the heights slightly to the east had already been ordered.

Bitter fighting raged along the whole of the Fisher Neck for the next 24 hours. The death toll was rising, and Colonel Nake took an unpopular decision. He suspended the attack against the Kutovaja base area.

'An attack with the limited forces I have available would lead to major losses,' he reported to General Dietl about 7 p.m. on Tuesday 2 July. 'The enemy has constructed strong defensive positions on the terraces in the hills on the other side of the isthmus and brought two light and three heavy batteries into position. The Fisher Neck is now blocked. Occupying the whole of the Fisher Peninsula would take up a significant amount of the corps' resources.'

In the village of Titovka, terrible scenes had been witnessed in the hours following the German attack.

'We were billeted in six or seven little wooden houses near the river bank and took in the first casualties during the morning,' Nurse Varvara Bichik of the 75th Medical Battalion recalled. 'A few hours later, the houses were full of young men groaning and dying. We had nobody to bury the dead, and the corpses were piled up at the roadside.'

Titovka was abandoned in the middle of the day on Monday 30 June. The bridge to the tongue of land with the area's only airstrip was blown up and the stores thrown into the river. 'The retreat came as a devastating shock. The road to the Fisher Peninsula was blocked, and the first salvoes of the German machine guns could be heard on the other side of the river. We managed to transport some of the wounded to the damaged quay, where with great difficulty they were taken on board a waiting trawler. The vehicles were set on fire, even though the field hospital was still sheltering a hundred wounded. A machine gun suddenly started firing nearby. Battalion Commander Vasiljev grabbed a white sheet and ran to the river bank, waving it. *Don't shoot! We have wounded here!!* It may sound strange, but the shooting stopped. We encouraged everybody who could walk, to make their way over the hill to the Litza Valley. It was a dreadful sight: Some of the soldiers had had arms and legs amputated and were trying to crawl to safety. There was nobody to help them, and few made it. The bodies of our dead lay strewn all the way to the Litza.'

In April and May 1941 the codebreakers at Bletchley Park had asked the Royal Navy to make new raids on German shipping to secure up-to-date Enigma manuals. In the course of a few weeks in the North Atlantic, the navy captured the U-boat *U-110* and the weather ships *München* and *Lauenburg*. The boarding parties retrieved an intact Enigma machine, code books and several packing cases with documents, which vastly improved the capacity to understand the encrypted German radio communications.

'There can be no doubt that at this stage the battle was won,' wrote codebreaker Patrick Mahon, who replaced chess master Hugh Alexander as head of Hut 8. 'The problem was simply one of perfecting methods, of gaining experience and of obtaining and above all of training staff.'[7]

The results soon became apparent. In mid-June the listening station at Scarborough had copied a series of Morse signals to and from the Luftwaffe's new base at Kirkenes on the Soviet border which confirmed in detail that the *Barbarossa* attack was just round the corner.

'The weakest link in Germany's security chain was her need to resort to W/T for last-minute communications with North Norway,' wrote Professor Hinsley in *British Intelligence in the Second World War*.

> On 14 June Bletchley Park decrypted messages which issued code-names to *Luftflotte 5*, apparently for operations against Russia from Norway and Finland. On 15 June an aircraft reporting unit at Kirkenes was instructed in the GAF Enigma to prepare to cross into Finland but under no circumstances to occupy its posts there until authority was given. Three further GAF Enigma messages decrypted on 20 June dealt with the crossing of the frontier. One lifted the ban on flying over the prohibited frontier zone but limited flying there to the movement of aircraft to airfields near the frontier. Another warned the special operations staff at Kirkenes that, since mine laying was to be carried out before the crossing, surprise would not be possible. In a third, Kirkenes was instructed that any aircraft flying over the frontier before the general crossing must do so at great height.[8]

When the attack was launched on Sunday 22 June, Bletchley Park was on the alert. A triumphant statement sent by Admiral Dönitz to the German U-boat captains on Monday was on desks in the Admiralty and 10 Downing Street a few hours later.

> Army advancing everywhere according to plan. Enemy everywhere withdrawing with little show of fight. Luftwaffe reports enemy's total losses on Eastern front up to morning of the 23rd as 1,800 planes and estimates that it has thus destroyed half of the effective Red Air Force. Our own losses amount to 36 planes.[9]

For Churchill and the few top officers who knew about the Enigma source, the developments appeared dramatic. Large parts of Belorussia and the Baltic were under German control after only a few days of fighting. A report to the War Cabinet on 30 June stated that 'Russia's military situation must be considered extremely serious.'

The reports strengthened the majority who wanted to support the Russians in word but not in deed. The Chiefs of Staff therefore had little difficulty composing a reply to Mason-Mac who had sent from Moscow a list of requests for immediate supply of equipment and raw materials: 3,000 modern fighter planes; 3,000 bombers; 20,000 light anti-aircraft guns; as many one and two ton bombs as possible; plus incendiary bombs, flame-throwers and detailed technical information about asdic, magnetic mines and night flying. In addition, the list included 10,000 tons of rubber, 70,000 bales of wool and 500 tons of tin.[10]

'If transport can be arranged, a specimen night fighter with war equipment will be provided for the Russians,' said the reply from London. 'We will do everything we can to release a limited supply of our latest bombs of large size. We are sorry that we cannot promise a supply of incendiary bombs as we have none to spare. It is regretted that the Russian request for modern fighter and bomber aircraft cannot be met, as intensive operations now being carried out by the RAF, are absorbing our entire output.'

The telegram reflected the attitude of Churchill and his closest military advisers, who thought that the Red Army would fall apart within two months. Operation *Barbarossa* had given the Allies breathing space, but all forces would need to be in full readiness again by 1 September to meet a feared German invasion of the British Isles. To give away weapons which would very probably fall into German hands would not be wise.

Mason-Mac continued to be left to support the Russians with vague promises. His task was to make the breathing space last as long as possible.

In the Mountain Corps HQ in Petsamo, General Eduard Dietl was in no doubt about the final outcome either. True, only 80 prisoners had been taken and the total Russian losses in the fighting along the frontier probably didn't amount to more than 500 men. This indicated that the main part of the Russian 14th Rifle Division had got away, which the increasing resistance on the west side of the River Litza seemed to confirm.[11]

However, he seemed overall to agree with an analysis from the 2nd Mountain Division on Tuesday 1 July expressing great optimism: 'The opposition which Gruppe Hengl has met consists of exchanges of fire with isolated groups of fleeing Red Guards. The 14th Division is defeated. Unless new forces are brought into action by the Russians, there is little reason to fear noteworthy resistance before we reach Murmansk.'

What caused greatest concern was the supply situation and the transport of heavy weapons. The route from the depots in Parkkina to the main position in the hilly terrain between Titovka and Litza was still not passable, despite the non-stop work of Finnish auxiliary workers, veterans from Construction Battalion 405 and the herd of 17-year-olds from the Reich Labour Service.

Armoured vehicles became stuck and moving artillery through bogs and over rocks was laborious toil. The corps consumed more than 300 tonnes of ammunition and supplies every single day, and it took columns of horses and mules three days to cross the stretch from Parkkina to the front line.

'The route snaked through swamps and over ridges,' wrote Hans Rüf. 'Despite the major contribution of the Labour Service people, some stretches were in a dreadful condition. Wheels were smashed to pieces. Vehicles and horses sank till they were stuck fast and had to be dragged out with the help of extra personnel and teams of horses. Many draft animals never got out of the mire and had to be killed on the spot.'[12]

To resupply the front-line troops would in a normal situation take at least eight full days. But Dietl was under pressure from Falkenhorst and didn't want to give the Russians a chance to regain their balance. All available men were therefore assigned to the supply units with a demand that ammunition and supplies to last three days were to be in place before the end of the week.

'By Sunday 6 July all units will be supplied with sufficient provisions for the days up to Thursday 10 July,' he wrote in his diary on 2 July. 'As soon as this objective is attained, the main attack across the Litza will be launched.'

In Moscow, Stalin was back as leader of a new war cabinet after his nervous breakdown the last weekend in June.[13]

On the evening of Thursday 3 July the despot's voice could be heard for the first time in a broadcast from Moscow: 'Comrades! Citizens! Brothers and sisters! Men of our army and navy! I am addressing you, my friends!'

He exhorted his listeners to merciless struggle against the invaders and praised Great Britain and the United States who had declared themselves willing to give help.

> The historic utterance of the British Prime Minister Churchill regarding aid to the Soviet Union and the declaration of the United States Government signifying its readiness to render aid to our country, can only evoke a feeling of gratitude in the hearts of the peoples of the Soviet Union. Comrades, our forces are numberless. The overweening enemy will soon learn this to his cost. All our forces for support of our heroic Red Army and our glorious Red Navy! All forces of the people – for the demolition of the enemy! Forward, to victory!

Behind the scenes, the mood was less friendly. Mason-Mac and his staff had received their first solid information about the situation in the North at a meeting that same day.

'German forces estimated three to four mountain divisions in the areas of Kirkenes and Petsamo,' he telegraphed to the Chiefs of Staff in London. 'Maximum GAF employed so far about two hundred aircraft. These belong to 5 Air Army under General Stumpff and are operating from Finnish aerodromes. Russians fear seaborne and/or airborne attack on Fisher Peninsula and Murmansk. They suggest action by our fleet and fleet air arm against enemy transport concentrations mentioned above. They also suggest assistance of bomber units operating from Murmansk area.'

But the rejection of the requests for supply of arms had come as a cold shower, and the Royal Navy emissary, Rear Admiral Geoffrey Miles, had nothing to add but utter gloom and pessimism: 'It would be suicide for any naval forces to operate when German dive-bombers are present, unless they have fighter cover. I have not much hope of an aircraft carrier being used, as suggested by the Russians, and I have no news about other naval units.'

It didn't much help that he was preoccupied with quite another question: the evacuation to Great Britain of the 30–50 civilian and military vessels which were in the Murmansk region.

> I impressed on Admiral Kharlamov the necessity of moving the 100,000 tons of shipping reported to be in northern waters to a safer place. The meeting was hardly satisfactory; the Russians being evasive. Their attitude to the question of shipping was that it was in a safe place already.

Confidence in Mason-Mac and his men was at a low ebb when Stalin decided to intervene. On the evening of Saturday 5 July the British Ambassador was called in to see Molotov and informed that a *Russian* military mission would be sent to London.

'Apologise for this very fast ball but this is typical example of Russian procedure,' said a Most Immediate telegram that same evening. 'Russian General Staff refuse to give me any more details tonight as names of Mission have not yet been announced by the Kremlin. As Russians accepted our Mission on basis of reciprocity we must presumably accept theirs, and in view of importance they attach to reaching a quick decision on Petsamo, it seemed to Ambassador and self that we should accept regrettable delay in departure of Catalina.'

The two Catalina flying boats would be ready for take-off from Archangel at 8 a.m. the next day. The Soviet Military Mission could therefore reach London on Monday 7 July, the same day as Dietl's major offensive across the Litza would be launched.

Would that give time enough to mobilise any effective British assistance?

CHAPTER 6

The First Attack

The Litza Front, Sunday 6 July to Saturday 12 July 1941

At first, it looked as if the optimists in the intelligence staff were right. Gruppe Ritter von Hengl was again given the major role, and the 43-year-old ardent Nazi from Bavaria assembled the three battalions of the 137th Regiment in the shadow of the Herzberg Hills just west of the Litza River on the evening of Saturday 5 July.

'We have achieved a great victory in reaching our first goal, and we honour those of our comrades who have sacrificed themselves on the battlefield,' he told the troops in his order of the day. 'Now we face the challenge of attacking a new target. I am confident everyone will do his best. *Heil unserer Führer!*'[1]

The new objective was the 120-metre steel bridge over the River Litza, which led directly to the main road across the tundra. The high ground to the east of the river was the last line of defence before Murmansk, and there was little evidence that the Russians had had time to establish fortifications in any depth. Returning scouts estimated the enemy forces to be a reinforced regiment with artillery support, comparable in strength to what the corps had already defeated at Titovka.

So von Hengl didn't anticipate any great problems when he went through the plans with his battalion commanders for the first time. The 1. Battalion was assigned to the key action. About 800 men under Major Wolfgang Fuschlberger would cross the river north of the bridge in rubber boats and storm Height 183, which dominated the area of operations. In a parallel manoeuvre on the west bank, the 2. and 3. battalions under Majors Vielwerth and Kräutler would follow the road south and capture the bridge in a frontal attack *before* the Russians had time to detonate possible explosive charges. Two kilometres to the south, Colonel Wilhelm Weiss, renowned for his victory at Trondheim, would establish a bridgehead with two battalions from the 3rd Mountain Division to stop the arrival of reinforcements from Murmansk.

It was a simple plan, which in the initial planning phase had led to intense discussions between General Dietl and the staff of 2nd Mountain Division. An augmented company had advanced eastwards along the coast two days earlier and taken a Soviet military camp by storm. The camp had well-stocked arms stores and 150 new lorries which had been delivered by boat to Litza, direct from the factory. Major General Schlemmer wanted to take advantage of this sudden surprise and thrust further east along the coast with the *whole* of the 137th Regiment, which would then wheel south to attack the Soviet defence line from behind.

'A frontal attack on the bridge will inevitably entail heavy losses,' Schlemmer had maintained. 'A rapid advance along the coast will require three or four days' preparation at the most, but won't meet significant resistance.'

He had been supported by the division's operations officer, Major Eduard Zorn, who pointed out that there were good, well-trodden paths to the settlement at Ura-Guba, 15 km further east. 'From Ura-Guba the regiment can advance southwards, into the wildernesses *behind* the Russian lines. Then our mission will have been accomplished. The road to Murmansk will lie open.'

This was an ambitious proposal, which took both Dietl and his Chief of Staff, Lieutenant Colonel Karl von Le Suire, aback. They had been struggling day and night with the troublesome logistics and they knew that an advance deep into the trackless tundra would not be possible until lorries could drive on the new road from Parkkina to Litza.

'In the current situation it will not be possible to provide adequate supplies for an extensive encirclement of the Soviet forces,' Dietl replied. 'The attack along the road must therefore proceed as part of a smaller pincer movement. Bigger operations can be set in motion only when the Litza area is secured and the supply depots built up.'[2]

Like Zorn and Dietl, le Suire had supported Hitler's failed coup in Munich in 1923 and belonged to the Führer's circle of old Nazi comrades. He agreed with the main idea, but was worried about the terrain and pointed out that the Russians would not let themselves be surrounded by a force of infantrymen with mainly small arms. 'The forces at our disposal are too small for us to successfully surround large forces spread over vast areas. The country is too difficult for that.'

The corps commander's word was law, and Schlemmer and Zorn had to give way. At 8.30 p.m. on Saturday, Fuschlberger led his mountain troops over the River Litza without resistance. An hour and a half later, Vielwerth and

64 • MIRACLE AT THE LITZA

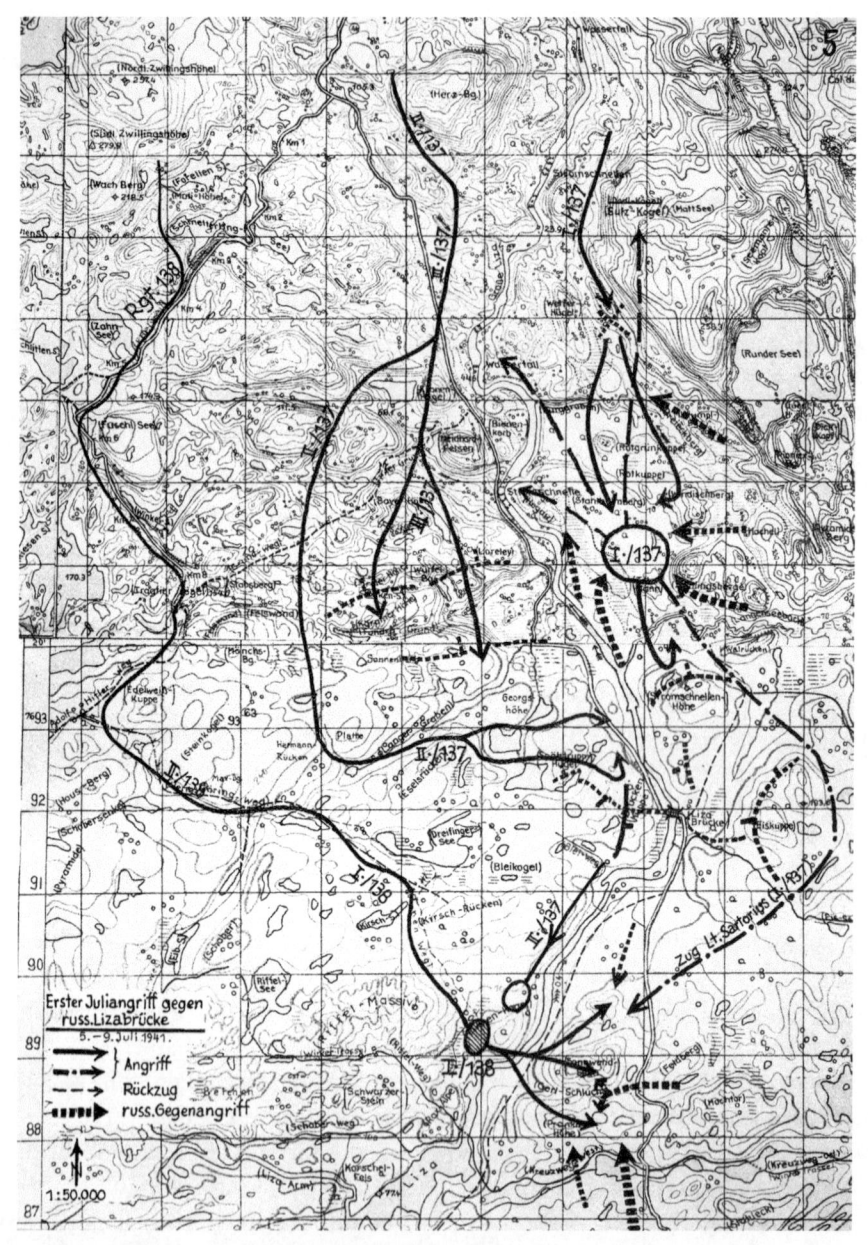

The first attack on the Litza: The 2. and 3. Battalions of the 137th Regiment advanced south from Herzberg (top of map, centre) along the main road to Murmansk, but were stopped before the Litza Bridge (brücke). The 1. Battalion crossed the river and was surrounded and decimated below Height 183. Two battalions from the 138th Regiment crossed the river south of the bridge. They were forced to a halt on the Brandl and Prankh Heights and in the Devil's Gorge between them (bottom of map). (Rüf: Gebirgsjäger vor Murmansk)

Kräutler mustered the second and third battalions in the hollow which came to be known as *Hexenkettel* ('The Witch's Kettle') and started marching through the scrub towards the bridge 5 kilometres to the south. A hot July day was coming to an end, and the soldiers were sweating under their heavy packs. There were no Russians to be seen, and the river meandered its way towards the sea in gentle curves, through a landscape never before disturbed by war. The idyll would not last.

Watching the bridge from a well-camouflaged cave in the hills to the east of the Litza, Major General Nikolai Nikishin had understood for several hours that something was about to happen. The mustering of troops around Herzberg had been observed from the air, and German prisoners had declared with great self-confidence that Murmansk would fall in the course of three days of *marvellous victories*. That was what they had been told, and that was what they believed.

'Everything indicates that Dietl will attack again soon,' wrote Major Khariton Khudalov, the commander of the independent 62nd Reconnaissance Battalion. 'As never before we must gather our strength and prepare to strike back.'[3]

Army Commander Frolov's order for a rapid deployment of the 52nd Rifle Division from the mining town of Montsjegorsk to the River Litza had come in the nick of time. The 205th Regiment and some artillery were already in Murmansk. Now the rest of the division was sent by train to the port, for onward transport either by ship or on foot. The vanguard, consisting of parts of the 112th Infantry Regiment under Major Fedor Korotkov, had crossed the mountain plateau on Sunday 29 June and reached Titovka about the time the bunker line was being attacked, but had suffered badly at the hands of the Luftwaffe and had lost many of their heavy weapons.

Two intact regiments comprised the division's main strength: the 58th Infantry Regiment under young Captain Pjotr Gromov; and the 205th Infantry Regiment under Lieutenant Colonel Sergej Govorov. These were two strong, well-trained units built around a core of revolutionary communists and seasoned veterans from the Winter War.

'The 205th and 58th Regiments are among the elite units of the Red Army,' Major Eduard Zorn wrote in a later report. 'The 205th have the honorary title *Red Banner Regiment* and earned great distinction in the Winter War. In March 1941 all incompetent personnel were replaced with fresh, first-class men. They have all been through rigorous training and have high status as soldiers. The 58th have the honorary title *Standard-Bearer Regiment* and are of similar quality. The personnel are recruited mainly from European Russia, including Moscow, St. Petersburg and Smolensk, whereas the 112th and 95th regiments have a large proportion of people from Siberia and the Caucasus. In the 58th and 205th Regiments, moreover, there are very many fanatical defenders of the Bolshevik regime. These dyed-in-the-wool Red Guards are the backbone of the division, and it is worth noting that there are *none* of them among our prisoners.'[4]

These two regiments reached Litza by a forced march in the days around 1 July, and Division Commander Nikishin posted them on the high ground on both sides of the bridge, with field guns, howitzers, and heavy mortars in the hollows further east. The 112th Regiment was regrouped after its retreat from Titovka and placed in well camouflaged positions in the scrub on the west bank, with a battalion of the 58th Regiment as extra security in the terrain immediately in front of the bridge.

By Saturday 5 July the road to Murmansk was blocked by a force of 10,000 men supported by almost 80 guns of 45–122 mm calibre.

'It was an anxious wait,' wrote Khudalov. 'I spent Saturday evening on the crags overlooking the bridge. The enemy was nowhere to be seen, but I had painful forebodings, as if we were facing a sudden Armageddon. One of the lads asked, "Why isn't the Luftwaffe coming? The sky is clear, but we haven't seen the planes all day." I was amazed. He was right. For the first time in several days, Murmansk had not been bombed. Were the planes being saved for other objectives, or were we coming to the start of the three *marvellous* days which were supposed to bring the mountain troops to Murmansk?'

Khudalov called divisional HQ. He needed to share his concerns with someone. Forty-five-year-old Major General Nikishin was an experienced campaigner. He had been a lieutenant in the Tsar's army and had fought many hard battles on the side of the Reds in the Civil War. He had had the same thoughts, and his advice was: 'We're coming to the same conclusion. Be alert! The utmost attention is needed!'

In Moscow at about the same time, General Filipp Golikov and Admiral Nikolai Kharlamov were hastily packing their bags. The bald 40-year-old infantryman had until recently been commander of the GRU, the military intelligence service, and had now been selected to lead the Soviet Military Mission to Great Britain, with Admiral Kharlamov as his deputy.

Stalin had made Golikov's priorities clear in a two-hour audience on Saturday morning: He was to request the opening of a new combined front with a landing of several British and Soviet divisions supported by air and naval forces behind the German lines in Petsamo. Stalin also wanted military operations in France and the Balkans, but the operation in the North was *a minimum which needed to be done as soon as possible.*

'Bring it home to the Western Allies that we will fight to the last ditch, and that the Nazi invaders will never be able to crush us. Yet, the Soviet Army needs effective assistance from the Allies. It can be rendered, first of all, through launching war operations against the Germans in the West and by supplying us with war materials.'[5]

The suffocating heat of July lay like a blanket over the Russian capital when a Douglas transport plane took off from Khodynka airfield with the six-man delegation on board. After a short stop in Archangel, the journey continued soon after midnight on Sunday 6 July in two British Catalina flying-boats.

'In the dusk we flew towards the crimson strip in the sky. We passed the neck of the White Sea and saw the outline of the Kola Peninsula,' Admiral Kharlamov wrote in his memoirs, *Difficult Mission*. The 35-year-old had lived both in Murmansk and in Polarnoje, and he knew many of the leading officers personally. 'Looking out of the window, I thought that not far away, General Frolov's soldiers were waiting in their trenches and dugouts for the enemy's sortie, and that somewhere quite near us the marines, in their black pea-jackets and peakless caps, were preparing for an attack. I felt guilty about leaving them at a time like this. I knew I was indebted to them. Would I ever be able to repay the debt?'[6]

The idyll was broken a few hours later. Early on Sunday morning Korotkov's regiment caught sight of the long column of German attackers approaching the bridge. All weapons opened up at close range.

'A storm of fire struck Kräutler's battalion (III/137) from a terraced ridge penetrated by deep clefts,' wrote Captain Vilhelm Hess. 'There were snipers hidden among the boulders, and the machine guns hammered at us from well camouflaged positions on the summits. Every single emplacement had to be taken in hand-to-hand combat before we could advance any further.'[7]

At the corps' forward command post near Titovka, Dietl received the first disturbing news slightly before 8 a.m. on Sunday. It was Major General Ernst Schlemmer on the field telephone. 'Soviet artillery has put the troops under heavy fire. I fear significant losses and request an immediate order to attack.'

The attack on the bridge was to be coordinated between von Hengl's frontal assault and Weiss's outflanking manoeuvre by units of the 3rd Mountain Division two kilometres to the south. But Dietl's celebrated Narvik Division under their new commander, Major General Hans Kreysing, had had an unfortunate campaign so far. The division had been deployed on the corps' southern flank, but by Sunday 29 June they had already become stuck in the swamps and woods around Titovka. The supposed inland route to Murmansk didn't exist, and Kreysing had ordered the division to turn back. Over the next few days the main part of the division was moved north along the Arctic Road and assigned to a position *behind* the 2nd Mountain Division. Kreysing was in his fifties and from the university town of Göttingen in Central Germany. As a paratrooper he had been awarded the Knight's Cross of the Iron Cross for his part in the airborne landings in Holland in the spring of 1940, and he and the other Knight's Cross-holders in the division found a secondary role intolerable. When Dietl enquired whether the attack on the Litza could be brought forward, he immediately answered a gleeful yes.

'If the 2nd Mountain Division's situation make it necessary, we can be ready in two hours.'

There were obvious flaws in this statement. The two forward battalions had been struggling through the wilderness for four full days. To keep time, the heaviest of the rubber boats had been dumped along the way. So Kreysing added: 'Till now, only a few small dinghies have been brought to the edge of the river. An immediate crossing with heavy weapons will not be possible.'

The absence of artillery was a major problem. But Dietl was in a hurry and ordered a combined main assault on the bridge at 10 a.m. on Sunday. It was a hasty decision, made under pressure.

Early that morning, a Fiesler Storch had landed on the airfield at Titovka with Colonel Rudolf Schmundt on board, and 44-year-old Schmundt from Metz in the Mosel Valley was not a man who could wait. He was Hitler's Principal Adjutant and the tyrant's loyal adviser in all matters military. Now he had come to the northern flank of the Eastern Front as the Führer's personal envoy. This was too good an opportunity for Dietl to miss, and he grasped it with both hands.

'Colonel Schmundt arrived at the command post at 07.20,' he noted in his war diary. 'The Führer wants a personal briefing on the corps' situation.'[8]

There can be no doubt that Dietl felt extremely isolated at the edge of the Arctic Ocean after the arguments with the army's top brass over Operations *Renntier* and *Platinfuchs*. Falkenhorst, his superior at Army HQ in Rovaniemi, wanted to prioritise the line of attack in mid-Finland. Their increasing rivalry expressed itself in ever more bureaucratic ways. Dietl had been denied reinforcements. He had been relieved as overall commander of Northern Norway only *after* the offensive began. Despite strident protests, he had been deprived of the command ship *Black Watch*, and at the beginning of July the Luftwaffe squadron in Kirkenes had been moved to the Salla Front.[9]

'Not one single dive-bomber is available for the corps despite many urgent requests to Falkenhorst,' he complained. 'I earnestly request you to arrange for a Stuka squadron to be assigned to us immediately.'

For Schmundt, Hitler was a military genius to be worshipped with flattery and servile adoration, and he conveyed without reservations the Führer's very latest intuitive revelations. 'Hitler believes there is reason to fear a British landing at the Petsamo Fjord, the Fisher Peninsula or the Motovskij Fjord. He has no solid evidence for this. It's more a question of a foreboding on the part of the Führer. He thinks the British will exploit the situation in the Arctic in the hope of achieving a cheap victory.'

Hitler's growing obsession with the High North as the war's *Schicksalzone* (Zone of Destiny) was about to become a fixation, cleverly fed by British disinformation in later years. This gave Dietl his chance to make further requests.

> The Mountain Corps has no means of repulsing an attack on the Fisher Peninsula. The further east the corps advances, the more vulnerable our supply lines become. A landing in Petsamo would therefore be a significant threat which could only be met by the transfer of new and powerful forces. At the moment, important parts of the corps are committed to the defence of the north flank. Fresh troops could relieve them from these duties and free the whole corps for the march to Murmansk.

If Hitler had had access to the inner circles of the Government in London, he would probably have brushed aside his premonition of an Allied landing in the north. The flying boats with Golikov and Kharlamov's military mission landed in Great Britain on Sunday evening. Soon after, the two Soviet officers were presented to Foreign Minister Anthony Eden, who welcomed them with great charm and many empty words.

'He looked extremely elegant in his navy blue suit,' Kharlamov wrote. 'Tall, slim with grey temples and moustaches, he was a classic specimen of an English gentleman. His manners were impeccable, and his ability to avoid a direct reply was well known … We discussed the problem of joint military operations in the Barents and Norwegian Seas, the possibility of more massive British air raids on important centres in Nazi Germany, and the prospects for the opening of a second front in the north of France. Eden was warm and hospitable, at least outwardly. He said: I am not competent enough to speak about military matters.'[10]

Golikov and Kharlamov were referred to the hard-boiled and reactionary Secretary of State for War, David Margesson, who had been the Tory Party's Chief Whip in the 1930s. Margesson could hardly conceal his disdain for the two Bolsheviks.

> He did not shake hands with us. Nor did he offer us a seat. Throughout our nearly 20-minute-long talk he remained standing, and there was nothing left for us to do but to follow his example.
>
> Margesson listened to us absent-mindedly. When he started talking we realised that he believed neither in the Red Army's victory nor in the viability of the Soviet political system. For him, there was no sense at all in a British-Soviet alliance.

Things didn't go any better in a meeting with the British service Chiefs of Staff:

> The First Sea Lord, Admiral Pound, assumed the leading role in the talks. He was a corpulent man, and balding. He dragged his foot as he walked. Pound gave us to understand that he was in a hurry and had more important things to see to than hare-brained talks with the Bolshies. It seemed to me he was terrified by our very presence.

As the historian Gabriel Gorodetsky wrote: 'The next morning Pound easily induced the Chiefs of Staff to reject the Soviet proposal for operations in the north which, he said, *amounted to a considerable commitment*. It was felt that the Russians seemed to be oblivious to *the magnitude of the administrative problems involved*. The ingenious ploy decided on was to present them with a questionnaire which would not only provide the Chiefs of Staff with information, but would help *to educate the Russians in the problems involved*.'

In the meantime the German Mountain Corps and the Russian 52nd Division had clashed in mortal combat around the bridge over the Litza. The 3. Battalion's frontal attack soon ground to a halt, and Major Vielwerth led the 2. Battalion through a dip in the ground towards the riverbank in an attempt to take the defenders by surprise in the flank.

'Vielwerth himself stormed down over the last scree towards the river,' wrote Captain Hess, 'but only a handful of his men followed and under the hail of small arms fire from the east bank and the bombardment of artillery from Height 183, the troops were driven into cover.'

Kräutler and Vielwerth's combined forces spent Sunday afternoon crouching in a half-circle round the western end of the bridge, but the last 500 metres had become a death-trap of machine gun bullets, hand-grenades and shrapnel. Smoke whirled up from numerous grass fires started by the red-hot fragments.

Whimpering and cries for help could be heard from the injured who were beyond reach of assistance. But the mountain troops clung on firmly in the hope that Major Fuschlberger's battalion would come in from the north, clear Height 183 and open the road to the bridge.

'The major had become involved in several skirmishes on his way southward along the east bank, and had left several platoons behind to secure his rear,' Hess wrote. 'When he came to the point of launching the final assault on the Soviet position, he was no longer able to muster a sufficient force. Instead, his troops were lying in isolated pockets under murderous fire. The situation soon became critical, as the battalion lacked heavy weapons and had little ammunition.'

Three kilometres further south, Colonel Weiss had sent the first company across the Litza in rubber boats soon after 10 a.m., as agreed with Dietl. During Sunday morning the whole of the 1. Battalion under Major Josef Brandl and the 2. Battalion under the ageing anti-Semite and aristocrat, Baron Hans Freiherr von Pranckh, were ferried over to the east bank.

'The crossing place was well chosen,' Hess reported. 'A sandbank several hundred metres wide led to the river, and the site was hidden from the artillery on Height 183 by sheer cliffs on the other side. The enemy was nowhere to be seen, and the troops quickly advanced eastwards towards the main road to Murmansk.'

Major General Nikishin had concentrated his forces around the bridge and the German advance in the south came as a nasty surprise.

'A dangerous situation was developing,' wrote Major Khudalov. 'If the attackers managed to secure their position, the way east would lie open and the whole of the 52nd Division risked being surrounded.'[11]

The 2. Battalion under the fearless Major Nikolai Soldatov was despatched in a forced march to the bridgehead and launched a violent counter-attack after midnight. 'Soldatov was a daring leader who always led from the front. He was strongly built, icily cool and an outstanding example to all. In fierce close fighting throughout the night, the battalion was surrounded. Communications with the division were cut, and the German mountain troops attacked repeatedly. All feeling of time disappeared. The men were totally exhausted. The toll of dead and wounded rose, and the ammunition had almost run out. Nevertheless, the battalion found the strength to hold on.'

The fighting around the bridge continued all night and into Monday 7 July. Dietl left his headquarters in Titovka about 7 a.m. and moved to 3rd Division's forward command post near Herzberg. Four hours earlier, the Russians had caused a surprise by withdrawing across the bridge and blowing it up. The west bank was in German hands, but Dietl's units in the bridgeheads on the other side of the river were in a desperate situation.

Fuschlberger's battalion on the north flank was surrounded and decimated. On the south flank, the 138th Regiment was still clinging onto the Brandl and Pranckh Heights, but Nikishin had rushed armoured vehicles and artillery into the front line and was bombarding the positions constantly. Despite repeated calls for emergency support, the Luftwaffe was nowhere to be seen. Morale was fading.

'The enemy is preparing for a new attack and has begun to seize the initiative,' Chief of Staff Le Suire wrote in the corps' war diary at 10.20 a.m. on Monday. 'Our troops on the east bank have no artillery, and the lack of rubber boats capable of carrying heavy loads makes resupplying impossible. According to the reports, the situation is swiftly deteriorating. The troops will need to be withdrawn to the west bank.'

Behind Le Suire's assessment there lay a dramatic realisation. In the years before, Dietl's mountain troops had been victorious from Poland in the south to Narvik in the north. They had fought and beaten the Polish, Dutch, French, Norwegian and British armies. The general and his men had been hailed by Goebbels' propaganda machine as warriors of a truly historical calibre. They had regarded the Russians as primitive *Untermenschen* and had been convinced that the advance over the tundra would be just another parade march.

Instead, the Red Army had shown itself to be a tough, stubborn and capable opponent, despite the sufferings Stalin had inflicted on the Russian people. Now the Soviet 52nd Division was busy subjecting the Narvik Corps to its first painful defeat. Dozens of mountain troops lay dead on both sides of the River Litza. Several hundred had been wounded and were attempting to crawl to safety. Their self-confidence was about to fall apart, and that was more than Dietl could bear.

He immediately challenged Major General Kreysing and his regimental commander, Colonel Weiss: 'Is it really necessary to abandon the east bank, or can the position be held with infantry weapons?'

The two cocky officers refused to face reality: 'The nature of the terrain is on our side. We can hold the bridgeheads!'

They were wrong. Despite being given a respite when the Luftwaffe's Stukas finally turned up around 4 p.m., the situation quickly turned critical. Nikishin's men attacked in wave after wave and steadily forced the German battalions back towards the edge of the water.

At 11 p.m. on Monday, Dietl gave up. The remains of Fuschlberger's battalion, which had been completely isolated for almost 24 hours, were told to retreat immediately. Twelve hours later the same order was given to Kreysing. The two battalions from the 138th Regiment were to leave the Devil's Gorge, evacuate the bridgehead and take up a defensive position on the west bank of the river.

The first attack on the Litza position had failed. Weiss and Fuschlberger's battalions had in the course of two brutal and bloody days lost several hundred men. Mentally, the mountain troops found themselves in a completely new situation. They were no longer invincible.

Meanwhile in Moscow and London, attitudes were beginning to change.

As early as 3 July, Mason-Mac had expressed his increasing frustration at the restrictions placed upon him by his superiors.

> Evidence available here indicates that these people mean to go on fighting. This is surely of maximum value to us. They are however saying that in spite of Germany's main effort being directed against them, we are doing practically nothing to help them either by action to relieve pressure or by giving them intelligence of an operational value. Fully realise difficulty with multiple operations to relieve pressure, and with full knowledge of risk to our source involved [a reference to Enigma], but still I earnestly ask permission to receive and pass on intelligence of immediate value. I will rephrase, water down and break up the information so long as I can convey something which is sufficiently near the truth to help Russian staff work and give them the impression we are trying to assist.

The chief of the British Military Mission had come to the conclusion that a revision of the strategy was needed. He was supported by Sir Stafford Cripps, the politically radical patrician who was British Ambassador to Moscow.

'What is required now above all things is some *action* by us to demonstrate our desire to help even at some risk to ourselves if necessary,' he wrote in a personal appeal to Churchill on 6 July. 'The Russians are very hard pressed all along the line, but they are putting up a fight better than anyone expected .... It may be that we can do no more than make a demonstration at Murmansk or on the coast of France, but such a demonstration made quickly would I am convinced bring in a huge dividend in the morale and determination of these people ... We are in danger of encouraging the collapse if we do not fully and frankly give the Russians everything possible to help and strengthen their resistance.'[12]

Churchill kept an open mind, and the very next day he sent a new declaration of support to Stalin.

> We are all very glad here that the Russian armies are making such strong and spirited resistance to the utterly unprovoked and merciless invasion of the Nazis. There is general admiration here for the bravery and tenacity of the Soviet soldiers and people. We shall do everything to help you that time, geography and our growing resources allow. The longer the war lasts, the more help we can give.[13]

Churchill revealed that several hundred bombers had attacked targets in Germany, something that would contribute to easing the pressure on the Red Army.

> Besides this, the Admiralty have at my request prepared a serious operation to come off in the near future in the Arctic, after which I hope that contact will be established between the British and Russian Navies. We welcome the arrival of the Russian Military Mission in order to coordinate future plans. In the meantime all we can do is to go on fighting to beat the life out of these villains.

Churchill's promise had obvious reservations, but it was nevertheless a promise. Officers at the top of the military hierarchy were well accustomed to Churchill's rhetoric, and still dragged their feet.

'The general trend of our conversations with the Russians both political and military, shows that we are being manoeuvred into a false position and may be forced to undertake unsound military action for political reasons,' said a note by a senior staff officer in the War Department on 10 July. 'It is the Russians who are asking for assistance; we are not. If they are going to fight they will fight – but for their own lives and not to help us defeat Germany.'[14]

'Accordingly I feel that the line we should take is as follows: We are doing quite nicely against Germany, particularly in view of ever increasing American aid and the practical certainty that USA will sooner or later come into the war. All our forces are now being devoted to the accomplishment of a definitive strategy for winning the war without having allowed for Russian aid.'

'If we are to divert forces from this major strategy in order to give Russia direct assistance, then we must be quite sure that these forces are not going to be wasted. In other words, we want more than assurances that Russia will not be rapidly defeated by Germany. We want concrete evidence.'

At the Mountain Corps' HQ, the retreat over the Litza had created an air of crisis.

'Dietl and his officers were worried that the Russians would exploit the situation by mounting an immediate counter-attack,' wrote Hans Rüf. 'A noticeable anxiety spread through the ranks, and at the command post at Herzberg the signals staff, clerks, cooks and all other non-combatants were hastily issued with rifles and told to prepare themselves for battle.'[15]

However, the Russian 52nd Division was totally exhausted after the bloody fighting and didn't have the capacity to carry out offensive operations. Instead, General Frolov initiated an alternative strategy that brought the Germans new worries: Destroyers and auxiliary vessels landed more and more fresh troops in uninhabited bays on the Litza Fjord. These were hastily enlisted reservists, sailors from the Northern Fleet without infantry training and personnel from the NKVD's border forces.

For the time being these landings were being checked by mobile patrols, but the threat to the German north flank was permanent and the losses were high. A Russian ammunition dump exploded, killing 70 men from a company of the 136th Regiment. Lieutenant Rohde's company, which had murdered the prisoners after the assault on Height 122, lost 36 men during two days of fighting.

Meanwhile, the casualty lists from the attack at the Litza were slowly being verified. In Fuschlberger's battalion, only 500 men had managed to make their way back to safety on the west bank, most of them without weapons or equipment. About 300 men had been killed, wounded or taken prisoner, including 13 officers. In the two battalions from the 138th Regiment, the losses were estimated at 15 per cent, which amounted to about 350 men.

These were uncomfortable figures, and Dietl was dismayed. In increasingly urgent telephone conversations with Falkenhorst's Chief of Staff in Rovaniemi, Colonel Erich Buschenhagen, he tried to justify the losses.

'My troops have proven that they are capable of attacking *without* the support of the Luftwaffe and with the enemy controlling the air space. But it can't continue like this. Murmansk cannot be reached if the corps is denied the aid of dive-bombers. The same applies to the growing threat against the north flank, where the landing vessels need to be attacked from the air. It is essential to expand and reinforce the corps with fresh troops to secure the flanks; a regiment at least, but preferably a whole division.'

He criticised Falkenhorst's strategy and maintained that all the army's resources now needed to be concentrated along one line of attack. 'The army cannot sustain two centres of gravity and attack Salla and Murmansk simultaneously. Instead, all the forces should be concentrated in the north. If I get sufficient back-up forces and air support, the capture of Murmansk will be guaranteed.'

Criticism was the last thing Falkenhorst wanted from the Nazi nest in the north, and the *Starosten* behaved with cold Prussian arrogance when he visited the Mountain Corps on Saturday 12 July. The confidence crisis had been overcome, and Dietl had already given orders for another attack the next day.

Falkenhorst, however, was interested in something quite different; he wanted to know who was to blame for the high losses in the first attack.

'The Army Commander is demanding an enquiry into the losses and how I/137's attack went wrong,' states an entry in the war diary. 'He is also calling for the dismissal of the battalion commander.'

Dietl tried to protest: 'Investigations are already underway. We must await the results before we denounce the person concerned.'

It was no use. Major Wolfgang Fuschlberger was made the scapegoat for the fiasco. He was dismissed, demoted and sent to the Central Front, where he fell outside Moscow a few weeks later.

Dietl earnestly requested air support for the attack the following morning.

'I can't promise anything,' Falkenhorst replied. 'I have no suitable resources available.'

In the United States, President Franklin D. Roosevelt had persisted in his struggle with the isolationists and in the spring of 1941 he signed the Lend-Lease Act, the huge aid programme which saved Great Britain from bankruptcy and grew to 50 billion dollars before the end of the war.[16]

In late June he followed Churchill's example and declared support for everybody who opposed Hitler, including the Soviet Union.

'On 9 July he directed Secretary of State, Sumner Wells, that substantial aid must be sent to Russia before 1 October,' Joan Beaumont wrote in her book, *Comrades in Arms*. 'He confirmed this with the Soviet ambassador on the following day. Fighter aircraft, he said, should be able to be delivered rapidly.'

As soon as Churchill learned about Roosevelt's generosity, the change in British strategy was implemented. He would not be left on the side-line if the Americans opened their arsenals.

'It seems absolutely necessary to send a small, mixed squadron of British ships to the Arctic to form contact and operate with the Russian naval forces,' he wrote in a sharp *Action this Day* memo on 10 July to Dudley Pound, the First Sea Lord:

> The effect upon the Russian Navy and upon the general resistance of the Russian Army of the arrival of what would be called a British fleet in the Arctic might be of enormous value and spare a lot of British blood.

The advantage we should reap if the Russians would keep the field and go on with the war, at any rate until the winter closes in, is immeasurable. A premature peace by Russia would be a terrible disappointment to the great masses of people in our country. These people have shown themselves worth backing, and we must make sacrifices and take risks even at our inconvenience, which I realise, to maintain their morale.[17]

Even Pound did not dare to sabotage a direct order from the great warlord himself. On Saturday 12 July the Commander of the Home Fleet was instructed to assemble a squadron which could operate in the Arctic.

The following day, one of the Royal Navy's most colourful and gallant officers was sent to Archangel by plane. Rear Admiral Philip Vian's name had become immortal after the raid against the prison ship *Altmark* in the Jössing Fjord in Norway in the winter of 1940.

Now he was to make sure that Churchill's *serious operation* got underway before it was too late.

CHAPTER 7

Bloody High Summer

The Litza Front, Sunday 13 July to Wednesday 16 July 1941

Only a few days into the attack, General Eduard Dietl realised that he was facing another defeat. Group von Hengl was pinned down by deadly fire in a mountain hollow known as the Ura Kettle 6 kilometres east of the River Litza and risked being totally wiped out if the troops continued their assault.

'We waited for night, knowing that night never came,' wrote Karl Springenschmid in his book *Es war ein Edelweiss*. 'It was still light in the Arctic, and we were bleeding to death under the onslaught of all types of weapons from every angle. We had ended up in a sort of witch's cauldron. Was it night or day? We didn't know. Sleep was impossible. Grenades rained down continually. More and more new crises had to be overcome.'[1]

The mood had been much lighter on Sunday 13 July when the Mountain Corps' core troops gathered again near the bank of the stubborn and blood-stained River Litza. High atmospheric pressure was building up over the polar regions. It was high summer in the Arctic, and the temperature rose towards 30°C.

'The mood before a major attack always seemed inspiring,' Hans Rüf reported. 'Troops marching and bivouacking, artillery being moved into position, huddled conferences with staff officers: everything testified to a gathering of strength. The soldiers no longer had the feeling of being abandoned. They were not alone. Men from unfamiliar units lay under every bush, ready to take part in the attack. Confidence in the success of the enterprise rose hourly.'[2]

The daily victory bulletins from the central Eastern Front stimulated optimism. The Panzer armies were already advancing towards Smolensk, hundreds of thousands of Russians had been killed or taken prisoner, thousands of planes and tanks had been destroyed. Neither Dietl nor his key officers wanted to achieve less than their rivals in Belorussia, who were reaping one honour after another as the whole world looked on in awe and horror.

> The whole corps felt a compulsion to continue the attack towards Murmansk. Morale was high despite the initial set-back. Nobody had a shred of doubt that the breakthrough would succeed.

Colonel Schmundt's personal report to Hitler had had an immediate effect. The motorised Machine Gun Battalion 4 with almost a thousand men, 55 machine guns, and 350 lorries and motorcycles had been transferred from the Salla Front, together with the 14th Finnish Infantry Regiment. A squadron of Stuka bombers had been ordered to take up a permanent station at Høybuktmoen, and five destroyers from the 6th Destroyer Flotilla plus four U-boats were on their way to bases in Tana and Varanger with orders to attack the Northern Fleet.

Encouraged by these significant reinforcements, Dietl had resurrected Schlemmer and Kreysing's plan for a major pincer movement around the main Soviet position east of the ruined bridge. An augmented battle group of about 6,000 men under Ritter von Hengl would advance towards the valley between Long Lake and Heart Lake, wheel south and take the Russians from behind. The important crags round the highway to Murmansk would at the same time be put under double pressure. A force of about 3,000 men under the Narvik veteran, Colonel Alois Windisch, would attack Height 183 north of the bridge. A similar force under Colonel Wilhelm Weiss would make a new attempt to capture the Brandl and Pranckh Heights in the south, along with the Devil's Gorge which lay between them.

> The four-man tents were pitched in the shade of the birch trees. It was oppressively hot, and thunderclouds were building up on the horizon. The troops ate, and oiled their weapons carefully. Artillery units hurried past, and the signals people dragged heavy reels of cable. Horses, mules and their attendants rested side by side on the moss-clad plain, and mortar ammunition was handed out. Each man had to make space in his rucksack for a heavy grenade. On a height nearby, Hengl and the officers were studying the maps.

Lieutenant Colonel von Hengl's real civilian name was Georg Hengl, and he was the son of an elementary school teacher. At the age of 17 he had almost been killed by a French bayonet during World War I. He had been wounded a further four times and in 1918 he had been transferred to the air force as observer for the flying ace Hans Baur, who later became Hitler's personal pilot. His courage as a youth had earned him both the Bavarian Order of Merit with Crown and Sword, and the Knight's Cross of the Order of Max-Joseph, which gave him the right to use the honorary title *Ritter* ('Sir') in front of his name. As a faithful Nazi he had made his career in the police and the SS under Heinrich Himmler before joining the mountain troops as an army captain, skier, mountaineer and member of the German team at the 1936 Winter Olympics in Garmisch-Partenkirchen. Like Dietl he was worshipped by the foot-soldiers, who had nicknamed him *Vater Hengl* (Papa Hengl).

'Unlike the ascetic and angular Dietl, von Hengl was a strongly built man who radiated health and joy,' wrote his admirer Springenschmid. 'Even in times of difficulty, he was always surrounded by an atmosphere of calm and common sense. He had a particular talent for giving the troops confidence. This was entirely because he expected the same of himself as he did of others. He had survived countless dangerous situations, had been wounded five times and he never lost his composure. In moments of danger he was to be found in the front line.'

On Sunday evening at 10.40 p.m. precisely, Hengl gave the signal to march off. The advance platoon crossed the Litza and secured a bridgehead on the east bank. Seven hours later the pontoon bridge was ready.

> At six o'clock on Monday morning 14 July the whole force was set in motion. First came the mountain troops with their steel helmets and packs; company after company at predetermined intervals. Then followed the pack animals, dismantled field guns, signals staff and pioneer troops, all disappearing into the scrubby woods like an endless brown-green sinuous snake.

Cold air from the north had suddenly struck Kola, and a violent thunderstorm broke out. The temperature fell towards freezing. The lightning flashed and the rain poured down.

> The storm happened in minutes. An icy wind came in from the sea, driving the rain ahead of it. The marshland soaked up water, and the rocks became as slippery as sheets of ice. The soldiers were sodden wet and laboured under the weight of their packs. The squalls brought only one benefit: The column was hidden from Soviet planes and artillery observers.

On the Russian side, the top officers were again late in understanding German intentions, partly because of the changes which had taken place.

Major General Nikishin had been dismissed as commander of the 52nd Division and been replaced by 44-year-old Colonel Georgij A. Vesjeserskij, a Polish-born former captain in the Tsar's army. The same had happened with Lieutenant Colonel Govorov, who had pulled back one of his battalions without permission and narrowly escaped a death sentence. His job was given to Major Nikolaj I. Shpilev from the 14th Division. Finally, Major Khariton Khudalov took over the 58th Regiment from Captain Gromov, who had shown himself too young and inexperienced to master the responsibilities.

'If the enemy succeeds in breaking through our right flank, our forces will be split and threatened from behind,' Chief of Staff Solovjov had told Khudalov during a staff conference. 'Army Commander Frolov has therefore given orders that the 58th and 112th Regiments should immediately be moved north together with the 208th Howitzer Regiment.'[3]

The problem was that this conference was taking place on Sunday 13 July, the same day as Hengl's battle group was assembling for the big attack. To be able to plug the gap in time, the newly appointed Khudalov would have to send the regiment on a forced march along the cart road east of the Long Lake.

> The weather was unusually bad, even for the polar regions. On the heights we were met by a downpour of rain and sleet, and the soldiers sank to their knees on the muddy track. On a rocky slope, we came upon a unit resting. The officers and men were exhausted and were sound asleep with helmets over their faces and their coats covered in snow.

Near the north end of Long Lake, explosions and small-arms fire were heard. The first machine-gun salvos hit the column.

> A couple of kilometres away, Soldatov's battalion had again been surrounded. Communications had been cut, but I knew the captain from a similar situation in the Devil's Gorge and I reckoned that he would cope. Nevertheless, I felt deeply uneasy. How could the enemy have managed to push so far east in such a short time? Two of our battalions were far ahead of the main force. What had happened? I gave orders to increase the pace and hoped to get there before it was too late.

In the meantime the newly appointed Rear Admiral Philip Vian and his entourage had landed in Archangel and travelled on to Moscow. On the morning of Tuesday 15 July, Vian was shown into the office of the Supreme Commander of the Soviet Navy, Admiral Nikolai Kuznetsov.

'Before leaving the Embassy for the Kremlin, Sir Stafford Cripps warned me that I should not find him easy: he was young, a politician of course, and would resent any views differing from his own,' Vian wrote in his memoirs, *Action This Day*. 'So I found. Sinister-looking, he received me politely, and said he was glad to meet the Commander of the British force which was to cooperate with the Russians in the far north against the Germans.'[4]

The meeting took place on Vian's forty-seventh birthday, and he had little sympathy for colleagues who played politics, whether they were in the Kremlin or elsewhere. The former destroyer captain was first and foremost a sailor and known for his ruthlessness and aggressive attitude. 'Both as a captain of a ship and as a flag officer, he burned to attack the enemy. He was the incarnation of fighting spirit and had an uncanny tactical sense,' said an article in the magazine *Naval Review* about the man who had spent more time at sea than anyone else in the Royal Navy. 'On the bridge, with his formidable eyebrows protruding from a gnarled face, he was an inspiring sight.'

Vian had not however come to the Soviet Union as head of a British force. He had come to investigate the *possibilities* of establishing such a force.

'I explained that I had been sent to examine the possibility of such co-operation. He showed surprise; he had it, he said, direct from Mr. Maisky, the Ambassador in Britain, that a naval force would be sent at once.'

Vian requested full authority for an unrestricted inspection of conditions at the docks in Murmansk and Polarnoje including anti-submarine barriers, anti-aircraft guns and other defence installations.

> He agreed, eventually, upon which I asked with what Russian naval forces we might expect to co-operate, and what command set-up he had in view. He gave no answer to these questions, and shortly afterwards we left.

Over the next few days Vian was shown round Archangel, Murmansk and Polarnoje, where he was welcomed by the Commander of the Northern Fleet, Vice Admiral Arsenij Golovko – without any more progress than in Moscow.

> In Polarnoje our time was divided between enormous and endless meals, and inspection of the so-called port defences, of which there were promises only, none being existent. There were no surface warships, only submarines, and these dived as each air-raid arrived. I asked the Port Admiral if he had not, in these submarines, the perfect answer to the interruption of German supply convoys; he replied, No, they were insufficiently trained; and this seemed to surprise the ever-present commissar.

Nor was Golovko very impressed with the visitor from Great Britain. 'Vian was tall and slim and behaved with nonchalant self-importance. He spoke in a high, staccato voice. Some of the questions he asked sounded odd to us.

For example he wanted to know whether we could provide a squadron with fresh vegetables, what quality the vegetables were and whether they could be inspected beforehand.'[5]

Vian also wanted to have detailed information about the fuel depots, something which was easy to answer. It was two quite different questions that aroused the young communist's indignation.

'Are you willing to build a military prison for British sailors, and what is the situation regarding brothels in the neighbourhood?'

Golovko answered stiffly: 'We will make vegetables available to the same extent as we supply them to our own seamen. But we will not set up a prison, and there are no brothels in our country. Nor will there be in future.'

The main German force reached the Round Lake about 3 p.m. on Monday, and von Hengl granted his troops a five-hour break. They had covered 5 kilometres, and the forming-up position for the attack was straight ahead.[6]

'The Ura Kettle opened up in front of the soldiers as a green hollow filled with tightly growing scrub,' Hans Rüf wrote. 'The dip was surrounded by bare hillsides. Height 322 on the Ura Mountain dominated from the south, and to the west were the steep slopes leading to Height 314. A moraine ridge littered with huge boulders rose towards Height 200 in the east, and the way forward ran between three lakes: the narrow Polyp Lake, Long Lake and Heart Lake.'

Hard fighting raged on the mountain plateaus on both sides. Two battalions had been sent out two days earlier to clear the way for the main force and were forcing their way eastwards in bitter fighting against Russian guard positions.

It was the noise from these skirmishes that Khudalov had heard as he led the 58th Regiment on towards the heights overlooking the Ura Kettle. The advance units from the 112th and 205th Regiments had been driven back, leaving a gap in the Russian defence line. Khudalov's mission was to close this gap before Group Hengl came through the Ura Kettle and reached the east bank of Long Lake with open access onwards to the area behind the main Russian position.

'Time passed terribly slowly,' wrote the newly appointed commander of the regiment, who waited impatiently for howitzers and 122 mm mortars to be brought forward. 'The fighting flared up, subsided, and then flared up again. The 1. Battalion was involved in an intense exchange of fire just 50 metres away. Captain Sjarov reported on the field telephone that two attacks had been repulsed. Five of the battalion's machine guns had been put

The second attack on the Litza ended in bloody hand to hand combat in the Ura Kettle between Long Lake and Heart Lake (Langer See and Herz S. on the map). Group Hengl reached the edge of the important Height 322, east of the north end of Long Lake, where a cart road led southwards to the Murmansk road (not shown on the map). The Narvik Regiment (139th) was stopped at Height 183, west of the southern end of Long Lake. (Rüf: Gebirgsjäger vor Murmansk)

CHAPTER 8

The Royal Navy Ventures North

Litza, Moscow and London, Thursday 17 July to Friday 1 August 1941

Rear Admiral Vian's journey to Moscow and Murmansk brought about a rapid clarification of the question of British help to the Soviet Union.

'A front in the north of France, besides diverting Hitler's forces from the East, would make invasion of Britain by Hitler impossible,' Stalin had written to Churchill in a detailed letter on Friday 18 July. 'It would be easier still to open a front in the North. This would call for action only by British naval and air forces, without landing troops or artillery. Soviet land, naval and air forces could take part. We would be glad if Great Britain could send thither, say, one light division or more of Norwegian volunteers, who could be moved to Northern Norway for insurgent operations against the Germans.'

As a supreme master of *Realpolitik*, Churchill still considered the Soviet chances of survival to be small. The Litza front was hard pressed, and Vian's inspection had shown that the defence installations in the Murmansk region were not good enough for the Kola Fjord to be used as a naval base. A Norwegian division as described by Stalin did not exist, and it would be madness to land large forces in regions where the Luftwaffe totally dominated the air. Churchill and his staff officers had bitter experience from the fiascos in mid-Norway during the spring of 1940. None of them wanted to take the risk of another defeat like the one at Namsos. The Russians would get help, but only on a limited scale.[1]

'Anything sensible and effective that we can do to help will be done. I beg you, however, to realise the limitations imposed upon us by our resources and geographical position,' Churchill wrote in his reply to Stalin the next day.

'One of our neighbouring companies was thrown back,' Lieutenant Gorjatsjik wrote in his diary. Lieutenant Kurjatsjev fell, and Lieutenant Kirejev was abandoned by his own men when they fled in panic. He was condemned to death by the Revolutionary Tribunal and shot. A German bomb exploded only 5 metres from our position. The whole trench collapsed. Four of my soldiers were badly wounded, and I was lucky to survive. I had gone to the field kitchen to fetch provisions.

Ritter von Hengl had planned to swing in behind Long Lake and begin the assault against the main Soviet position round the bridge at 5 p.m. on Wednesday 16 July.

But Major General Schlemmer had been following the development of the battle with increasing concern, and he reported to Dietl three quarters of an hour before the signal was due to be given.

> Hengl has two battalions stationed on Height 322, east of Long Lake. The rest of the regiment is still embroiled in heavy fighting in the Ura Kettle. The Russians are repeatedly launching new attacks, which make it impossible to gather the available forces for the final push. As long as all the forces are occupied defending the current position, it is pointless to consider going further.

The situation was deeply depressing for Dietl. Group Hengl had got stuck several kilometres from the objective, and Group Windisch seemed to be suffering the same fate as Fuschlberger's battalion had suffered in front of Height 183. A large area of the scrub along the approach route had been burnt, and Soviet artillery shot at anything that moved among the charred tree stumps. The losses were beyond anything he had previously experienced. In the 2nd Mountain Division alone, the casualties approached 3,000 dead and wounded.

General Frolov in Murmansk had shown himself to be a clever opponent. On Fisher Neck, the 135th Regiment was regrouping for another all-out attack against the German supply lines. Eleven vessels from the Northern Fleet had landed 1,300 men from the 135th Regiment, which had until now lain in reserve at the fishing station of Teriberka, plus a force of 250 volunteers from the navy. A powerful threat was developing against the north flank.

Late on the afternoon of 16 July, Dietl took the decision: the second attack on the Litza was to be called off. The corps was ordered to fall back and take up defensive positions around the bridgehead east of the river.

Vielwerth's battalion lost six officers and forty-six men in a short time and had to take cover in a hollow. Kräutler's force swung round and advanced further towards the plateau with the rest of the regiment just behind. They didn't get very far before a new hail of fire swept over the column. The Russians were brilliantly camouflaged and showed amazing discipline. They waited until the range was only a few tens of metres before opening fire. The effect was devastating. Dead and wounded fell all around, and the survivors threw themselves in panic behind the nearest rocks.

During the next 24 hours the battle developed into a series of close-quarter fights of increasing brutality. All chivalry appears to have been abandoned. Prisoners were taken only if they were needed to provide tactical information. Others were mercilessly shot down. The prior Nazi ideological campaign had convinced the mountain troops that the Red Guards were part of an inferior, Bolshevik-infested race who carried out vicious atrocities without hesitation.

'Several Russian air attacks against the field hospital on Herzberg, which was well marked with a red cross, created tremendous anger among our troops,' Hans Rüf wrote five years later when he tried to explain away the behaviour. 'It led to the war becoming inhuman. Injured Soviet prisoners would suddenly find means to shoot at soldiers from behind. Soon, no more prisoners were taken. The instinct for self-preservation led to barbaric counter-measures. Russian doctors carried mortar-bombs under their white coats. After that they were considered fair game and shot. The red cross armbands of the medical units disappeared on both sides. The brutality of war changed everybody.'[9]

The ideological campaign was just as intense on the Russian side. The Germans and Austrians were portrayed as scavenging animals under Fascism's yoke, who used cruel torture against prisoners-of-war. The soldiers were told that their ears and noses would be cut off if they allowed themselves to be captured. Terror was used to maintain discipline.

'Two men were lined up and shot in front of the cave which served as the regiment's command post,' Red Guard Viktor Andrejev said under interrogation. He had belonged to a unit from the 205th Regiment that had been surrounded and had suffered severe losses in the early stages of the battle. 'They were accused of panic-mongering, and so suffered the death penalty.'

Many others claimed that officers and political commissars shot soldiers who turned back – even in hopeless situations.

On Fisher Neck, Krasilnikov and Pashkovski had been sending wave after wave of Red Guards against the Germans on Mustatunturi and Height 122 throughout July, without gaining any ground.

out of action by German mortars. The western flank was being threatened by troops stalking from boulder to boulder.'[7]

Red Guard Ivan Lukjanov, who was taken prisoner two days later, gave a lively account of the situation. 'The German mortars had a devastating effect. It was like a cloudburst over us. We had to crawl forward, and the officers and NCOs followed us with their handguns cocked. They threatened to shoot anyone who turned back.'

By late evening on Monday 14 July, the 208th Howitzer Regiment was at last in position in the valley bottom behind the front line. About the same time, an orderly reported breathlessly to Khudalov. 'Lieutenant Schpak led a reconnaissance platoon and detected movements in the gullies below Height 314. An enemy column was advancing with mortars on pack animals. We were outnumbered, but we had an advantage: We controlled the heights.'

They had detected the main German force. Von Hengl had given the starting signal at 8 p.m. and sent Major Vielwerth's battalion (II/137) towards the narrow, stony pass leading into the Ura Kettle.

'Now it was a matter of reaching the exit point from the Kettle as quickly as possible,' Rüf wrote. 'Vielwerth and his mountain troops stormed through the gullies and on along the banks of Heart Lake before swinging to the right, into the hollow. The rest of the regiment followed behind in a kilometre long column.'[8]

Suddenly, a hail of fire broke out from the ridges overlooking the kettle. The German advance had been sprung at the very last moment. Troops from Khudalov's 58th Regiment and Korotkov's 112th Regiment opened fire with all they had.

'We lay stuck in the gully with Heart Lake on our left and the steep slopes under Height 314 on our right,' Springenschmid reported. 'Bursts of machine gun fire rained down on us from the flank and made movement impossible. Shells from field guns and mortars exploded among the rocks and showered us with splinters and shrapnel. Nobody could go any further until the nearby summits were cleared.'

Hengl sent two battalions into immediate action against the key heights. The guns of the 111th Mountain Artillery Regiment were unloaded from the pack animals, mounted and put into position. In the course of the night the forward Soviet positions were over-run. Nevertheless, Tuesday 15 July was a black day for the mountain troops, who suffered severe losses as they forced their way through the Ura Kettle and fought their way onwards towards the strategically important plateau east of Long Lake.

> You must remember that we have been fighting all alone for more than a year, and that, although our resources are growing, and will grow fast from now on, we are strained to breaking point both at home and in the Middle East ... It is to the North that we must look for any speedy help that we can give.

In the first phase, the previously announced naval operation was about to take place. 'The Naval Staff has been preparing for the past three weeks an operation by sea-borne aircraft upon German shipping in Northern Norway and Finland, hoping thereby to destroy the enemy's capacity to transport troops by sea to attack your Arctic flank. We have asked your staff to keep a certain area clear of Russian vessels between 28 July and 2 August when we shall hope to strike.'

Under pressure from Churchill the First Sea Lord, Sir Dudley Pound, had reluctantly assembled a naval task force with the cruiser HMS *Devonshire* as flagship and Rear Admiral Frederic Wake-Walker as commander.

'By force of circumstances this operation was carried out in a hurry,' wrote the cautious Wake-Walker, whose mission was to execute the hotly debated *political* gesture in support of the Soviet Union, using aircraft from the carriers HMS *Victorious* and HMS *Furious*.

> Neither *Victorious* nor *Furious* was really ready for such an operation, and some of the pilots had never deck-landed before. During the six days in which the operation had to be planned, *Victorious* was frequently at sea exercising, as also was *Devonshire* for some days. *Furious* was only available for two days and was at sea exercising for most of the time. This made it very difficult for any consultations to be held as to the details of the plan.[2]

Nevertheless, the strike power of the task force was formidable. Within minutes, the two carriers could deploy 64 aircraft, including 30 Albacore torpedo-bombers, 21 Fulmar fighters and some Hurricanes. The escort was made up of the heavy cruisers HMS *Devonshire* and HMS *Suffolk*, 10 destroyers, the oil tanker *Black Ranger*, plus the 7,000-ton mine laying cruiser HMS *Adventure*. As the very first tangible expression of willingness to help Stalin's hard-pressed regime, the minelayer carried a cargo of 320 magnetic mines and degaussing equipment, destined for the Soviet port of Archangel.

'*Adventure* was placed under my orders so she might make her passage to North Russia under cover of the forces taking part,' wrote Wake-Walker, who left Scapa Flow with the task force on 23 July and headed for Iceland.

The Rear Admiral's ultimate goals were the two small but heavily defended ports of Kirkenes and Petsamo, at the end of the long supply route along the

Norwegian coast from the main Wehrmacht depots in Germany to the isolated Mountain Corps on the tundra.

German freighters were being unloaded day and night at the local wharves, ships which would have been tempting targets for Wake-Walker's torpedo-bombers. But the British had no spies behind enemy lines in Northern Norway, and the Russians refused to share current intelligence from air reconnaissance.

Lieutenant Commander Norman Denning at the Admiralty Operational Intelligence Centre in London and the codebreakers at Bletchley Park had therefore been hard at work, hoping to piece together as accurate a picture as possible of German ship movements to and from Kirkenes and Petsamo.

For once, the codebreakers were at a loss. No recent decryptions of German radio traffic emanating from the High North were available. As the head of the Naval Section at Bletchley Park, Frank Birch, wrote to Denning: 'Harbour reports in North Norway ceased on 16/6 and W/T in extreme north has been un-readable since 12/6.'[3]

Birch's analysts had nevertheless put together a list of 32 ships which had been identified by Enigma in the spring of 1941. Many of them were among Dietl's old workhorses for the transport of supplies and troops: *Barcelona, Kerkplein, Donau 2, Barmbek, Nicole Schiaffino, Stamsund* and several more.

'There has been no sign of any of them moving south since last mention,' Birch wrote. 'Had they moved south, however, we would almost certainly have heard of some of them.'

The conclusion was optimistic, based on out-dated intelligence. No guarantees existed that the ships were still in the relevant ports, and Wake-Walker felt uneasy. The attack on Kirkenes and Petsamo was basically Churchill's operation, and the Rear Admiral had learned to fear the wrath of the former First Lord of the Admiralty. When the battleship HMS *Hood* was sunk by *Bismarck* in the Denmark Strait in May, Wake-Walker as the senior surviving officer had taken command of the remaining ships and decided to break off the engagement. In disappointment and rage, Churchill had very nearly accused Wake-Walker and his fellow-officers of cowardice and threatened a court martial. Only the intervention by the Commander of the Home Fleet, Admiral John Tovey, had saved him from disgrace. Now Tovey had appointed him leader of a new operation which the explosive Prime Minister was following with close interest. That thought could frighten the strongest, and the lack of clear and recent intelligence did nothing to help.

'I had information of various anchorages used by shipping in May and June,' Wake-Walker wrote. 'These seemed clearly connected with the assembly of forces in the Kirkenes area preparatory to the attack on Russia. For operations in this area to be effective in terms of material damage, far better intelligence than was available in this case is necessary.'

Meanwhile, high summer had returned to Kola as fast as it had disappeared. The sun dispersed the clouds, the wind died and the temperature climbed again to 30°C. The Litza Valley, once so green and tranquil, had been transformed in the course of three weeks into a smouldering Hell. Swathes of scrub had been consumed by fire and lay in ashes. Explosions rocked the air, and clouds of black smoke rose from bomb craters. Hundreds of dead horses and mules lay shot to pieces in no-man's-land, surrounded by the bodies of young men from Germany, Austria and Russia. All were decomposing rapidly in the roasting heat, and the stench of suffering and death filled the broken valley.[4]

'On the slopes between Height 314 and Heart Lake we found the bodies of 120 mountain soldiers,' Khudalov wrote. He also had to record his own troops' grim statistics after the fighting in the Ura Kettle. On Wednesday 16 July the 58th Regiment had been reduced to only 505 men, less than one sixth of the normal complement.

Rest and recuperation were out of the question. General Frolov in Murmansk had ordered fresh attacks on the German bridgehead, which was under continual bombardment by field guns and mortars. The three depleted regiments of the 52nd Division stormed over the rocks and drove the corps back. Heights 322 and 314 were abandoned after bloody fighting and the Germans concentrated their defence round a front line which extended in an arc south of Round Lake, from Height 258 to the summit known as Col de Lana.

'The Russian artillery suddenly opened up,' wrote Hans Rüf. 'We had redeployed, and Hell's dance began. Guns and mortars shelled the whole line systematically, from position to position. One unit counted over a thousand shells landing in the course of one single day. The bombardment continued day and night. The bogs below were ploughed up and the rocks above smashed to pieces. And in the midst of it all came the Russian attacks. The men leapt to their rifle and machine gun positions. The fighting lasted for an hour or two before the Russians pulled back, leaving ten or twelve men behind. Even before they had disappeared, the next wave came in. Hand grenades rolled down the hillside and exploded amidst the attackers. We heard grim screams of pain, but the Russians kept coming – again and again.'[5]

The situation was becoming more and more challenging for Corps Commander Dietl and his senior officers. The losses continued to mount, and some units in Group Hengl were reduced to a handful of men. The last reserves were spent, and the north flank was in flames from Mustatunturi in the west to the Litza Fjord in the east. The Russians seemed unstoppable, and some officers were already in favour of pulling the corps right back to the Titovka Valley to shorten the supply lines and stabilise the situation. To Dietl, this was unthinkable. If the bridgehead were given up, the hope of reaching Murmansk would be abandoned for good. All the blood spilt by the heroes of Narvik would have been in vain.

'It is impossible to continue the attack without significant reinforcements,' Dietl had told the recently promoted Chief-of-Staff of Army Command Norway, Major General Erich Buschenhagen as early as 17 July. The corps is without reserves on a front 60 kilometres long, with open flanks to north and south. The troops are exhausted and have suffered heavy losses. The number of pack animals is so severely reduced that many units can no longer be supplied with their daily needs of food and ammunition.'

The following day he repeated the request in a telephone conversation with Army Commander Falkenhorst in Rovaniemi, adding another demand:

> The attack can only be resumed if the corps is provided with reinforcements of at *least* one new division. That will make it possible to sort out the flanks and secure the lines to the rear.

Falkenhorst appeared to have agreed with this request. So it came as a nasty surprise to Dietl's Chief of Staff, Lieutenant Colonel Le Suire, when Buschenhagen two days later gave a quite different account of the conversation. 'Falkenhorst was glad that Dietl assessed the situation calmly and confidently and that he had no thoughts whatever of abandoning the attack.'

Falkenhorst's insincerity was showing again, and Le Suire replied angrily: 'The conversation was not at all like that. Dietl said that he could and would resume offensive operations as soon as he was supplied with a new division. He also said that he needed reinforcements immediately just to maintain the current position.'

Le Suire argued again that the army's centre of gravity should be moved from Salla to the Litza Front. This further poisoned the relationship between the army headquarters in the luxurious Pohjanovi Hotel in the capital city of Northern Finland and the corps headquarters in the tents on the tundra at Kola.

An hour later it was Dietl's turn to try: 'The Russians are also worn out. So now is the time to transfer a fresh division that can over-run the positions at the Litza! One regiment is not enough, but a new division will guarantee the outcome.'

Neither argument had any effect. 'It's quite impossible to move a division from Salla to Litza,' Buschenhagen explained. 'We have no forces to spare.'

This ill-tempered discussion went on for three days. The provisional reply came on the evening of Wednesday 22 July. Falkenhorst was considering sending two battalions to the exhausted corps, but he wouldn't weaken the defence of Norway without consulting higher authority. So he had asked for approval from Wehrmacht Supreme Command. Until a reply had been received, the unruly corps commander would just have to manage as best he could.

Two battalions were not nearly enough, but Dietl was nevertheless relieved. Wehrmacht Supreme Command consisted of the Führer's own staff. Hitler would have the last word, and Hitler was Dietl's friend.

While these discussions were going to and fro on the telephone line between Rovaniemi and Titovka, a Catalina flying boat passed by, far out at sea. The head of the Russian Military Mission, General Filipp Golikov, had given a report to Stalin and was on his way back to London with new instructions.

'Russia is fighting and will fight to the bitter end,' Golikov said when he met Foreign Minister Anthony Eden together with Ambassador Maisky and Vice Admiral Kharlamov. 'I must however renew my plea for concrete assistance without delay. I also ask for information in regard to the progress of the operations planned in the North.'[6]

Like Churchill, Stalin clearly understood that the industrial might of the United States could ultimately decide the outcome of the war. Furthermore, his confidence in Great Britain's willingness and capacity to help had worn very thin. Golikov had therefore been given a new mission: the general was to travel to America to acquire all the weapons the British wouldn't provide.

'I hope to go almost immediately to the United States in connection with the supply questions and hope I will enjoy the assistance of His Majesty's Government in this matter,' he explained as he put forward an astonishing additional demand, obviously inspired by the scheming despot in the Kremlin.

'I emphasise the importance of the route Greenland–Iceland–Spitzbergen for the transit of supplies to Russia. There is already a considerable Russian colony at the mines in Spitzbergen which could be armed for defence. If that proved insufficient, regular troops could if necessary be sent, including I hope, Norwegian troops. That of course will have to be arranged with the Norwegian government. I insist on the necessity of occupying Bear Island also in order to deny it to the Germans. We would be prepared to put a small garrison there with two batteries.'

Golikov's temerity opened up a new dimension in the discussions about military help to the Russians in the North. A new player found an opportunity to enter the negotiations within the great anti-Nazi alliance that was being created: the Norwegian Government-in-Exile, which had struggled to find its place in the Allied coalition since its escape from occupied Norway in June 1940.

When Eden forewarned Foreign Minister Trygve Lie of the Russian demands a few days earlier, Lie had pointed out that the Spitsbergen archipelago was under Norwegian sovereignty. 'An occupation by the British or the Russians would be a serious infringement of the rights of the Norwegian Government.'[7]

The Svalbard Treaty gave Norway control over Bear Island and Spitsbergen, and Article 9 forbade the establishing of military bases on the islands. Forty-five-year-old Trygve Lie was a quick-thinking man who had taken over the post of Foreign Minister from the ageing and compromised Halvdan Koht a few months earlier. He was right to be concerned about possible long-term effects of an occupation. But he was also a pragmatist, and he added: 'If the Russian Government is willing to take part in the defence of Svalbard against the Germans as part of a combined allied war effort, we shall almost certainly be willing to discuss the matter.'

There was however an insurmountable obstacle. In early May 1941, Stalin had broken off diplomatic relations and expelled the Norwegian Ambassador from Moscow, claiming that Norway had ceased to exist after the German occupation. This had further contributed to the government in exile's isolation. Now the cards were suddenly being reshuffled as a result of *Barbarossa* and the negotiations about aid to the Soviet Union.

'The condition for any discussion must be that the Russian side gives full and complete recognition to the Norwegian Government in London,' Lie specified. 'A mutual diplomatic representation must be set up.'

Ambassador Maisky quickly saw to it that the diplomatic relationships were re-established as soon as 8 August; an obvious indication of the importance Stalin attached to securing the shipping route through the Barents Sea.

In the meantime, discussions among the staff officers had pointed out that a military occupation of Spitsbergen would be at least as challenging as a landing in Northern Norway. Almost 3,000 miners in the mining communities around the Ice Fjord produced nearly 600,000 tonnes of coal, which were shipped to ports in north-west Russia and Northern Norway and used for domestic heating in winter.

A loss of this supply would require the Quisling administration to increase the import of coal from Germany, which would put further pressure on the Nazi economy. That could lead to a German counter-attack against Spitsbergen supported by long-range bombers from the Norwegian mainland. The consequences could be dramatic as the island group was surrounded by metre-thick ice for half the year.

If the wooden buildings in the mining communities were destroyed and burnt, it would be impossible to rescue the civilian population and a possible military garrison. They would be trapped behind pack ice that no Allied ship could penetrate.

Anyway, a detailed plan could not be made until a thorough reconnaissance had been carried out. That gave Rear Admiral Philip Vian a new task. He had just returned home from his exploratory trip to Moscow and Murmansk. Now he was being sent north again to Barentsburg and Longyearbyen.

'My force consisted of the cruisers *Nigeria* and *Aurora*, together with the destroyers *Tartar* and *Punjabi*, and sailed from Scapa Flow on 27 July,' Vian wrote in *Action This Day*.[8]

Despite its newly won recognition, the Norwegian Government-in-Exile was not officially informed of the expedition. The Norwegian Admiral Commanding, Henry Diesen, did however send Lieutenant Ragnvald Tamber with the expedition as interpreter and liaison officer.

Diesen, who had failed miserably during the German invasion in April 1940, now seemed much more belligerent. 'The admiral was rigid in his views and advocated castrating all the Nazi leaders after the war. When the extent of the Nazi atrocities became known, he extended his condemnation to the whole population, women included.'

In his 'Wolf's Lair' headquarters in East Prussia, Hitler had become involved in new feuds with the Army chiefs von Brauchitsch and Halder. More than two million Soviet soldiers had been killed, wounded or taken prisoner in less than seven weeks. The Wehrmacht's losses in the same period amounted to barely more than 200,000 men. The German string of battlefield victories had been overwhelming despite the scale of losses, but the Red Army was not defeated. Whenever a Soviet formation was destroyed, another appeared. Stalin's reserves seemed endless, and behind the triumphant façade, concern was growing.

'The mood was tense,' Wilhelm Canaris, the head of German military intelligence reported after a visit to Wolfsschanze at the end of July. 'The campaign is obviously not going according to the book, and it is steadily becoming more apparent that the Bolshevik regime will *not* collapse from within as predicted but rather seems to be closing ranks and increasing its resistance.'[9]

Thousands of planes had been shot down. Eight thousand tanks were destroyed in the middle of July. Fourteen days later the tally had risen to 12,000, but new and heavier varieties kept rolling out of the Soviet factories. 'If I had known that Stalin had so many tanks available, I would have thought twice before attacking,' Hitler told the panzer commander, General Heinz Guderian, at the beginning of August.

The Nazi leaders still had unshakeable belief in final victory. Their dispute arose from the question of *how* to carry the attack forward. Brauchitsch and Halder wanted a direct attack on Moscow. Hitler wanted to secure Leningrad and the raw materials in the Ukraine and Caucasus first.

In a private letter in July, Halder wrote: 'He is playing the warlord again and plaguing us with so many absurd ideas that we risk throwing away everything our glorious victories have secured. The Russians are not like the French. They don't give up when they are tactically defeated. No, they have to be picked off one by one in a terrain which is a mixture of forest and bog. This takes time, and Hitler doesn't have the nerves for that.'

In a sense, the situation on the Litza Front was a miniature picture of the situation on the Central Front, with one important difference; Dietl had got stuck and was going no further. There is every reason to believe that Hitler's desire to support his party comrade's unsuccessful campaign in the North was among the 'absurd ideas' which angered Halder. He and Brauchitsch had been opponents of the attack through Finland and were supported by Falkenhorst and Buschenhagen. But the Mountain Corps was led by some of the army's most ingrained Nazis and the Führer would not leave them in the lurch.

On Thursday 24 July he gave approval for the transfer of two battalions from Norway to the Litza Front.

For Dietl, this reinforcement was a first show of support after many weeks of fruitless wrangling with 20th Army Headquarters, but it was not enough.

'The two battalions are only enough for a tidying up action on the north flank,' he replied the same evening.

The ageing Colonel Albin Nake had been dismissed as commander of the 136th Mountain Regiment and been replaced by another ardent Nazi from within the corps, 49-year-old Colonel Georg Hofmeister, whose wife was a close friend of Frau Marga Himmler, the estranged wife of the SS boss. Hofmeister was to lead the regiment and the new battalions in a merciless attack on the Soviet forces which had landed around the Litza Fjord.

'The action will start in a few days,' Dietl wrote. 'But to continue the attack on Murmansk the corps needs *at least* a full division and strong artillery support.'[10]

In Rovaniemi, Falkenhorst and Buschenhagen were requesting more and more written reports from Dietl to support his demands.

Dietl was ready for this request and replied the next day: 'An allocation of 1,000 mountain troops and 100 mountain artillerymen is needed immediately. Neither this reinforcement nor the two new battalions will be enough. If I am to hold a 60-km-long front against constant Soviet attack, I really need an augmented regiment and artillery. That is only to hold the position. A renewed attack on Murmansk would need a whole new division.'

Hitler had in the meantime side-stepped Brauchitsch and Halder and forced through a prioritisation of Leningrad in the north and the Ukraine in the south as objectives, rather than Moscow. On Wednesday 30 July he followed this up by reinforcing Dietl's corps with a new division.

It wasn't just any division that Hitler wanted to send north. It was one of the Wehrmacht's absolutely elite formations, the highly trained 6th Mountain Division under the fire-breathing Nazi General Ferdinand Schörner, who had captured Athens a few weeks earlier and planted the swastika on the top of the Acropolis.

Rear Admiral Wake-Walker had sailed north, and on 30 July he was approaching the Eastern Bank, about 100 nautical miles north-east of the objectives, under cover of thick fog.

'The weather was favourable, overcast, low cloud and visibility not too good,' he wrote in his report. 'About 1200 the clouds thinned and finally cleared away with good visibility. Still, the Force had not been sighted and there appeared every reason to hope that the attack would be launched without it being detected.'[11]

Churchill's operation was about to be put into action after several weeks of doubt and disagreement, but Bletchley Park had still not managed to identify which ships were in Petsamo and Kirkenes, apart from five destroyers from the 6th Destroyer Flotilla, thought to be stationed in the area.

At 2.30 p.m., just as the first planes were taking off from the decks of HMS *Victorious* and *Furious*, the good luck came to an abrupt end. The clouds cleared, and a Heinkel reconnaissance plane flew right past.

'An enemy report was made by the aircraft, and from that moment the German destroyers operating off Tana Fiord ceased to transmit. I considered it was too late to call off the attack and it was accordingly launched as originally arranged.'

About 40 minutes later, 20 Albacore torpedo-bombers and nine Fulmar fighters reached the coast. But the harbour at Petsamo lay empty and in Kirkenes the auxiliary cruiser *Bremse* and the minelayer *Bali* were leaving the Bøk Fjord as escorts for two impounded Norwegian ships, the local steamers *Sandnes* and *Karen*, which were being used as accommodation ships for Luftflotte 5 and the German navy.

Anti-aircraft guns opened intense fire, and Messerschmitt fighters were on their way from Høybuktmoen.

'The enemy reconnaissance aircraft sighted us at the most unfortunate moment, and gave the enemy plenty of time to prepare for the arrival of the strike force,' wrote Captain Henry Cecil Bovell of HMS *Victorious*, who was one of the Royal Navy's most experienced aircraft carrier captains. 'With all chance of surprise gone, and with a cloudless sky, heavy casualties were inevitable, yet the attack was pressed home with great determination and gallantry. I consider that the conduct of all who took part is deserving of the highest praise,'

The biplane, single-engine Albacore torpedo-bombers were very out-dated, with low speed and scant capacity to withstand modern weapons. Nevertheless, the pilots launched the attack fearlessly and the torpedoes were fired into Kirkenes harbour. But none of them hit their targets, and on the way out of the fjord 11 Albacore bombers and two Fulmar fighters were shot down.

The resistance in Petsamo was weaker, but no cargo ships were to be found and the torpedoes were wasted on old wooden quays, oil tanks and a 100-foot fishing boat.

Churchill's first goodwill gesture to Stalin had ended in total fiasco. The Fleet Air Arm had lost 13 aircraft, 11 others were damaged and 38 pilots and navigators had been killed or taken prisoner.

'The object of this attack, which was to make a gesture in support of our Allies and create a diversion on the enemy's northern flank, was achieved,' the Admiralty stated in a later commentary. 'There is reason to believe that the moral and political repercussions had some effect on the enemy's dispositions.'

That was mostly untrue, as Dietl noted dryly in his war diary: 'A shed on land burnt down, a few dead and wounded, a 74-tonne vessel sunk.'

Rear Admiral Golovko in Polarnoje expressed himself in similar terms: 'Unfortunately the losses that the British suffered were significantly greater than the damage they inflicted. They had seriously underestimated the air defences in Kirkenes and Petsamo.'

CHAPTER 9

Red August

The Litza Front, Saturday 2 August to Sunday 7 September 1941

Despite the failure of the raid against Kirkenes and Petsamo from a military point of view, tangible aid to the Soviet Union developed steadily from the beginning of August 1941.[1]

'So proceed,' Churchill wrote on a memo from the Air Ministry on 27 July about two squadrons of Hurricane fighters that were being prepared for transport to Murmansk. 'We must give what help is possible.'

The 39 planes with 350 pilots and ground staff from RAF No. 155 Wing were originally intended to provide air support for a British naval force in the Kola Fjord, but that project was abandoned. Instead, the two squadrons were to be used against the Luftwaffe on the Litza Front and were sent north with the very first Russian convoy, codenamed *Dervish*. The six Allied freighters also carried two million leather boots; significant quantities of tin; rubber; aluminium; machine tools; jute; woollen jackets; and other products and raw materials.

On Saturday 26 July the submarine HMS *Tigris* took to sea from the Holy Loch and set course for Polarnoje, followed a week later by her sister ship, HMS *Trident*. With a displacement of 1,500 tons, a range of 4,500 nautical miles, 16 torpedoes and a 4-inch gun on the foredeck, each of these two vessels was in effect an underwater cruiser, intended to take up the fight against the Germans on the Finnmark coast. The skippers were Lieutenant Commanders Howard Bone and Geoffrey Sladen, both among the most outstanding submariners in the Royal Navy.

'Rendezvous was fixed for 10.00 on Monday 4 August in position 69.30N 35.10E, and *Tigris* was sighted at 10.45 two miles north of this position,' reported 56-year-old Captain Richard Bevan, who a few days earlier had been appointed Senior Naval Officer Polarnoje. 'The submarine had encountered fog for a large part of her journey and had obtained no sightings for three days until that same morning. This negligible error was a remarkable feat by the Commanding Officer of *Tigris* in terms of accurate navigation – with which the Soviet authorities were greatly impressed ... Contact was made with *Trident* at 04.30 on 10 August within half a mile of the rendezvous position, thus keeping up the reputation set by *Tigris*.'[2]

In his headquarters in the Titovka Valley, General Eduard Dietl was embroiled in a new and bitter conflict with Falkenhorst and Buschenhagen. In addition to the 6th Mountain Division, Hitler had extended the support to his old Nazi friend with a further two regiments: the reinforced Bavarian 388th Infantry Regiment under Colonel Wilhelm Daser and the motorised 9th SS Infantry Regiment under SS-Obersturmbannführer Ernst Deutsch.[3]

To Falkenhorst's chagrin, his rival's corps would in the next few weeks receive reinforcements amounting to 25,000 men, and the wily army commander soon came up with a new idea: would the corps with the support of the two fresh regiments be able to complete the initial stage of the attack on Murmansk *before* the arrival of the 6th Mountain Division at the beginning of September?

Despite misgivings, Dietl and his divisional commanders, Schlemmer and Kreysing, reluctantly accepted Falkenhorst's proposal a few days later. With the assistance of Daser's infantry and Deutsch's SS-troops they would annihilate the main Soviet forces on the east side of the Litza, to create a favourable starting point for the 6th Mountain Division's subsequent push towards Murmansk. For a third and final time, the corps would try to surround and crush the enemy hiding in the accursed ravines, with the whole of the 2nd Mountain Division attacking along the coast in the north, and the 3rd Mountain Division moving in from the south.

The subsequent quarrel stemmed from the interference of Falkenhorst and his chief of staff with the tactical appreciations of the Mountain Corps. They wanted Kreysing's division and Daser's motorised infantry regiment to abandon the road leading to the blown-up bridge and cross the Litza 6 kilometres further south, in the wild, trackless terrain near Lake Knyrk.

'To eject the enemy from his positions in the hills by a frontal attack is in my opinion absolutely impossible,' said Buschenhagen, who strongly advised the corps to shift the main thrust of the attack further south.

Dietl and Le Suire resented Army Command Norway HQ's meddling in their tactical evaluations and rejected the proposal, insinuating that the desk-bound and torpid generals in Rovaniemi did not understand the difficulty of the terrain.

'You can't imagine how impenetrable the land is just by studying the maps,' claimed Le Suire when he met Buschenhagen on the Arctic Road for an open-air crisis meeting on 18 August. 'It will be impossible to bring forward and make use of artillery in the jungle of scrubby woodland. Further north, the thrust will have the support of all of the corps' and the divisions' artillery. That would not be the case in the south.'

Dietl considered the interference almost as an attack on his personal reputation as a tactician, and he completely refused to listen. 'The 3rd Division and the company commanders have unanimously said that an assault over the Pranckh and Brandl Heights will offer the best chance of success. That route leads directly to the highway to Murmansk, and the artillery will be able to provide fully effective support. A regrouping would require road-building and further loss of time without any guarantee of success. The corps' plan is the best one, based on all our experience from the campaign so far.'

He categorically refused to move Kreysing's force south, and he made an angry entry in his war diary: 'As the general-in-command, the demand has laid a heavy additional burden on me. If I refuse and the attack fails, that will obviously be used as another black mark against me and my leadership.'

A full-scale crisis of confidence had arisen between the rivals in the northern theatre of war. The war diary would be sent to Berlin and to Wolfsschanze and would undoubtedly be shown to Hitler. That was more than Falkenhorst could risk. On Wednesday 20 August, he invited Dietl to a conciliatory meeting in Rovaniemi.

On the Russian side, 14th Army Commander Frolov had for weeks been insisting on repeated counter-attacks, from Mustatunturi in the north-west to the bridgehead near the mouth of the Litza in the east. The exhausted battalions in the 52nd Division and the partly reconstituted 14th Division were thrown against the German positions again and again without *apparent* effect.

'Divisional Commander Vesjeserskij was convinced that the Germans were preparing for a major new offensive,' Major Khudalov wrote. 'To improve our own position, we had to attack first. I was ordered to take Height 275, three kilometres west from us.'[4]

The three battalions of the 58th Regiment had advanced into the Ura Kettle, with Soldatov's Red Guards in the gloomy Valley of Death and the rest

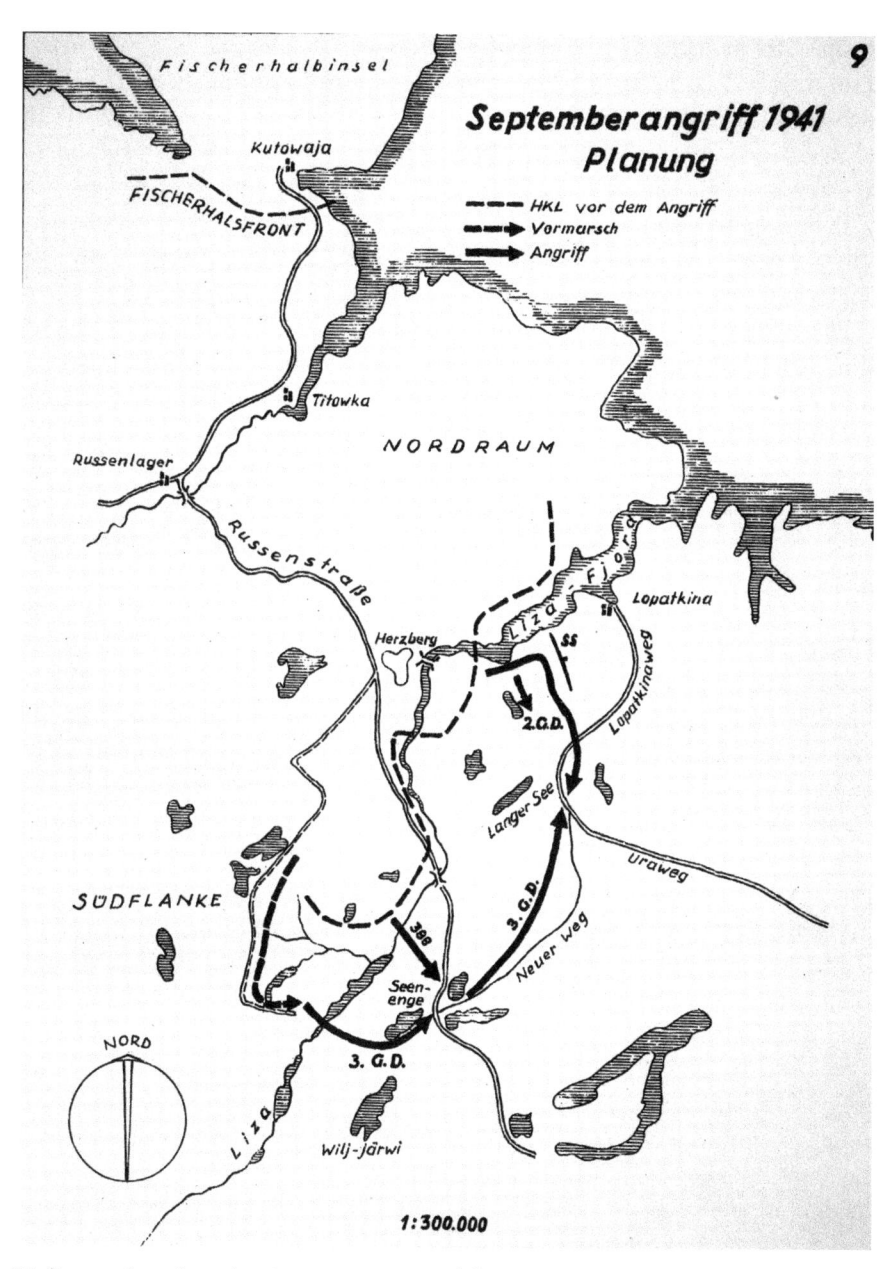

Dietl's corps planned a major pincer manoeuvre round the Soviet main position, with the 2nd Mountain Division and 9th SS Regiment in the north (2. G.D.) and the 3rd Mountain Division with 388th Regiment in the south (3. G.D.). The two arms of the pincer would come together when the forces from the north and the south met at Height 322, north-east of Long Lake. (Rüf: Gebirgsjäger vor Murmansk)

grouped on the surrounding ridges. The dominating Height 275 rose steeply up from Round Lake and gave von Hengl's mountain troops all the advantages of the terrain.

'We tried to storm the height time after time without success. Every time we got halfway up the cliff, the Germans threw a shower of hand-grenades down on us. I got help from the army's artillery commander, who personally controlled the bombardment from the regimental command post. That was no use either. The mountain troops clung on firmly to their position.'

The last major effort was made on the night of Wednesday 13 August, when Khudalov assembled the whole regiment to storm the summit. But just a couple of hours before the starting signal was due to be given, two deserters from his 1. Battalion had betrayed the plan to the Germans.

'On 11 or 12 August everybody except the sentries was gathered together and told that the decisive attack would take place right after midnight.'

In the positions occupied by Vielwerth's battalion and the 111th Mountain Artillery Regiment, the news led to a full state of alert.

'We were informed of a huge attack at 11 p.m. and had only an hour to prepare,' says the entry in *Bericht GAR 111 juni-oktober 1941*. 'We didn't know if the deserters were telling the truth, but we didn't take any chances. A major attack meant that the Russians would advance on a broad front, and right enough: Soon after midnight it was as if the heavens were raining down fire upon us. The height was immediately enveloped in tongues of flame as if a volcano had erupted. Clouds of smoke obliterated all visibility, but the mountain troops were ready. Four hours of intense fighting followed before the Russians withdrew. By then our batteries had fired off 1,875 rounds.'[5]

The deserters Kamil and Akabar were Avars from Dagestan in the Caucasus. They hated the Bolsheviks who had forcibly collectivised the old Muslim population. 'There are hundreds of Avars in the regiment who don't want to fight, but the political commissars are well aware of their attitudes and keep a close eye on them.'

The German interrogators were given a disturbing picture of the situation in the Ura Kettle after several weeks of fighting. 'The losses have been extremely high, and the ravines and surrounding hillsides are covered with the bodies of officers and men alike, because the topsoil is too thin to bury them. The bodies have started to decay and are making a horrible stench.'

According to the deserters, some companies were reduced to 20–25 battle-hardened Red Guards. Only a handful of the veterans from the opening phase of the battles had survived, and the combined strength of the 1. Battalion amounted to barely more than 100 men. 'The replacements are coming less and less frequently, and have recently been made up of political prisoners and miners in their fifties without military training or experience.'

The situation was hardly better on the German side. Even though the daily Russian attacks seemed to be a senseless waste of life, their effect was significant.

'The troops were worn out, impassive and depressed, wrote Hans Rüf. 'The mental and physical strains had left deep scars. Many of the men sat apathetically at their posts with sunken cheeks and unshaven faces. The constant bombardment and the hail of projectiles from field-guns and mortars necessitated constant vigilance and forced the soldiers to crouch in hollows and trenches. Anyone who wasn't careful risked being killed by Russian snipers. Nobody could allow themselves to lower their guard.'[6]

The losses had reached frightening levels. Up to 12 August the 2nd Mountain Division alone had 671 dead, 151 missing and 2,257 wounded. This amounted to 3,079 men, 36 per cent of the fighting force, the highest losses among the divisions operating on the Eastern Front in the summer of 1941.

These were critical days, and Hengl, Vielwerth and the other officers in the front line were concerned that the bridgehead might collapse. They moved among the units every day with words of encouragement, but the reality could not be hidden. Even the hard-bitten mountain soldiers in the 137th Regiment were reaching the limits of their endurance and desperately in need of rest. Dietl appeared to be staking everything on the arrival of reinforcements to restore morale. Lower down the hierarchy another question was being whispered: Would the 6th Mountain Division arrive before it was too late?

A fortnight earlier, on Thursday 31 July, the cruisers *Aurora* and *Nigeria* with Rear Admiral Philip Vian on board had sailed into the Ice Fjord in Svalbard in radiant Arctic summer weather. Vian had to work out whether the demilitarised island group should be used for military purposes as Stalin wished.

As it was still unclear whether the Germans had occupied Longyearbyen and the other mining communities, Vian landed an advance patrol under the polar explorer Arthur Godfrey, who was a major in the Royal Engineers, and Lieutenant Ragnvald Tamber who had been seconded from the Norwegian Navy.

'Everything appeared calm and peaceful,' Tamber wrote about the landing at Cape Linné. 'We jumped ashore and ran towards the radio station. The only sign of life was seven or eight huskies who ran towards us, obviously happy to see people. Because of the racket the dogs were making, we didn't go right up to the station until the door opened and one of the telegraph operators met us on the threshold. He turned out to be a man I knew from the campaign in Norway in 1940. I was very glad and relieved to see him again.'[7]

The telegraph operator told them that there were no Germans on the archipelago, and Godfrey signalled the good news to Vian. 'Courageously taking the bull by the horns, they achieved their objectives,' Vian wrote. 'Fortunately the settlement was clear of the enemy.'

The shipping season had begun, and more than 400,000 tonnes of coal lay in stock-piles near the quays. The islanders were awaiting the arrival of several cargo ships from the mainland, bringing passengers, post and provisions north for the coming winter season and returning south with coal to the fuel depots in Harstad, Hammerfest and other North Norwegian towns.

For the 60-year-old District Governor Wolmer Marlow and Managing Director Einar Sverdrup of the Great Norwegian Spitzbergen Coal Company, Vian came as an unexpected and unwanted guest. First and foremost, they were responsible for the safety of the 800 Norwegians on the island. But they were also expected to take care of the economic interests of the mining company *and* the political interests of Norway, at the moment occupied and at war with Nazi Germany. Their position was unenviable – caught, as they were, between the Quisling regime in Oslo, which had ordered and paid for coal supplies for the civilian population, and the government-in-exile in London, which had no independent military means to maintain Norwegian sovereignty. Not having received any form of instructions, they chose to defend the status quo – as defined in the Spitzbergen Treaty.

'A naval action as carried out by you is in conflict with Article Nine of the Treaty (which makes Spitzbergen a demilitarised area),' Marlow maintained in a strong exchange of words with Vian in the admiral's quarters on HMS *Nigeria*. 'As soon as your force has left Longyearbyen, I have to send a telegram to Oslo reporting your intrusion.'

Vian replied coldly: 'In that case I have no choice. I have to shoot you. The radio stations will be destroyed. It's essential to keep the fleet's visit secret.'

These were harsh words, to which Marlow replied: 'If the stations are destroyed and the daily radio correspondence ceases, the Germans will soon become suspicious and start enquiries. Then they will not only shoot me, but everybody else who ought to have reported the matter.'

In Marlow's and Sverdrup's opinion, the only solution was for Spitzbergen to be occupied as soon as possible by a British garrison.

Vian had neither troops nor full authority to accommodate their wishes. Instead, a high-risk compromise was entered into whereby the 28-year-old

Tamber was appointed Provisional Military Governor, issued with two revolvers against a note confirming receipt and allocated a volunteer guard force of 18 miners.

Vian and the British squadron left Longyearbyen the same evening and set course at full speed towards the Norwegian coast, in the hope of carrying out new attacks on German shipping. The following weeks would be nerve-racking for young Lieutenant Tamber. He had orders to impound all coal ships and deceive the Quisling Government with false radio reports. The hope was that Vian would return with an adequate occupation force before the Germans discovered the deception and sent the Luftwaffe northwards.

In the meantime a new series of troop movements was underway along the coast of Norway, following a strict timetable. Ordinary replacement troops for the Mountain Corps were on their way from Austria, and the 388th Infantry Regiment was to be transferred from South Norway to arrive in Kirkenes in the middle of August.[8]

The troops of the 6th Mountain Division faced the longest journey. They were to move in several stages from the southern to the northern edge of Europe. General Schörner's mountain soldiers had left Greece in sweltering heat in the beginning of July. Their weapons and equipment had been refurbished during an eighteen-day stay in Semmering in Southern Germany. As soon as all leave had ended, the signal to depart followed. On Saturday 23 August the trains rolled north towards Stettin in Poland, where the units separated. The division's main force, consisting of the horses and all the foot-soldiers, would be sent by ship to Oslo and then on by train to Trondheim where the convoys to Kirkenes awaited them.

All the motorised units took the route through the Baltic: by ship to Vaasa in Finland and then by train to Rovaniemi for transport onwards along the Arctic Road. The operation was code-named *Nordlicht I* and *II*, and it operated within tight time frames. Twelve days after their departure – between 5 and 15 September – the division was to be mustered by the Litza to join Dietl's attack against Murmansk.

Naval Intelligence Division and Bletchley Park had come in for harsh criticism after the catastrophic Kirkenes operation, which had dealt the Fleet Air Arm a psychological knock and led to the almost total destruction of one of their best squadrons.

'The presence of a strike force in this area must always be an embarrassment to the enemy,' Rear Admiral Wake-Walker wrote in his report of the battle. 'But without intelligence it is like looking for a needle in the haystack to try and locate the small amount of shipping that may be strung out along the inner leads and open sea between Narvik and Kirkenes. That much can be done in this way I am certain, if the appropriate force is employed and routine reconnaissance can be made.'[9]

Norman Denning in the Operational Intelligence Centre at the Admiralty in London was in regular contact with Frank Birch, the leader of the codebreakers' naval department, but the task was not easy. Even though the mathematicians working with Alan Turing had analysed and mastered the German Navy's Enigma cipher, capacity was limited. The war against the U-boats had top priority, and the batteries of computing machines designed to speed up the deciphering process were still being installed. Atmospheric disturbances made it difficult to hear stations in the Arctic, and the radio listeners in north-east England couldn't deliver a steady flow of intercepted messages.

The situation seems to have stabilised eventually on 11 August, after two difficult months. There were still blank periods, and it could take up to 60 hours before an intercepted telegram lay in plain text on Denning's desk. But a steady stream of decryptions was again being delivered and soon revealed an interesting picture: the five German destroyers from the 6th Flotilla which operated from bases in the High North had received new assignments. They were increasingly being used as escort vessels for cargo ships trafficking between Tromsø and Kirkenes, supported by the artillery training ship *Bremse* and several armoured trawlers. Another German convoy operation had obviously been initiated, comparable to the ship movements preceding *Barbarossa*.

A telegram sent on the evening of Monday 11 August from the *Admiral der Norwegischen Polarküste* to the 6th Destroyer Flotilla was decoded as follows: 'Provide destroyer escort for hospital ship *Stuttgart* from Magerøsund to Kirkenes because of an increasing threat from U-boats. *Stuttgart* will reach the sound 05.00 hrs. Return to Tromsø for new duty after escort ended.'

The following day the new duty was described in a telegram to the destroyers *Z-7 Hermann Schoemann* and *Z-20 Karl Galster*: 'The troop transport ship *August Bolten* will be in Magerøysund 11.00 hrs. on 13 August. Escort the ship to Kirkenes with one or two destroyers. Speed 11 knots.'[10]

Galster took over the escort in Honningsvåg and reached Kirkenes on 14 August with *August Bolten* and the cargo ship *Bretagne*. The flagship of the 6th Flotilla, *Hermann Schoemann*, returned to Tromsø and picked up a new convoy to Kirkenes on 15 August: the tanker *Weissenburg*, the troopship *Barcelona*, the steamer *Hans Leonhardt* and the armoured trawler *Gote*.

CHAPTER 10

A Very Effective Offensive along the Coast

The Finnmark Coast and the Litza Front, Tuesday 19 August to Monday 8 September 1941

Lieutenant Commander Geoffrey Sladen started the underwater offensive against the German supply lines on Tuesday 19 August when he fired two torpedoes against the merchant ship *Levante* due south of Hjelmsøy in West Finnmark.

'The vessel, which was flying the Nazi flag and camouflaged, was similar to *Birka* of about 2,500 tonnes and very light with propellers thrashing the water,' Sladen wrote. He was angry and disappointed when he saw the cargo ship quickly change course and set full speed towards the nearby fishing station of Havøysund. The torpedoes had missed, but the 37-year-old hothead wasn't nicknamed 'Thrasher' without reason. He took HMS *Trident* to the surface, opened fire with the canon on the foredeck and pursued the 5,000-tonne vessel almost into Havøysund Harbour.

> Enemy immediately altered course around Gavlodden Point into Havøy Sound and away to the south. 9 rounds HE and 12 rounds SAP were fired before he went out of sight. Fire was opened by ship and a shore station with machine guns, but fire was erratic and not close. I followed around the point but enemy was making a good speed and was at long range. If I followed I should be taken at least another 10 miles from the open sea before I would bring him to action so I allowed discretion to override my desire to follow and retired to seaward, having to be content with a most unsatisfactory action.[1]

Sladen moved the submarine to the Kvænangen Fjord, where two days later he fired four torpedoes at the artillery training ship *Bremse* and a further two at the old oil tanker *Tripp*, still without making a hit. 'I was sure that personal assessment of the land south of the ruined Litza Bridge, accompanied by Major General Kreysing.

'Dietl will once again consult with the 3rd Division,' states the entry in the war diary. 'His opinion is still that we must choose the line of attack that the troops think is best.'

However, Dietl's shoulder was dislocated in a traffic accident on his way home from Rovaniemi. He was treated promptly in the nearest field hospital but had to leave the final assessment to Chief of Staff Le Suire.

To Dietl's dismay, Kreysing and Le Suire had lost the will to resist the pressure from Rovaniemi, especially after studying the new Russian defences through field glasses. With Kreysing's agreement, Le Suire recommended moving the direction of attack to the south. 'The terrain is difficult, but not impossible. The scrub will be as big a problem for the defenders as it will for the attackers.'

When Dietl came back from the field hospital on Monday 25 August, the decision had in effect been taken. 'The chief of staff told the commanding general that Kreysing would move the division to the south in accordance with Falkenhorst's wishes. As both Army HQ and the 3rd Division are in agreement about the move, the general decided to back down.'

Frolov and his retinue had come to the regiment's field headquarters on the blood-stained Height 304, after visiting the Red Guards in the Ura Kettle just a few hundred metres from the German bridgehead.

'I apologised that we hadn't managed to push the Germans back over the Litza. I added that the losses had been great and that we often suffered from a shortage of ammunition.'

'That's alright,' replied Frolov. 'I'm amazed that the 58th Regiment still has enough marrow in its backbone to stand against the enemy.'

The two reduced divisions on the front line had gone onto the defensive after the bitter fighting on 14 August. Frolov gave orders that the troops should dig themselves in and prepare to face a new assault towards Murmansk. 'Take care to build extra protection for your positions with barbed wire, trenches and minefields. Ensure good communications between the units, and above all be on the lookout for surprises.'

Even though Frolov and his staff had spread self-confidence and calm during their visit, there can hardly be any doubt that he was a very worried man. The Red Army had suffered enormous losses on the Central Front, just as they had at the Litza. The Kremlin sent encouraging words, but not much more. He would just have to do the best he could with the weapons, equipment and fit men available in North-west Russia. Several thousand reservists had already been sent to the front along with all the recruits and sailors the Northern Fleet could spare. The sources were beginning to run dry, and the situation could quickly become critical if the mountain troops launched a massive new attack.

In August Frolov made a last desperate roll of the dice: About 15,000 political prisoners and forced labourers who had been employed in the mines in Montsjegorsk before the war were transferred to the barracks in 'The Little War Town' in Murmansk and rapidly given improvised weapon training.[12]

As a last resort, Stalin's Gulag convicts were to be thrown into the cauldron to prevent a German breakthrough.

On the other side of the River Litza, Dietl had been forced to give way to Falkenhorst and Buschenhagen. He had travelled to the summit meeting in the banquet hall of Hotel Pohjanovis in belligerent mood, but had been pushed from pillar to post. The two rivals had not managed to agree, but neither of them had dared to push to the limit. Falkenhorst would avoid open revolt and complaints to Hitler. Dietl would not risk charges of insubordination. Instead, before a final decision was made, he agreed to undertake a new and final

```
ADM
TO I D 8 G
FROM N S                                    ZIP/ZTPG/5556

7825 KC/S                                   T O I ZZZ 2256/11/8/41
        T O O 2140

FROM: ADMIRAL COMMANDING POLAR COAST
TO: 6TH D.F. (TO BE ACKNOWLEDGED)

IMPORTANT.
    ARRANGE DESTROYER ESCORT FOR HOSPITAL SHIP STUTTGART FROM
HAGEROESUND TO KIRKENES BECAUSE OF DANGER FROM SUBMARINES OFF
HAGEROE. STUTTGART WILL BE AT HAGEROESUND AT 0500. THEN PROCEED
TO TROMSOE.


1305/12/8/41+++
```

When it again became possible to read the German radio messages after 11 August 1941, the codebreakers discovered that the Germans had started significant convoy traffic between Tromsø and Kirkenes with destroyers from the 6th Flotilla as escorts. (National Archives, London)

Close study of the intercepts made it apparent to Denning that a major build-up of Dietl's mountain corps was underway, although no mention of the 388th Infantry Regiment and the 6th Mountain Division was found in the texts. The tension in the OIC rose, but Denning kept a cool head and chose to wait. He wanted to have more accurate and recent information before he sent clear instructions to the submarines HMS *Tigris* and HMS *Trident* in Polarnoje.

About the same time, the commander of the Soviet 14th Army, General Valerian Frolov, was on a tour of inspection among the exhausted troops east of the Litza.

'I still think of him with great respect,' Khudalov wrote many years later. 'He combined an iron will and determination with concern for his subordinates. He was approachable, sociable and calm. I never saw him lose self-control.'[11]

I had *Bremse* in the bag, and the miss can only be put down to the torpedoes passing under.'

Sladen was almost six and a half feet tall. He was one of the pioneers of submarine warfare and had developed the rubber suit which the divers riding 'human torpedoes' with their robust sense of humour called 'Clammy Death.' In his free time he played rugby with such finesse and vigour that he had been a member of the English national team four times. Sladen liked to win, and he hated the thought of turning back to Polarnoje without having achieved anything. A few days earlier his rival, Howard Bone in HMS *Tigris*, had sunk the *Hurtigrute* ('coastal express') ship *Håkon Jarl* with 9,000 bales of dried fish on board. That was no great victory, but it was better than nothing.

'The normal draught for a cruiser of *Bremse*'s type is nine and a half feet, but she may have been low in fuel, being southbound,' he noted in his log with increasing frustration. 'Set course to seaward, but returned to Kvænangen Fiord as it seemed a good place.'

On Saturday 23 August his patience was rewarded. From a position near the little fishing village of Brynilen he fired six torpedoes at the cargo ship *Ostpreussen*, which was en route to the foundries in Germany heavily laden with iron ore from the Sydvaranger mines.

'The first three hit *Ostpreussen*, which disintegrated and completely disappeared within five minutes.'

Armed trawlers dropped depth charges, supported by bombers from nearby airbases. 'One HE 115 wave-hopping close by,' Sladen noted at 10.30 p.m. 'Being now twilight and likely to get no darker I surfaced and continued seaward charging, where I was left in peace. It was a brilliant clear night and conditions were ideal for the enemy to have continued to harass me with aircraft or surface ships. Fortunately they did neither.'

At the Admiralty in London, Denning had made a breakthrough in the analysis of the German radio traffic. The intercepted telegrams showed that the destroyer *Hermann Schoemann's* convoy of 15 August had reached Kirkenes unscathed two days later. On Monday 18 August at 12 noon a new convoy with five troopships had left Tromsø and headed north at a speed of ten knots, escorted by *Bremse* and two armed trawlers. The artillery training ship had made a rapid return journey from Kirkenes and had been observed and shot at by *Trident* when passing Kvænangen Fjord at 9 a.m. on 21 August. Seven hours later she left Tromsø at the head of a new fast-moving convoy consisting of merchant ships and two U-boats.

Slightly before midnight on 23 August the radio monitors at Scarborough Head picked up a new telegram from the Naval Commander in Tromsø to the harbourmaster in Kirkenes. 'Transports *Bochum, Mendoza* and *Skramstad* for Kirkenes and *Bessheim* for Hammerfest will leave Tromsø at 0400/24/8 escorted by destroyers *Eckoldt* and *Galster* and patrol vessels *Windhuk* and *Nordwind*. Speed 10 knots.'[2]

But new problems had arisen at Bletchley Park, and the deciphered and translated telegram didn't reach Denning in London until 10 a.m. on Tuesday 26 August, 58 hours later.

That was hopelessly too late, and the convoy would probably long since have passed *Trident*'s area of operations. The pattern was however becoming clear. A big German logistical operation was underway between Tromsø and Kirkenes. The convoys were leaving Tromsø every third day as if by clockwork. Denning felt confident. As soon as the analysis was ready, he ran to the radio room. It was time to alert *Trident* and all other naval vessels in or on their way to the Barents Sea.

Denning's telegram reached Sladen at 00.51 on Thursday 28 August, when the submarine was on the surface at the southern end of Sørøy Sound.

'Decided to stay in the sound tonight and surface for 1–2 hours for charging and fresh air during the darkest part of the night,' the Lieutenant Commander wrote in the log book. 'Some small vessels seen burning navigational lights.'

Sladen had plotted the reported convoy's course and speed, and had come to a disappointing result. He was too late to carry out an interception. 'Admiralty's 1958A/27 stating convoys leave Tromsø every three days – last on 24th. I should therefore have seen one yesterday.'

But the sea had been empty, and the convoy had most likely sneaked past during the darkest hours of the night. His patrol was coming to an end, and Sladen had only two torpedoes left. He refused to give up, however, and took an inspired decision. He decided to remain in the operational area for a further two days, until 6 p.m. on Saturday 30 August. 'In case the convoy was a day late in starting I decided to remain inshore. It appeared perfectly safe provided I was well up the sound and could not be silhouetted against the very bright north-western horizon.'

Two days later he saw the smoke from several ships steaming up from the south. It was 2.09 p.m. on 30 August, four hours before his deadline.

For once, the Germans had decided to break the sailing pattern. The major assault on the Litza Front was approaching, and the naval commander in Tromsø

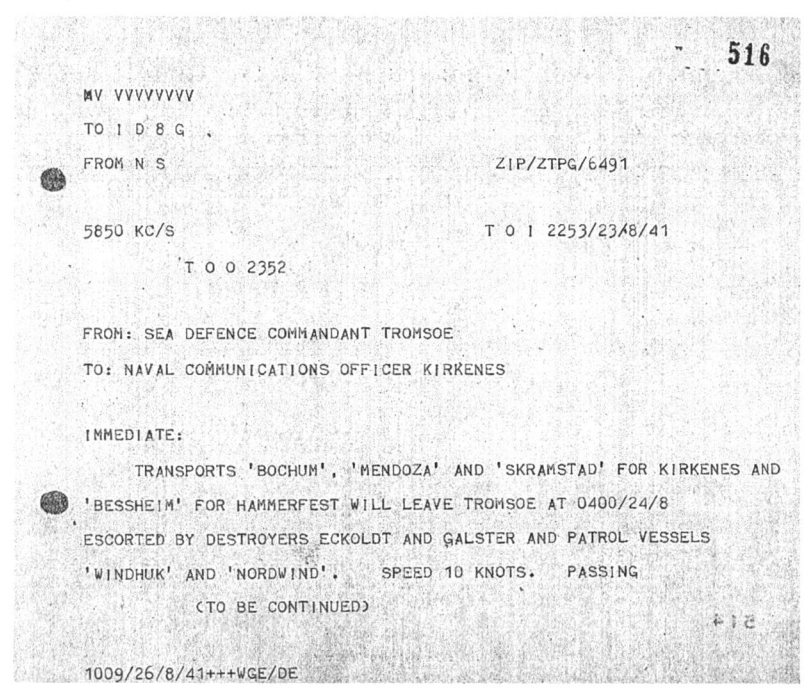

```
MV VVVVVVVV
TO I D 8 G
FROM N S                           ZIP/ZTPG/6491

5850 KC/S                          T O I 2253/23/8/41
     T O O 2352

FROM: SEA DEFENCE COMMANDANT TROMSOE
TO: NAVAL COMMUNICATIONS OFFICER KIRKENES

IMMEDIATE:
    TRANSPORTS 'BOCHUM', 'MENDOZA' AND 'SKRAMSTAD' FOR KIRKENES AND
'BESSHEIM' FOR HAMMERFEST WILL LEAVE TROMSOE AT 0400/24/8
ESCORTED BY DESTROYERS ECKOLDT AND GALSTER AND PATROL VESSELS
'WINDHUK' AND 'NORDWIND'.    SPEED 10 KNOTS.    PASSING
         (TO BE CONTINUED)

1009/26/8/41+++WGE/DE
```

Newly intercepted telegrams told the codebreakers at Bletchley Park that convoys were leaving Tromsø at three day intervals. But the deciphering took up to 58 hours (TOI 22.53/23/8/41, sent by telex from Bletchley Park to the Admiralty 10.09/26/8/41), which meant that the convoy escaped. (National Archives, London)

was under pressure from Mountain Corps Norway. So he had stepped up the pace and sent an early convoy to Kirkenes on 26 August. This was followed by the normal third day convoy on 30 August, leaving Tromsø at 4 a.m. and consisting of the vessels, *Donau II, Bahia Laura, August Bolten* and *Cornoauille*, all overladen with horses and replacement troops for Dietl's corps.

Heinkel reconnaissance planes scanned the sea ahead of the convoy. Three patrol vessels used ASDIC and the destroyers *Hans Lody* and *Karl Galster* circled continuously round the four merchantmen. At 4 p.m. the ships approached the entrance to Sorøysund.

Two cable lengths away, Sladen was studying the convoy through the periscope.

> Convoy consisted of 4 ships in line ahead approximately 2 cables apart, escorted by three trawlers, two large destroyers and one HE 115, so presumably it was valuable. I selected the second ship being the largest as my primary target, but having only two torpedoes I decided to fire them individually at the second and third ships.

While the orders were transmitted to the torpedo room, the nearest German destroyer suddenly changed course. 'I thought I must have been detected but it eventually passed about 100 yards clear on my starboard side and turned a complete circle. I now decided to shift my fire to first and second ship. On firing the first torpedo I was about 60 degrees on port bow of destroyer, range 400 yards and right ahead of port wing trawler, range 600 yards. I swung to starboard and fired second at second ship.'

Time had passed 4.40 in the afternoon and the cold-blooded submariner was surrounded by enemy escorts. In the control room all eyes were fixed on the stopwatches as the torpedoes sped through the water at more than 40 knots. 'Explosion of first torpedo was heard after 48 seconds and I saw, out of the corner of my eye, black smoke coming up apparently from the leading ship, the target. Explosion of second torpedo was heard after 50 seconds, and it seems certain it likewise hit its target.'

Sladen took the periscope down and ordered full speed towards the open sea. 'During next 2 hours 15 minutes I was attacked by 56 depth charges, the first 45 being unpleasantly close. I was very much impressed by the bearing of all hands during what was an unpleasant 40 minutes.'

Aboard *Donau II* and *Bahia Laura*, all hell broke loose. *Donau II* was hit in the engine-room and sank when the boilers exploded six minutes later. *Bahia Laura* caught fire after being hit amidships. More than 40 horses from a veterinary company were trapped aboard. To shorten the suffering, the ship was sunk by artillery fire after all hope had been lost.

'All officers and men had been given instruction in the use of life-saving equipment,' said the report of the Wehrmacht's subsequent enquiry, 'but nobody knew what to do after a torpedo strike, and 80 per cent couldn't swim. This caused panic, and many were annoyed that *Bahia Laura*'s crew were the first to take to the lifeboats. The rescue work had to be undertaken by the navy and people from the passing *Hurtigrute* ship *Midnatsol*.'[3]

During the next twenty-four hours 1,162 survivors and 132 dead were brought to Hammerfest and Tromsø. 'The people who had been shipwrecked were in a pitiful state. Most of them had no clothes and some had saved themselves by jumping overboard just in their stockinged feet.'

Almost 600 soldiers and seamen perished in the ice-cold waters outside Sildemylingen, and large quantities of equipment were lost.

When the news reached the Mountain Corps in Titovka at 11 p.m. it caused dismay and nervousness among the staff officers.

> Two steamers torpedoed 16.20 hrs. at entrance to Sørøy Sound. One sunk, another on fire. On board probably troops from 193rd Mountain Regiment. Warships and planes from Luftwaffe securing the site of the wreck.

The all-out attack on the Litza Front was due to begin on Saturday 6 September. The important 193rd Regiment was part of the 6th Mountain Division and was intended to play a key role in the assault. If the regiment was put out of action long before it arrived, the chances of military success would be dramatically weakened. So it was with considerable relief that the corps received further clarification a few hours later: '*Donau II* with reinforcements for Cycle Battalion 68, 138th Mountain Regiment and Pioneer Battalion 74 sunk. *Bahia Laura* on fire with Veterinary Company 702 and reserve troops from March Battalion Salzburg. Units from 193rd Mountain Regiment *not* affected.'[4]

The main force of the 6th Mountain Division was still aboard the troopships that had just left Trondheim or were about to do so. The outlook was however gloomy, as described by the transport staff:

> The torpedo attack shows that enemy naval forces could also put future troop movements in danger. We don't know whether British or Russian U-boats were behind the attack. There is reason to consider the possibility of losses and delays in the imminent transport of the main body of 6th Mountain Division. Both *Donau II* and *Bahia Laura* were to have taken part. The loss of these two ships alone will entail a limited delay.

This news was a further blow to Dietl. The German Navy's performance in supporting the Northern Front had so far been hugely disappointing. U-boats and the 6th Destroyer Flotilla were sent north to support the corps and stop the delivery of troops and supplies to the Russian forces on the Fisher Peninsula.

But Vice Admiral Otto Schenk in Tromsø and Flotilla Commander Alfred Schultze-Hinrichs in Kirkenes had been hesitant and over-cautious in their leadership of the war at sea. A few unprotected Russian coastguard vessels had been sunk, but they had refused to send their destroyers and U-boats into the Kola Fjord. During the air attack on Kirkenes the 6th Flotilla had put its tail between its legs and hidden in the innermost bay of the Tana Fjord.

Dietl was now facing the decisive test. His two depleted divisions were ready on the Litza, and the need for reinforcements was more urgent than ever. What would happen if the navy failed again and didn't manage to bring the 6th Mountain Division to Kirkenes? He didn't even dare to think about it.

Back in Longyearbyen on Spitzbergen, the local Norwegian commander, Lieutenant Ragnvald Tamber's situation was becoming increasingly difficult. He had hoped initially that Vian would return in a couple of weeks with the Royal Navy and a well-armed Allied force capable of occupying the islands and resisting a possible German attack. But the radio was silent, and the days passed in nerve-racking suspense without anything happening.

'As now 18 days have passed and no forces at all have been here the situation is becoming critical,' he wrote on 18 August in a desperate letter sent with a seal-hunting ship to Iceland. 'I have during this time impounded three big cargo ships, one sealer and 2 smaller craft, all waiting here, loaded and ready for sea. The Germans are growing suspicious, and if they now send a plane for reconnaissance they will understand at once that something is wrong. I must therefore ask that escort vessels *immediately* be sent to save the ships and that the problem of supplies be solved *forthwith*. I also point out that this behaviour towards the two allied nations concerned is very bad and has a very bad effect on the morale of the population.'[5]

As a seaman and an officer, Rear Admiral Vian was obviously concerned that the promises to Tamber had not been kept. Svalbard had become a minor thread in the wide-ranging debate about aid to the Soviet Union, and the powerful military and political leaders in London thought it was just as senseless to send troops to the icy wastes as it was to send them to Northern Norway.

'We operate a fleet in the far northern waters largely for political reasons,' said Vice Chief of Staff Charles Portal in a COS meeting on 5 August. He was very doubtful about the enterprise. The Joint Intelligence Sub-Committee had advised that the Germans could easily send a force of 10,000 men to Spitsbergen with the support of a pocket battleship, two cruisers and a flotilla of destroyers. An occupation would therefore require the deployment of a significant Allied force with anti-aircraft guns, which were already in seriously short supply along the Channel Coast. 'For ships to refuel at a naval base on Spitsbergen would require further strengthening of air defences.'

Vian's personal opinion following his reconnaissance at the turn of the month was crystal clear. He saw no strategic benefits in occupying an archipelago that was enclosed by ice for large parts of the year. The Royal Navy's needs could much more easily and practically be met by a tanker equipped for refuelling in open sea.

Churchill was in dialogue with Stalin and was due to meet Roosevelt a few days later at Placentia Bay in Newfoundland for the war's first big political conference. Churchill was impatient and wanted clarification.

'The Prime Minister, who was at Chequers, telephoned and demanded a plan, since he was receiving M. Maisky within the hour,' Vian wrote in *Action This Day*. 'He continued to telephone every few minutes, and a decision of some kind became urgent. Lord Ismay, who as Chief of Staff to the Minister of Defence who was also the Prime Minister, had to handle the calls, then produced a plan that Mr. Churchill accepted. The Force was to return to Spitsbergen, to collect any accumulated shipping, withdraw the Norwegian community to England and the Russians to Archangel and destroy the facilities for mining coal in both settlements.'

The Norwegian Government in Exile reacted pragmatically and gave its approval, and Ambassador Maisky did likewise on 16 August after consultations with the Kremlin.[6]

Vian took to sea three days later at the head of a force consisting of the cruisers HMS *Nigeria* and *Aurora*, three destroyers, four armoured trawlers, the oil tanker *Oligarch* and the 20,000-ton Atlantic liner *Empress of Canada*. The squadron also took a Canadian battalion of 650 men; a unit from the Kent Fortress Royal Engineers who were specialists in the handling of dynamite and in economic warfare against Nazi Germany; a symbolic support group of 25 Norwegian soldiers; and the dramatist Noel Coward, who wanted an adventure.[7]

'The plane flying me back to Scapa was stopped by weather at Invergordon,' Vian wrote. 'There I found Noel Coward, also bound for Scapa to stay with the Commander in Chief. I took him by car to Thurso, and during the long drive north he decided to shorten his visit to Admiral Tovey and sail with me.'[8]

The departure was coordinated with another operation of historic significance: the first Russian convoy. This was code-named *Dervish* and consisted of six vessels laden with rubber, tin, wool and other raw materials. The most important items however were 39 Hurricane fighter planes, some aboard the ageing aircraft carrier HMS *Argos* and some in packing cases on the cargo ships. The aircraft carrier HMS *Victorious*, the cruisers *Devonshire* and *Suffolk*, six destroyers, three minesweepers to be stationed in the White Sea and three armoured trawlers provided a powerful escort.

'The situation was unsound,' wrote Rear Admiral Wake-Walker. He had again been given the command despite the fiasco in Kirkenes and Petsamo. He obviously considered Vian as a rival and he made no attempt to hide these feelings in his report. 'Two separate forces were operating in the same area quite independently. I had only the vaguest indications of what Force A was doing. It was only by good fortune that one force did not lead enemy aircraft to the other.'

Vian didn't have time to respond. He had enough to do, dealing with the sensitive personal and political problems involved in an unannounced evacuation of Spitsbergen.[9]

Tamber and the mining company officials Wolmer and Sverdrup had been glad when the squadron steamed into Grønfjorden early on the morning of Monday 25 August. The tense wait had passed without a German invasion. But the reaction came when the miners heard about the Allies' proposed solution.

'Herr Sverdrup reacted violently to this and stated that the whole mine would be ruined by the burning. The cost of the loading and distributing gear at Advent Point had nearly broken his company, and the climate was such that it would take years to replace owing to the difficulty of transport.'

Vian was unyielding. There was a bigger political context that Sverdrup didn't understand, and his protests could not be accepted. In the course of a hectic week all the Norwegians were gathered together, including hunters who had wintered in the far north in Fairhaven. The mines were put out of operation and the coal stores set alight.

The evacuation of the Soviet mining communities of Barentsburg and Grumantbyen required equally firm diplomacy from the Canadian officers, especially because the Soviet Consul was reluctant to cooperate. The Russians had a stock of 600 live pigs and several hundred tonnes of supplies and personal belongings, which was more than the squadron's vessels could accommodate.

'The consul, who had a bottle of Caucasian brandy beside him, said that according to Mr. Maisky's letter he was to follow the instructions of Admiral Vian, but Vian had sent him no instructions,' said the Canadian report. 'Before a reply from Vian was received, the Consul had finished a further two bottles of Caucasian champagne and half a bottle of Caucasian Madeira and passed out. Meanwhile all the Russian heavy goods had been loaded. After allowing an extra half hour to work on the Consul in the lavatory, he was carried aboard on a stretcher covered by a sheet so that his own people should not know what had happened to him.'

Forty-eight hours after their arrival, HMS *Nigeria* and *Empress of Canada* set course for Archangel with about 2,000 miners and 200 tonnes of equipment and personal belongings on board. When the coal depots were set on fire, some of the buildings in Barentsburg had burnt down. The Russians had protested, and Vian was taking care to cover his back.

'At the Admiral's suggestion, the Consul and Vice-Consul from Barentsburg came on board *Nigeria*,' Potts wrote. 'In his presence and mine, they were asked if the arrangements made for their evacuation had been satisfactory. They said that they had.'

The ships returned on Wednesday 3 September and left Longyearbyen at 10.30 p.m. that evening with 700 Norwegians on board. The coal depots were in flames and the islands lay deserted – a sign that the war was steadily being extended to new territories.

Twenty-four hours later HMS *Nigeria* and *Aurora* left the convoy and set course at high speed towards the Finnmark coast. Denning's signal that the troopships were leaving Tromsø every third day had reached Vian, who wanted to take the opportunity to repeat *Trident*'s success.

The torpedo attacks on *Håkon Jarl, Ostpreussen, Donau II* and *Bahia Laura* had worried the German staff officers much more than London and the Kremlin realised. Following Colonel Schmundt's visit in July, Hitler had already ordered increased readiness against a British invasion, on the basis of *Der Führer*'s allegedly unsurpassed power of intuition. The air attacks on Kirkenes and the torpedo attacks seemed to confirm that Hitler in some mysterious way was right. When the Luftwaffe's reconnaissance flight discovered Vian's and Wake-Walker's fleets far north in the Barents Sea on 3 September, this was seen as a further indication of imminent danger.

'Our most important task will be to oppose the naval force which is operating between North Cape and Spitsbergen,' declared Colonel Andreas Nielsen when General Dietl asked for Stuka support for the major attack on the Litza Front a few days ahead. 'If the British fleet is to be attacked, only a few not-at-full-strength, sub-units can be spared to support the Mountain Corps.'

What was much more serious for Dietl was that Falkenhorst was showing his true colours again. The staff officers had thought for a long time that the army commander was jealous and wanted the 6th Mountain Division to be deployed on the Salla Front, where the attack on the Murmansk railroad had again become stuck.

'The navy has reported that the sea route between Tromsø and Kirkenes cannot be adequately secured,' Buschenhagen told Chief of Staff Le Suire in a telephone conversation on Thursday 4 September, two days before the great assault was to be started. 'The first transport ships are now lying on stand-by in Tromsø. It may be appropriate to hold them back, in which case the troops will be landed at the nearest port to march onwards on foot to Kirkenes.'

Buschenhagen's telephone call came as a shock to Dietl and Le Suire. The overland route through Finnmark to the Litza Front was 600 km long. If Falkenhorst persisted in this devious move the 6th Mountain Division would not arrive in time.

'The corps earnestly requests that Mountain Army Norway abandon the proposal unless absolutely necessary,' said an entry in the war diary. 'Marching the division on foot is an emergency solution which entails problems of a very serious nature for us.'

About the same time as this request was being telegraphed to Rovaniemi, a plane landed at Luostari Airport with two of Dietl's most prominent Nazi friends on board: General Alfred Jodl, who was the Führer's Chief of Operations at the Supreme Command of the Wehrmacht; and General Rudolf Konrad, who was looked upon as the father of the mountain troops. Both of them had Hitler's ear, and Falkenhorst wouldn't dare to challenge them.

The convoy that was waiting in Tromsø received orders to proceed to Kirkenes.

In the early hours of Saturday 6 September the troopships *Trautenfels* and *Barcelona* raised anchor and set course towards Kirkenes with about 2,000 mountain soldiers from the 6th Mountain Division on board, escorted by the artillery training ship *Bremse* and several armoured trawlers. Things were working out exactly as Denning and the intelligence analysts at Bletchley Park had anticipated, and Rear Admiral Vian on his flagship HMS *Nigeria* was confident.

'I received a signal from the Admiralty that a German convoy would pass on 7 September,' he wrote in his memoirs. 'It was suggested that it should be intercepted. I replied that we would certainly try. The difficulty, as on earlier occasions, was to make the approach to the coast without coming under observation of enemy aircraft. This time a northerly gale was blowing, bringing low cloud and poor visibility, while, since it was September, there were a few hours of darkness.'[10]

The two cruisers hurried south at 29 knots and approached land on Saturday evening. The contours of the mountain ranges along the coast appeared on the radar screen an hour and a half after midnight.

'At 0125 HMS *Nigeria*'s R.D.F. reported land ahead, range 5,000 yards. *Aurora* was then 5 cables astern. This was confirmed by lookouts and course was altered to starboard. Immediately afterwards and while the ships were still turning, *Nigeria* sighted a dark, blurred object on the port bow, bearing 250 degrees. The alarm was given and the guns started to train around.'

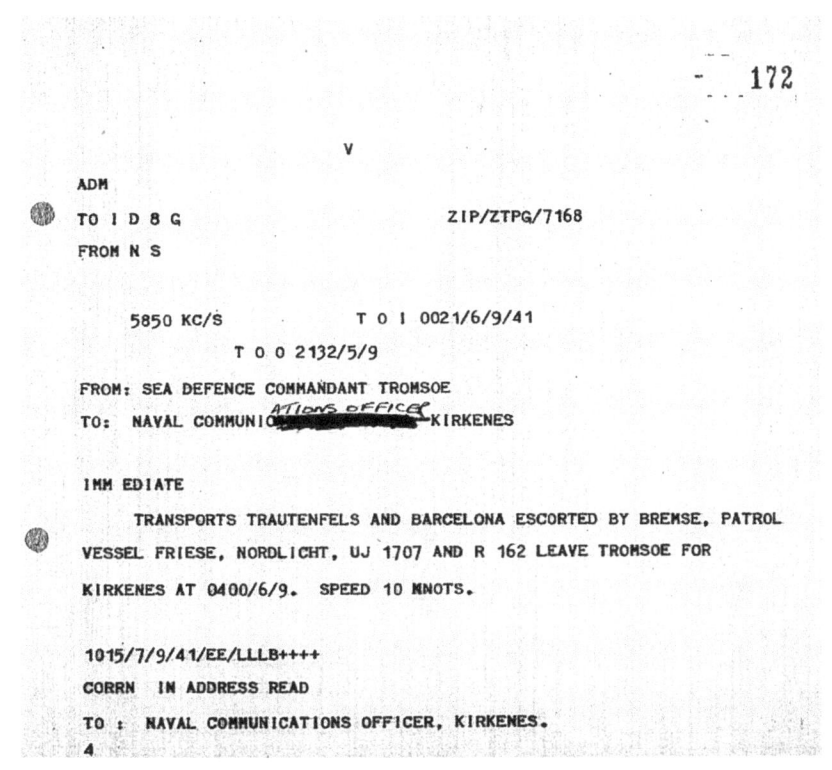

```
                                                    - 172
                    V
      ADM
   TO I D 8 G                    ZIP/ZTPG/7168
      FROM N S

         5850 KC/S              T O I  0021/6/9/41
              T O O 2132/5/9
      FROM: SEA DEFENCE COMMANDANT TROMSOE
                      ATIONS OFFICE
      TO:    NAVAL COMMUNIC̶̶̶̶̶̶̶̶̶̶̶̶KIRKENES

      IMM EDIATE
             TRANSPORTS TRAUTENFELS AND BARCELONA ESCORTED BY BREMSE, PATROL
      VESSEL FRIESE, NORDLICHT, UJ 1707 AND R 162 LEAVE TROMSOE FOR
      KIRKENES AT 0400/6/9.  SPEED 10 KNOTS.

      1015/7/9/41/EE/LLLB++++
         CORRN  IN ADDRESS READ
         TO :  NAVAL COMMUNICATIONS OFFICER, KIRKENES.
      4
```

The convoy with the first troops from the 6th Mountain Division left Tromsø at 4 a.m. on Saturday 6th September and was intercepted by Vian off the Nordkyn Peninsula soon after midnight on Sunday 7th September. (National Archives, London)

Vian's first thought was that the cruisers had chanced upon a solitary cargo ship on its way east. 'But other vessels were observed almost immediately, and it soon became clear that we were facing an enemy convoy.'

The exchange of fire which followed in the darkness and poor visibility was short and confusing. *Nigeria* and *Aurora* had intercepted *Bremse*, the armoured trawlers and the troopships *Trautenfels* and *Barcelona*, only twelve hours sailing distance from Kirkenes. The artillery training ship had sailed under Lady Luck's protective hand all summer and escaped the Fleet Air Arm's and *Trident*'s torpedoes without a scratch. Now it was all over in less than half an hour, as hundreds of shells and at least one torpedo struck *Bremse* at short range.[11]

'A powerful explosion was heard towards the stern,' reported Dr. Jebsen the ship's doctor, who was one of the 36 survivors. 'A big hole appeared in the hull and the ship heeled rapidly. We took continuous hits from both sides and the stern was completely shot away. A stoker sat jammed in the ladder to the petty officers' mess with his whole rib-cage smashed to pieces.'

The end came quickly. *Bremse* capsized about 1.15 a.m. and lay with her keel in the air. A few minutes later the wreck was rammed by HMS *Nigeria*, which suffered severe damage to the bow and had to break off the fight.

'The whole engagement from the time of first sighting to the time at which touch was lost was only 28 minutes. It was a confused melee in which accurate recording of events could not be made. To piece the whole thing together with any certainty is not possible. Targets suddenly appeared from different directions in the mist and disappeared again just as quickly. It cannot be stated definitively how many were engaged or how many were sunk.'

The final German attack on the Litza Front started at 3 a.m. on Monday 8 September, 48 hours late.

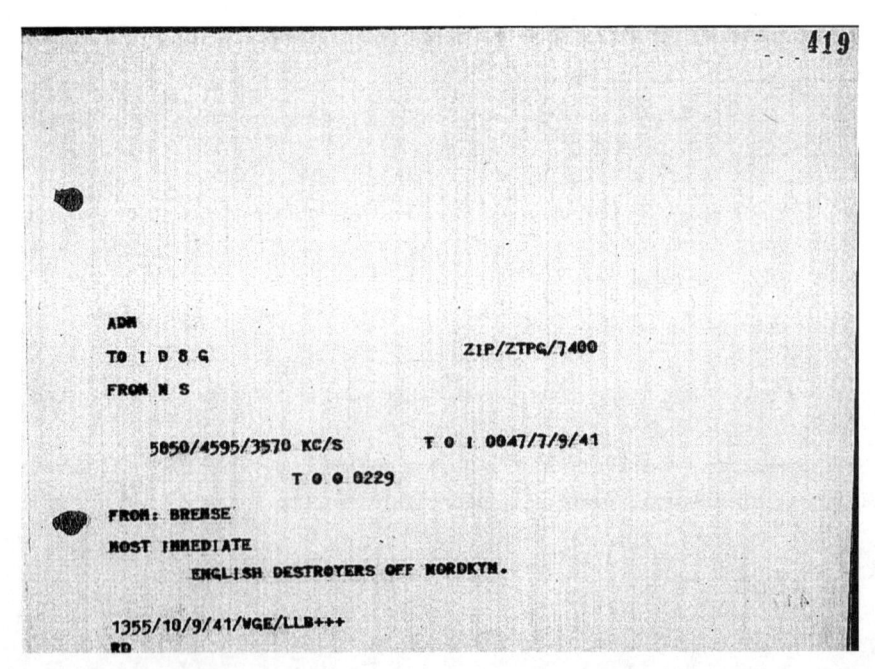

The only radio signal Bremse managed to send during the battle was intercepted immediately but only reached London after a delay of three days, at 1.55 p.m. on 10 September. (National Archives, London)

The first news of what had happened at sea reached Dietl six hours later. *Trautenfels* and *Barcelona* with the troops from the 6th Mountain Division on board had miraculously escaped into Honningsvåg under cover of the mist.

In the meantime, Falkenhorst had played his hand again. Army Command Norway had given orders that all further sea transport was to be suspended. The troops on the two ships were to land in the nearby Porsanger Fjord and march along National Highway 50 to the frontier.

'The navy's available forces are not sufficient to protect the sea route along the northern coast,' Dietl wrote disappointedly in the war diary. 'This means that we face further delays. The troops who are landing in Porsanger won't reach the frontier for several weeks. This confronts the corps with extremely serious new problems.'

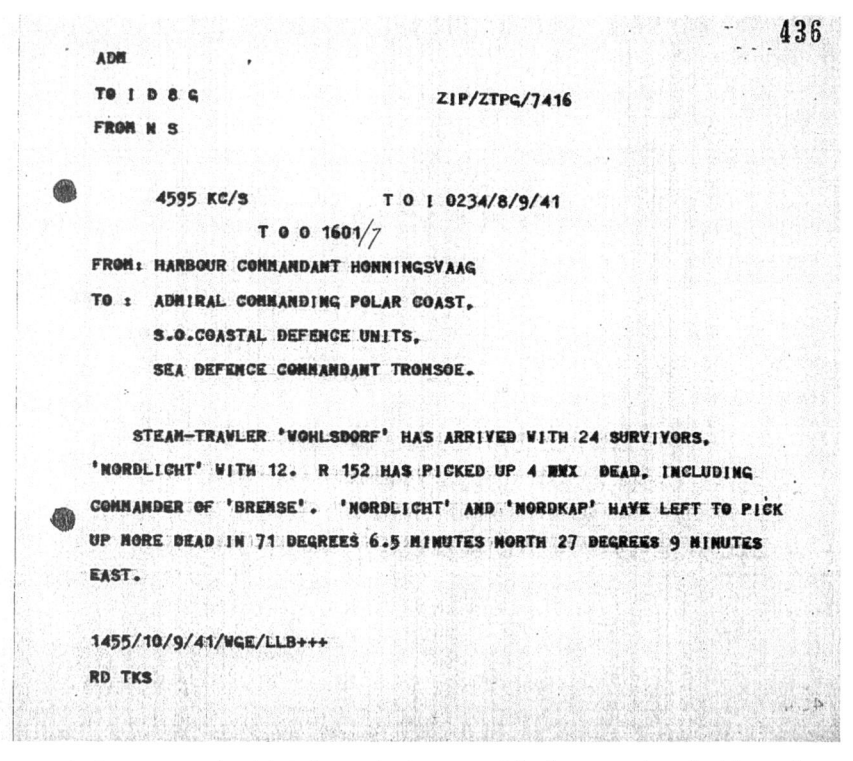

```
                                                                    436
    ADM
    TO  I D 8 G                    ZIP/ZTPG/7416
    FROM N S


         4595 KC/S              T O I 0234/8/9/41
                  T O O 1601/7
    FROM: HARBOUR COMMANDANT HONNINGSVAAG
    TO :  ADMIRAL COMMANDING POLAR COAST,
          S.O.COASTAL DEFENCE UNITS,
          SEA DEFENCE COMMANDANT TROMSOE.

          STEAM-TRAWLER 'WOHLSDORF' HAS ARRIVED WITH 24 SURVIVORS.
    'NORDLICHT' WITH 12.  R 152 HAS PICKED UP 4 MMX DEAD, INCLUDING
    COMMANDER OF 'BREMSE'.  'NORDLICHT' AND 'NORDKAP' HAVE LEFT TO PICK
    UP MORE DEAD IN 71 DEGREES 6.5 MINUTES NORTH 27 DEGREES 9 MINUTES
    EAST.

    1455/10/9/41/WGE/LLB+++
    RD TKS
```

Intercepted telegrams gave the Admiralty continuing news of developments along the Finnmark coast, including current details of the rescue attempt after the sinking of Bremse. (National Archives, London)

CHAPTER 11

Defeat

The Litza Front, Monday 8 to Friday 19 September 1941

The artillery barrage lasted ten minutes, turning parts of the Litza Valley into a burning inferno.[1]

'Tongues of flame suddenly ripped the darkness apart,' wrote Hans Rüf. 'The shells flew with a deafening roar over the heads of the soldiers as they lay crouched together, and landed on the Soviet formations on the east bank. None of us had experienced so intense and widespread a firestorm before.'

Throughout August, 111th Mountain Artillery Regiment and the corps' own gunners had been busy transporting 49 heavy guns to the front, and 112th Regiment had brought forward a similar number in the south. Most of them were standard 75 mm field guns, but a few monster 17-tonne, 21 cm calibre howitzers had also been dragged with great effort up onto the barren mountain plateau. This had been a massive operation involving almost 10,000 artillerymen and 4,000 horses, and the ammunition dumps contained 55,000 projectiles varying in weight from 6 to 113 kilograms.

'The terrain consisted of bare ridges up to 300 metres high, which in the north sloped steeply towards the sea and in the south were sliced and fragmented by ravines and hollows choked with scrub,' wrote Lieutenant Colonel Erwin von Mehlem. He had taken over as Regimental Colonel after Friedrich Kammel, the corps' previous artillery commander, had committed suicide in Parkkina. 'The landscape imposed tremendous toil on the logistic services and endless agonies on the wounded. The achievement of the porters and the beasts of burden cannot be praised highly enough.'

At 3.10 a.m. the troops in the northern pincer of the attack started their advance in three formations: Gruppe Hofmeister, Gruppe Hengl and Gruppe

Kräutler, who with the support of the 9th SS Infantry Regiment probably amounted to a force of around 10,000 men, despite the losses in July and August.

'The autumn rains had begun three days earlier. The supply roads and the tented camps were under water. The clouds hung low over the valley. Everybody was frozen and soaked through and longed to get started.'

At the 3rd Mountain Division's assembly area 16 kilometres further south the terrain was every bit as difficult as Dietl had maintained, and the huge combined attack had had to be postponed 48 hours for the cart road optimistically named 'Adolf Hitler Road' to be completed. It was about 5 kilometres as the crow flies to the crucial Murmansk Highway, which would need to be blocked before the Trondheim Regiment (138th) under Colonel Weiss could advance further north-eastwards along the 4-kilometre-long New Road which led into the territory behind the main Soviet position. As soon as Weiss and von Hengl met on Height 322, east of Long Lake, an iron ring would be cast round the stubborn 52nd Infantry Division, which would then be ground to pieces company by company.

The primeval forest on the division's right flank was assumed to be free of enemy troops. Much depended on the recently arrived 388th Infantry Regiment which was to storm the Brandl and Pranckh Heights, secure the Devil's Gorge and join up with the Narvik Regiment (139th) under veteran commander Alois Windisch on the left flank.

> Reconnaissance had shown that the woodland was thinly occupied, and the Litza was crossed without resistance. The bridgehead on the east bank was secured within twenty minutes. Two battalions were ready to lead the march towards the Murmansk Highway.

During the small hours of the night the alarm was sounded at Colonel Vesjeserskij's command post. The forward units of Korotkov's 112th Regiment on the north flank had been surprised by the artillery barrage and had retreated with huge losses. By 7 a.m. the coastal heights were in German hands.

'I made contact with Korotkov on the field telephone,' wrote Khudalov, who was still holding the Ura Kettle with the 58th Regiment. 'He was mortified because he hadn't managed to foresee the attack this time either. The enemy had driven a wedge between his battalions and was approaching the 158th Artillery Regiment's position.'[2]

Vesjeserskij acted quickly. The seriously exhausted 205th Regiment, which had been resting at the 'seaside resort' of Ura-Guba for two weeks,[3] was sent on a forced march to the front. All the reservists, who had been building defence works around Murmansk, were ordered to lay down their spades. They were divided into companies, equipped with rifles and put on lorries with the remainder of the available sailors from the Northern Fleet.

'At twelve noon we got orders to prepare for battle,' reported 32-year-old former joiner Andrej Kanarski from the Ukraine. He had stolen grain from a cooperative farm during a famine and had been condemned to four years' hard labour. 'We were told that the enemy had broken through the positions and had to be stopped. A political commissar stirred us up for battle and threatened to shoot anybody who turned back. Some of the oldest men knew nothing about using weapons and wanted to know how they were to defend themselves. He replied: "If you can't shoot, tear the enemy apart with your teeth."'

When Captain Bevan met Rear Admiral Golovko in Polarnoje in the morning, the Soviet naval commander was still unconcerned. 'A thick fog came down in the early hours of the morning and was followed by a strong gale. Under cover of the fog during the night, the enemy launched an attack with one battalion and advanced about 4 kilometres.'[4]

Golovko appeared to be unaware that the *whole* of the German corps had started marching towards Murmansk. He expressed satisfaction that 24 Hurricane fighters had taken off from the aircraft carrier HMS *Argos* and landed at the air base at Vaenga at the other side of the Kola Fjord before the fog set in, and that 290 ground support staff were already on site. The RAF worked intensively to prepare the planes, which were to be deployed over the Litza front a few days later under Wing Commander Henry Ramsbottom-Isherwood.

At the same time, the six steamers in the *Dervish* convoy were unloading at Archangel, and the first three ships had already left New York Harbour loaded to the Plimsoll line with machine tools, weapons and other supplies that Golikov's military mission had purchased in the USA. *Capira, North King* and *Ville d'Anvers* were bound for Iceland where they would join the first of the regular Arctic convoys, PQ 1, made up of 11 ships scheduled to reach Russia at the end of September.

The establishment of an Allied lifeline to Stalin and his fighting Red Army had taken time, and the negotiations had been hampered by doubt and suspicion. Supplies and various forms of military assistance were now underway on an increasing scale, but a worrying new question had arisen: what would happen if the Litza front broke and the unloading ports were put out of action?

As Bevan noted in his diary, 'Considerable fighting reported on the Murmansk front where the enemy have launched a strong attack with five battalions. This may be a prelude to a heavier attack with the capture of Murmansk as the objective.'

The Army Command in Zossen regarded the Waffen-SS with mistrust and hatred, and Brauchitsch, Halder and Falkenhorst had persistently opposed Hitler's wish to give 9th SS Infantry Regiment a place in the front line.

'Do you really have such great confidence in the regiment that you will deploy it again?' Buschenhagen had asked in August, referring to the SS troops' weak performance on the Salla front earlier in the summer.

But Dietl needed every last man who could carry a rifle, and he liked the flamboyant SS-Sturmbannführer Ernst Deutsch who was eager to overcome the army officers' scorn and disdain. So he accepted the regiment for front-line service.

At first it looked as if honour would be restored. Himmler's Aryan Guards stormed cheering and shouting through the morning mist on 8 September and rapidly eliminated the defenders from the heights assigned to them. But it was a long way from street terror against Jews and political opponents in Gdansk and other Polish cities to the unyielding granite around the Litza. As soon as the Russians counter-attacked and losses began to mount, their aggression evaporated. At the southern edge of the bridgehead the 2. Battalion of the 9th SS Regiment had to be rescued by Hengl's pioneers, and the 3. Battalion's advance in the north ended in a bloodbath.

'The battalion ran into a well organised counter-attack and was coming under murderous fire,' Hans Rüf wrote. 'Panic took hold. The soldiers streamed back in wild flight and didn't stop until they reached the sea. All the ground which had been won was lost. A serious crisis had arisen on the north flank. If the Russians grasped the opportunity and followed up, the road to the riverbank would lie open to them. They could fall upon 136th Regiment from behind and put the whole attack in danger.'

Von Hengl, who had recently been promoted to colonel and had been awarded the Knight's Cross of the Iron Cross for the capture of the bunker line, threw the reduced 1. Battalion of 137th Regiment into the breach and avoided a breakthrough.

Major General Schlemmer's judgement was harsh. 'The SS troops attacked boldly on the first day but suffered very great losses and lost a lot of their self-confidence and fighting spirit during the retreat. If a further attack is to take place, the battalion is not even mature enough to undertake a defensive role.'

These reports from the north flank were disturbing, and a few hours later the telephone lines from General Kreysing's command post in the south started buzzing with similar reports about the other reinforcements the corps had been given.

The Bavarian 388th Infantry Regiment had followed up a powerful artillery bombardment by sending 1,600 men across the Litza and advancing boldly straight towards the gap which the mountain troops had named 'The Devil's Gorge' back in July. On the surface, it all seemed calm.

'The Russians lay well hidden in stone hollows behind barbed wire and minefields without giving themselves away,' 58-year-old Colonel Wilhelm Daser later wrote in a humble report to Dietl.[5]

The remains of the 95th Regiment from the Russian 14th Division had fortified the Brandl and Pranckh Heights. The border regiment had been shattered in the battles in the Titovka Valley, but had been partly reconstituted and was eager for vengeance. 'The Red Guards wanted to surround us and engage us in close fighting. They allowed our troops to pass by and then opened fire from all directions with rifles, machine guns and mortars.'

The first of the distress calls reached corps HQ at 2.45 p.m. '*Gruppe Daser* has suffered severe losses and requests permission to withdraw to the west bank before the whole force is eliminated.'

Dietl had allowed himself to be persuaded to start the big attack before the arrival of the 6th Mountain Division precisely because the 9th SS Infantry Regiment and the 388th Infantry Regiment had been put at his disposal. These two units were to have given the corps the extra punch necessary to secure a breakthrough. The SS regiment had been put to flight a few hours into the battle, and Daser's regiment was begging to be relieved. Both had failed unforgivably, and Dietl took a hard line: '*Gruppe Daser* must unconditionally hold the position in consideration of the situation of the rest of the corps.'

Nor had he forgiven Kreysing's weakness in the power struggle with Falkenhorst, and he added 'The responsibility lies with the divisional commander. I shall not interfere with his dispositions.'

Further distress calls followed throughout the afternoon. All the company commanders were put out of action. The troops fought in isolated pockets with steadily declining supplies of ammunition and they feared they would be completely destroyed.

At 5.15 p.m. Kreysing gave permission. '1. Battalion to withdraw back over the Litza immediately. 2. Battalion must wait till darkness falls before the retreat can take place.'

This shocking setback weakened the south flank, and Daser was depressed and unhappy when he reported to Dietl at the 3rd Division's command post. The ageing colonel was an ardent Nazi, but he was first and foremost a soldier, true and brave. As a young officer he had fought in the Kaiser's army in the great battles on the Western Front: Somme, Aisne, Ypres and Verdun. But the slaughter in the Litza Valley had been different and more intense, and the two battalions in the front line had lost 380 officers and men from a force of 600. That was more than 60 per cent, and the percentage losses among the officers and NCOs were even higher.

'We have done our duty and paid with blood,' Daser said. 'Lowland troops without pack animals accustomed to the hills cannot fight and survive in this terrain. They can only die.'

In Murmansk, it had gradually become clear to the new Army Commander[6] that the major attack had begun, with the 2nd Mountain Division in the north and the 3rd Mountain Division in the south. If the pincer closed on Height 322, the supply lines would be cut off and his main force – the 52nd Infantry Division under Colonel Vesjeserskij and parts of the 14th Infantry Division under General Nikishin – would be surrounded. As soon as the stores of food and ammunition were finished, they would have to lay down their weapons and the road to Murmansk would lie open again.[7]

In 'The Little War Town', the last reservists and prisoners were being conscripted and armed to make up a new division consisting of 13,000 untrained men, mostly prisoners from the Gulags. The division was called *Polarnoje*, and it was far from being ready for battle. However, it was the last available resort and there was no other way. The Polarnoje Division was ordered to march to the front.

At the same time, Frolov ordered the forces on the Fisher Peninsula to make a renewed attack against the German rear lines. Colonels Mikhail Pashkovskij and Daniel Krasilnikov didn't need to be asked twice.

The battalions of the 135th Regiment were dug in on the Fisher Peninsula and had throughout the summer been throwing themselves in turn against the German positions on Height 122 and Mustatunturi, encouraged by Regimental Commander Pashkovskij who dashed to and fro across the isthmus on a captured German motorcycle, and by Area Commander Krasilnikov and his political commissar, Pavel Shabunin.[8]

The dominating Mustatunturi (Finnish: 'The Black Mountain') lived up to its name. It was strewn with German, Finnish and Russian bodies. During a powerful assault in the middle of July, Pashkovskij had prematurely announced that the peak had been captured, and immediately been awarded a prestigious decoration. The announcement was false. The colonel, who was considered by many to be cold-hearted and inconsiderate, had forced the troops back up the hillside under heavy German shelling.

'Mustatunturi had to be recaptured at any price, so that the colonel could keep his medal,' Lieutenant Paul Savtsjenko explained during interrogation. The 28-year-old from Riga in Latvia was the only officer who deserted to the Germans during the fighting at the Litza, and he gave them several useful pieces of information. 'The result was further painful losses. My company shrunk from 140 to 26 men.'[9]

During the fighting on 31 July the young Lieutenant Ivan Loskutov was sent as artillery observer to one of the summits near Mustatunturi. He held out for six full days and finally had to call down fire on his own observation post to prevent a German breakthrough. He survived though badly wounded and was later acclaimed in one of the war's great propaganda poems, *A Gunner's Son*, by the Stalinist writer and war correspondent Konstantin Simonov.

> The radio report said: 'The Germans are around me Fire 1, 4, 10. Have no mercy.'
> The major blanched. 1, 4, 10. That was his son's position. His Lionel was there.
> He said nothing. He forced himself to forget he was a father.
> 'Fire!' And the shells flew!
> 'Fire! And reload faster!'
> There was silence for an hour before Lionel's voice was heard again: 'The salvoes made me deaf, but I am unharmed. Fire! The Germans are fleeing. Surround them with a sea of fire.'
> The major heard the words. He couldn't restrain himself. He screamed on the radio: 'Can you hear me? Death can never conquer men like you!
> 'Be calm, my boy. Never lose courage.'
> Those were the major's words.

This heroic poem was published in a children's book in 1941 and moved the hearts of millions. The reality in the trenches and gun positions was rather different, as the attack in September showed.

'A unit of border guards with support from the 135th Regiment was sent to attack the Germans from the rear and capture the summit,' wrote Commissar Shabunin, who obviously regarded Krasilnikov and Pashkovskij as savages. 'The Germans left, but hit back violently. Our troops had to make a hasty retreat with severe losses. Krasilnikov arrived as the survivors were streaming back to our positions. He had expected to see the red flag with hammer and sickle flying on the top of Mustatunturi but found instead a group of about 30 defeated men in flight. He was furious, and threatened to shoot them all. That was how he usually stopped people from spreading panic. They all thought he was serious in his threat, and many of them sought refuge among the nearest rocks. He calmed down when I intervened. I was able to stop the madness and explained that the blame lay with Pashkovskij, who had failed to send reinforcements. That set off a new outburst of rage. Krasilnikov gave the colonel an earful and promised that he personally would lead a troop up the mountain and recapture the summit. The people he had been going to execute were given dry clothes and two hundred grams of vodka.'

In a nearby trench, Lieutenant Gorjatsjik was more despondent than he had been for a long time. He had been demoted from company to platoon commander, and the Communist Party had refused to accept his application for membership.

'It's raining constantly,' he wrote in his diary. 'The water gathers in the communication trenches, and everything is soaked through. We go on watch at night and try to sleep by day. I got 200 grams of bread, brewed tea and at last received a long-awaited letter at 04.00. I couldn't take my eyes off the picture of little Svetlana, who must soon be four months old. Then the thought struck me: we can all die here in an instant! Life hangs on a thin thread, and that is a fact that makes me infinitely sad. *I want to live, live, live!* I'm still young. I'm not yet 21 and I have hardly lived. I have only married – nothing else. Oh, that damned Hitler! We are willing to endure everything if we just survive and win! And we'll smash this accursed enemy. The whole people has arisen, and our reserves are endless.'

The reinforcements sent to the corps had shown themselves unfit for battle, but Dietl refused to give up. In progressively colder and more atrocious autumn weather, the assault was continued using the troops who had suffered defeat in the middle of July.

On the evening of Friday 12 September, with horrendous effort and with the support of repeated Stuka dive-bomber attacks, Gruppe Hengl managed to cut off the lateral-connection between the coast and the Murmansk Highway, and capture the northern edge of the mountain plateau known as Height 322. But the Russians had moved their artillery east, and the 58th Regiment with Soldatov's battle-hardened battalions in the van launched constant new counter-attacks.

'If our Stuka bombers had turned the Ura Height into a Hell earlier in the day, it was now the turn of the Russian heavy artillery to continue the endless bloodshed and death,' wrote Rüf. 'There was nowhere to take cover on the plateau, and the losses mounted from hour to hour. The shells fell incessantly on the green hollows where the soldiers huddled together. Other troops were being assembled a few kilometres away for a renewed attack.'[10]

According to Dietl's plan the 138th Mountain Regiment was to advance along the lateral-connection from the opposite direction, make contact with Gruppe Hengl and thus seal off the ring of death around the main Soviet force.

The Knight's Cross winner's mountain soldiers looked southwards in vain for advancing German troops and realised in the course of the morning that the attempt to surround the Russians had failed for the third time.

'Seeing how the situation was developing, von Hengl refused to let his soldiers bleed needlessly to death. He established a new position and allowed the troops to draw back from the Ura Height and the New Road before the next firestorm swept across the plateau.'

The cause of the fiasco was plain. Kreysing's Narvik Division was halted by the Russian counter-attack 300 metres from the Murmansk Highway and could go no further until further supplies arrived.

'Why is the 3rd Mountain Division's assault going so slowly?' Falkenhorst had asked, even though he himself had insisted on relocating the spearhead of the attack into the impenetrable terrain near the lakes. Continuous rain and sleet had turned the Adolf Hitler Road into a sea of mud. It was a further eight kilometres through marsh and scrub from the end of the road to the front line, and the porters were already over-stretched. When Buschenhagen expressed his bewilderment over the slow progress, Dietl had had enough. He wrote explosively in the diary: 'Unfortunately, it appears as if Army Command still lacks the necessary understanding of the difficulties of the terrain. Otherwise, the staff would have understood why bringing up supplies takes so long, despite all our efforts.'

The pressure was beginning to wear the corps commander down. He was exhausted and depressed and appeared to be losing self-control increasingly often. His contemporary Bavarian rival, Major General Ferdinand Schörner, who was supposed to lead the 6th Mountain Division to Murmansk, was worried about Dietl's condition when he visited the front line for the first time on 9th September.

'The man is totally worn out,' he reported to the staff officers who were still hoping to capture the Litza position before the winter.[11]

That was not how it was going to be. To Dietl's fury, the final attack on the Murmansk Highway was repeatedly postponed and didn't begin until the early hours of Sunday 14 September.

DEFEAT • 135

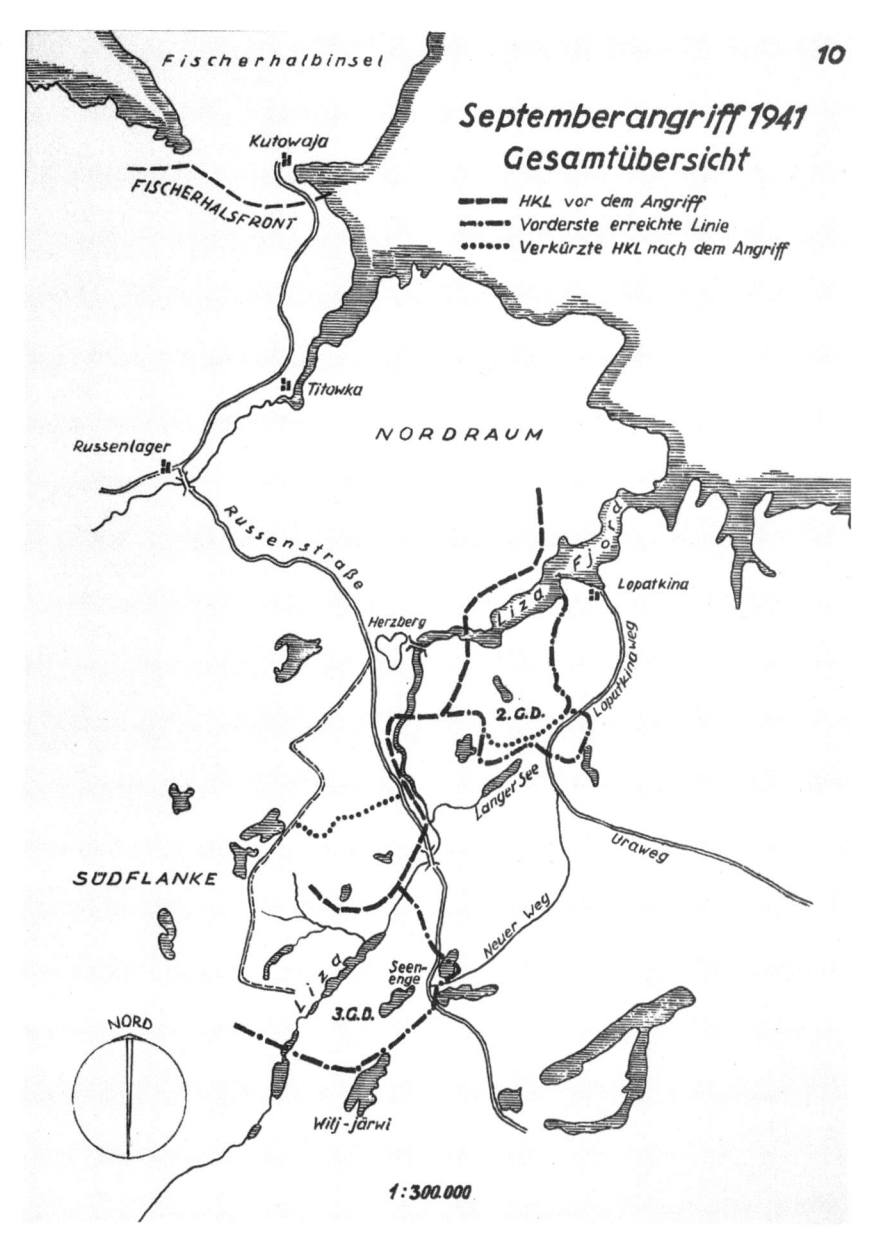

The third attack on the Litza also failed. The dotted line shows that the 2nd Mountain Division was again stopped in the Ura Kettle. The 3rd Mountain Division succeeded in cutting off the Murmansk Highway but was stopped by Russian counter-attacks by the new Polarnoje Division among others. The mountain division was prevented from advancing along the New Road (Neuer Weg) to Height 322, where Gruppe Hengl was waiting in vain for the pincer to close. (Rüf: Gebirgsjäger vor Murmansk)

'The delays led to sharp confrontations between the staff officers, Dietl and Divisional Commander Kreysing,' according to the war diary. 'The fact that the Stuka bombers couldn't be deployed because of the weather is no excuse. German troops must be expected to attack even if the enemy counter-attacks. In this instance not a single assault was attempted, despite the corps allowing the division a four-day pause from 9 to 13 September to replenish supplies of food and ammunition.'

German troops crossed the Murmansk Highway within the next forty-eight hours, and two battalions from the Narvik Regiment under Colonel Windisch captured the heights overlooking the lateral road. It was only 5 kilometres to Height 322, but they were 5 kilometres too many. The lorries bringing Soviet troops and ammunition from Murmansk had trundled back and forth day and night, and the Russian 95th Regiment fought heroically, with increasing support from the Polarnoje Division which advanced towards the lake area and threatened Kreysing's flank.

'We had wanted to capture Height 322 as foreseen in the original plan,' Kreysing reported to Dietl on Wednesday 17 September. 'Unfortunately it couldn't be done. The division just wasn't strong enough.'

The end came the next day. Falkenhorst had been to Wolfsschanze and got the Führer's permission to cancel the attack if necessary. The Soviet submarine *SC-422* and HMS *Tigris* under Howard Bone had in the meantime torpedoed and sunk the cargo ship *Ottar Jarl* and the express freighter *Richard With*, with the loss of another hundred lives. This setback further spooked the German Army Command, which immediately ordered the four troopships waiting in Tromsø to return to Trondheim. The *whole* of the 6th Mountain division was to take the detour through the Baltic and wouldn't reach the Litza front until the end of October.

> The fact that the supply route along the coast is now completely blocked, and that the navy cannot promise any improvements, entails an end to the Mountain Corps' operations. The 6th Mountain Division will not arrive in time. The army has therefore decided to break off the attack on Murmansk.

Winter frost had started, and the first snow settled over the bloodstained tundra by the Litza. The casualty lists were grim. The Germans had lost 12,490 men killed, wounded or missing, and the Russian losses were similar.

Falkenhorst and the army command gave Dietl and the corps 'full credit' for their effort and planned a new attack in the summer of 1942. These were fine and flattering words, but they could not hide the bitter reality.

Hitler had suffered his first defeat on the Eastern Front.

A German 10.5 cm gun from 2. Battery, 730th Artillery Regiment firing at Soviet positions on the Litza front. *(Arkiv Rune Rautio)*

The fighters of the increasingly famous Arctic Ocean Squadron at Høybuktmoen were in the air every day, but never won total air dominance over the Litza front. *(Arkiv Rune Rautio)*

Despite desperate attempts, the Germans never managed to take and hold the steel bridge over the Litza. The Russian 52nd Rifle Division held strong positions on the hills to the east, and the bogs and scrub on the flat land near the river became a killing field. *(Rüf: Gebirgsjäger vor Murmansk)*

Soldiers from the 136th Mountain Regiment honour the dead around the first graves. One company alone lost 18 men in the initial attack, and the mountain troops began to realise that the march to Murmansk would be far more demanding than anything else they had experienced. *(Rüf: Gebirgsjäger vor Murmansk)*

The wounded had to be carried from the front line to the nearest field hospital. *(Rüf: Gebirgsjäger vor Murmansk)*

Soldiers who were wounded at the Litza received initial aid at a forward dressing station and then carried to the nearest field hospital. This journey took hours and days under enemy fire, and many died on the way. *(Rüf: Gebirgsjäger vor Murmansk)*

The German hospital ship *Stuttgart* at anchor in the Neiden Fjord. In the foreground, casualties are being taken from ambulances to a launch. *(Erling Skjold collection)*

Khariton Khudalov took command of the heroic 58th Regiment, which deserves much of the credit for the successful defence of the Litza front. He went on to become a general and was present at the liberation of Kirkenes four years later.

Major General Nikolai Nikishin led the Russian 52nd Rifle Division to the Litza, but was transferred to the reconstituted 14th Rifle Division after the battles in July.

SS-Obersturmannführer Ernst Deutsch with SS Brigadenführer Karl Herrmann and his adjutant, Untersturmführer Martin Nissen, who fell during the assault on Monday 8 September. *(Arkiv Rune Rautio)*

The mountain troops in the Narvik Regiment (139th) had been hailed as heroic warriors, but their self-image took a knock during the hard fighting in the Litza Valley. *(Arkiv Rune Rautio)*

The commander of the Narvik Regiment, Knight's Cross holder Colonel Alois Windisch (1892–1958, wearing a helmet) during a conversation with his officers beside the River Litza on Sunday 13 July. Nearest to him (bending over the map) is Major Anton Holzinger (1901– 89), who also won the Knight's Cross after the Narvik battles. Windisch was dismissed and sent home when he refused to carry out the last attack on the Soviet positions in September. Holzinger was severely wounded and spent a year in a hospital in Germany. *(Rüf: Gebirgsjäger vor Murmansk)*

A chaplain leads prayers prior to a new attack on the River Litza. *(Rüf: Gebirgsjäger vor Murmansk)*

Major and Political Commissar Konstantin Novikov of the 181st Border Battalion was captured during a raid behind the German lines. He gave away no information and on Dietl's orders he was executed on 5 August, in accordance with Hitler's criminal 'Guidelines for the Treatment of Political Commissars'. *(Rüf: Gebirgsjäger vor Murmansk)*

Mountain troops from the 136th and 137th Regiments stormed a height near the Litza Fjord at the end of July 1941 to secure their exposed seaward flank. The Russians lost several hundred soldiers and machine guns during hard fighting. *(Rüf: Gebirgsjäger vor Murmansk)*

On 1 July, mountain troops from Lieutenant Hans-Wolf Rohde's company executed two prisoners who had been captured on Height 122 at Fisher Neck. The misdeed was recorded both in Rohde's report and photographically. *(Rüf: Gebirgsjäger vor Murmansk)*

An Albacore bomber at the entrance to Petsamo Fjord in high afternoon light on 30 July 1941. There were no ships in the fjord, and the attack failed.

Rear Admiral Philip Vian commanded British naval operations in the Barents Sea in the summer of 1941. When his fleet sank the artillery training ship *Bremse*, the German convoys were suspended. *(© Imperial War Museum, A1595)*

Rear Admiral Frederic Wake-Walker led the attack on Kirkenes and escorted the first convoy to Russia. *(© Imperial War Museum, A 23581)*

The Fleet Air Arm suffered serious losses during the attack on Petsamo and Kirkenes. 24 planes were damaged or destroyed and 38 aircrew were killed or taken prisoner. The picture shows an Albacore torpedo-bomber taking off from HMS *Victorious*. *(Erling Skjold collection)*

German prisoners of war being landed at the naval port of Polarnoje, supervised by Russian guards. Of the 425 members of the corps declared missing, many ended up in Russian prison camps. *(Arkiv Rune Rautio)*

Spitzbergen was evacuated in late August/early September 1941 and the coal stocks set on fire. *(© Imperial War Museum, H 13604)*

The artillery training ship *Bremse* (1,435 tonnes) was used as a convoy escort and was sunk outside Nordkyn on 7 September 1941 in a decisive Enigma-assisted strike against the German supply lines. The picture was taken in the Long Fjord near Kirkenes at the end of August. *(Erling Skjold collection)*

One of Captain Sladen's torpedoes hit the steamer *Bahia Laura* (8561 BRT) in Söröysund on 30 August 1941. *Donau II* (2931 BRT) is already sinking, having been hit shortly before, while *Cornouaille* (3324 BRT) alters course to starboard to avoid possible further torpedoes. Almost 600 soldiers and seamen drowned. The sinkings alarmed the Germans and led to them suspending the convoys a short time later. The most important reinforcements didn't reach Dietl in time. *(Erling Skjold collection)*

Mountain soldiers from the Narvik Regiment marching across the swamps in the south on their way to the jungle of scrubby woodland which was the site of bloody battles in September 1941. Dietl was strongly against locating the line of attack so far south, but was overruled by Falkenhorst. *(Rüf: Gebirgsjäger vor Murmansk)*

Infantrymen from the 388th Regiment advancing towards the Brandl Height on Monday 8 September. Soon after, the soldiers walked into an ambush that inflicted losses of 60 per cent on the front-line units. The regiment sent reinforcements, but the troops were forced to retreat after a few hours. *(Rüf: Gebirgsjäger vor Murmansk)*

Mountain soldiers at the bridgehead by the Litza on the morning of Monday 8 September 1941, waiting for the signal to attack. They had won victories from Poland to Narvik and were expecting to take Murmansk swiftly, but they were brought to a stop in the Litza valley and suffered a series of humiliating defeats at the hands of the Red Army, which fought heroically for every single position. The exhaustion and dejection following two months of intense fighting are obvious. *(Rüf: Gebirgsjäger vor Murmansk)*

Major Josef Brandl of the 138th Mountain Regiment led the bloody fighting around the heights just south of the Litza bridge. *(Rüf: Gebirgsjäger vor Murmansk)*

A badly wounded company commander in the 2nd Mountain Division and his men taking refuge in a hollow among the boulders on Height 200 near the Ura Kettle. The soldiers had reached the limit of endurance, and the final attack ground to a halt by 10 September. *(Rüf: Gebirgsjäger vor Murmansk)*

Major General Hans Kreysing was Dietl's successor as commander of the 3rd Mountain Division and had won the Knight's Cross in Holland, but during the fighting in September he fell out with the corps commander and was severely reprimanded. *(Rüf: Gebirgsjäger vor Murmansk)*

The controversial and brutal General Ferdinand Schörner (left) came too late to save Dietl's attack on Murmansk. He later became a field marshal and Hitler's last Chief of Staff. He is seen here with Dietl (centre) and von Hengl (right). *(Arkiv Rune Rautio)*

Golovko gave the reindeer Pollyanna to Commander Sladen as thanks for his support. The reindeer was taken to England on HMS *Trident* and given to London Zoo. *(Royal Navy Submarine Museum)*

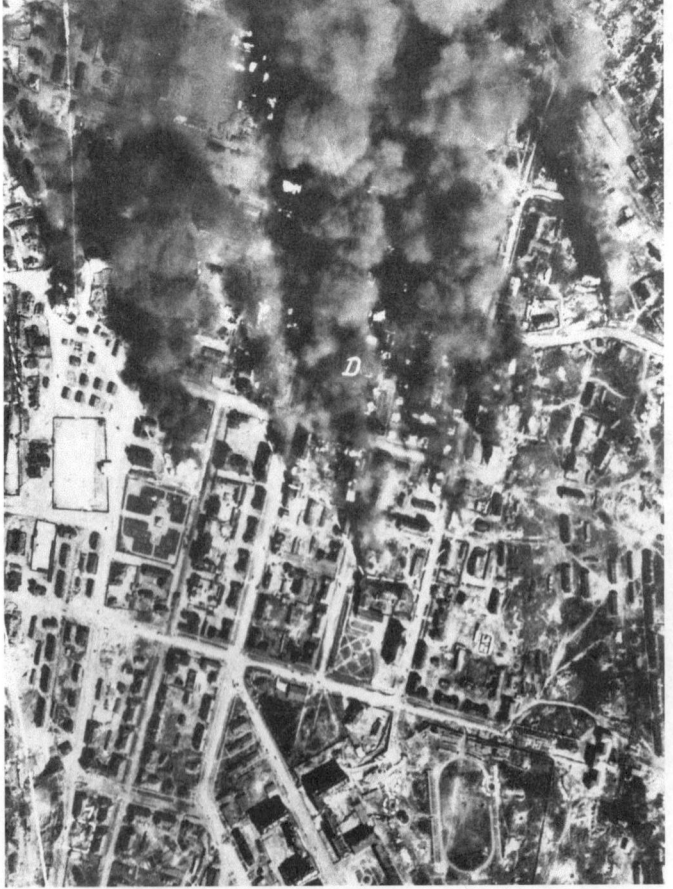

There were 8,000 crosses in the war cemetery in Parkkina when the war in the Petsamo region ended in the autumn of 1944. The cemetery was flattened by bulldozers soon after, illustrating the hatred between the Russians and the Germans after four years of bloody war. *(Rüf: Gebirgsjäger vor Murmansk)*

Murmansk had over 100,000 inhabitants and was bombed with increasing intensity by the Germans in 1941 and 1942. Large parts of the town were reduced to rubble, but the convoys continued arriving and four million tons of arms and equipment reached the Red Army before the end of the war in 1945. *(Arkiv Rune Rautio)*

EPILOGUE

A Heroic Struggle

There is no doubt at all that it was the Russian 14th Army that prevented Dietl's Mountain Corps from reaching Murmansk. The soldiers of the 52nd and 14th Rifle Divisions and finally the Polarnoje Division fought heroically and never allowed the corps to penetrate more than 5 kilometres beyond the River Litza.

Compared with the massive battles on the central part of the Eastern Front, the operations in the Litza Valley were on a comparatively small scale, with altogether about 100,000 men involved. The fighting was very brutal and intense, and the losses amounted to 35 per cent of the fighting troops, among the highest losses on the Eastern Front in the summer of 1941. Between 6,000 and 10,000 men lost their lives in a short time in the remote, green valley.[1]

What makes these battles particularly interesting, however, is the strategic perspective. The German corps' attack on Sunday 29 June worried Stalin, and the demand for a second front in the North was made the very next night. The dialogue between Churchill and Stalin – and eventually Roosevelt – during the catastrophic opening weeks of *Barbarossa* laid the foundations for the alliance which ultimately won the war, and the question of emergency aid via the Arctic was an important issue.

This dialogue led to the British naval operations in the Barents Sea, which very effectively impeded shipping between Tromsø and Kirkenes from late August onwards, with direct tactical support from the codebreakers at Bletchley Park.

At 10.04 p.m. on Saturday 6 September, Norman Denning (later Admiral) at the Admiralty received a telegram that had been sent from the German Admiral of the Polar Coast in Tromsø to Sub-chaser 1701: 'Take over *Bremse* convoy at 0600/6/9 south of Karlsoy at the eastern end of Grotsund for passage to Kirkenes.'[2]

A second telegram a few hours later told that the convoy consisted of the troopships *Trautenfels* and *Barcelona* and had left Tromsø at 4 a.m. on Saturday and was now approaching the barren Nordkyn peninsula. These deciphered reports confirmed that the hypothesis formed in August about the German logistic operation was correct: Merchantmen laden with troops and supplies left the town of Tromsø every third day with clockwork precision.

Denning felt no need to give Vian further updating. The admiral was already underway from Svalbard to Nordkyn with the cruisers HMS *Aurora* and *Nigeria* and would soon be in position to intercept the convoy. The conclusion of this series of messages came during the night, when the radio listeners intercepted the following distress call from the artillery training ship *Bremse*: 'Under attack from surface vessels in sector 7367.'

The subsequent silence said it all. *Bremse* was going down and the troopships were running for shelter in the nearby fishing port of Honningsvåg.

The sinking of *Håkon Jarl, Ostpreussen, Donau II, Bahia Laura, Bremse, Ottar Jarl* and *Richard With* alarmed the Germans, increased Hitler's fear of a British landing in Northern Norway and delayed the arrival of the 6th Mountain Division by six weeks.

It is obviously impossible to be sure in retrospect whether the corps would have broken through at the Litza and captured Murmansk had Schörner's mountain troops had arrived in time. The Russian defences were at breaking point, and Rear Admiral Golovko was unable to hide his apprehension when he met Captain Bevan during the tense and decisive days between 12 and 15 September.

'The enemy has launched a heavy attack on the Murmansk Front and advanced three to four kilometres in a south-easterly direction,' Bevan wrote in his diary. 'Lack of Russian reserves in this district gives cause for anxiety should the enemy receive the reinforcements of a further division which is believed to be on its way. 3,000 naval ratings sent to the front. These are the only available troops at present. The Commander in Chief admitted that the situation would become serious if the enemy receives reinforcements as no further Soviet reserves are available. The Murmansk hospital is stated to be full of wounded. The Polarnoje hospital is also receiving wounded from the front who arrive here by sea.'[3]

The front held, and the 6th Mountain Division didn't reach Litza until the end of October, after a long diversion though the Baltic and Northern Finland. Murmansk remained a free city and from December 1941 onwards, when the White Sea froze for the winter, it became the main receiving port for supplies from the west. Over the next four years, more than four million tons of weapons and equipment were unloaded from 800 Allied ships to aid the Red Army, which against all odds resisted Hitler's murderous onslaught.

We cannot assert that the outcome of the war would have been different if Murmansk and the Fisher Peninsula had fallen into German hands. However, the vital Western supplies to Russia would have had to find another and more difficult route. If the 14th Soviet Army had succumbed, the course of the war would have been changed and it might have taken longer and cost more lives to defeat Hitler and the evil Nazi regime.

The events on the Litza Front were particularly significant for the weak and isolated Norwegian Government in Exile, which in June 1940 had decided to continue the fight against Hitler as guests of the UK government.

Stalin's request for a second front in Northern Norway and an occupation of Svalbard ended the isolation. The government was brought into the negotiations between Great Britain and the Soviet Union, which led to a rapid restoration of diplomatic ties with the USSR.

Free Norway had at last become a small but respected member of the winning alliance – with more than a thousand ships carrying Allied supplies across the oceans.

On the German side, Falkenhorst was called back to Norway in December 1941 and replaced as head of what was to become the Lapland Army in January 1942 by Dietl. The relationship between these two rivals was frigid. Some of the staff officers thought that Falkenhorst had diverted the 6th Mountain Division because he wanted to inflict a humiliating defeat on Hitler's favourite and would have preferred to use Schörner's mountain troops on the Salla Front.

Falkenhorst himself didn't mention the power struggle with Dietl at all in the scanty memoirs he wrote after the war.

> The outcome of the fighting in the north was highly unsatisfactory, as the objective was not achieved despite huge losses. My initial fears were fully and completely confirmed. It would have been better to drop the whole operation and put the six divisions into the Central Front, as recommended by the Chief of the Army, General von Brauchitsch. Now the Lapland Army was stuck in the Karelian wilderness to no purpose. Providing it with supplies was an enormous logistical exercise, and it was unavailable for service on the main front, which badly needed as many troops as possible. Seldom has an unwise splitting of forces been more damaging than in Northern Finland.[4]

Falkenhorst didn't acknowledge any personal responsibility, laying the blame instead on Hitler and his supporters. Dietl did the opposite. He blamed Army Command Norway, in other words Falkenhorst.

'The tragedy which has ruined my efforts here is that I have never had nearly enough troops available for such difficult fighting,' he wrote in a bitter and self-pitying note to Hitler's chief of operations, Alfred Jodl, in the autumn of 1941. 'The army failed to establish a real centre of gravity which could provide the foundation for an attack of overwhelming strength. Therefore we have missed out on the final victory despite enormous effort and self-sacrifice.'[5]

The army in Lapland eventually grew to 230,000 soldiers and auxiliaries. Dietl continued as commander until the summer of 1944, when he died in a plane crash in the Austrian Alps.

Falkenhorst survived as senior army commander in Norway until December the same year when he was dismissed and sent home. At the end of the war he was arrested by the British Army and sentenced to death for having carried out Hitler's notorious *Kommando-befehl* in Norway, ordering the execution of forty British and Norwegian commandos who had taken part in raids against German shipping and the Vemork heavy water plant.

However, the smooth-talking general escaped the hangman. The sentence was commuted to 20 years in prison, and Falkenhorst was released in the summer of 1953. He died of a heart attack in 1968 at the age of 83.

Schörner's division moved into the bridgehead at the Litza in October 1941, several weeks after Hitler's envoy, Colonel Schmundt, had ordered Dietl to go on the defensive.

'The importance of the Petsamo region lies first and foremost in the nickel mines which are essential to German warfare, something the enemy also recognises,' said the Führer's new directive. 'We must assume that the English will establish themselves securely around Murmansk and Kandalaksja with strong air forces, possibly in conjunction with Norwegian and Canadian troops, and will make every effort to deliver large quantities of material by sea to Murmansk.'

That was the reason for resuming the offensive against Murmansk in the spring of 1942, but the plan was never realised. 'What you have started with great self-sacrifice, we shall complete next year with new and powerful forces,' Jodl had written in a letter of consolation to Dietl.

But in December 1941 the German army was halted in front of Moscow and gradually driven back. Hitler had suddenly got more pressing problems to solve, and Litza became an inactive front. The 2nd and 6th Mountain Divisions held the bridgehead for three long and frustrating years until the autumn of 1944, when the Soviet 14th Army launched an attack with superior forces and liberated Petsamo and Varanger.

The 3rd Mountain Division was transferred to the main Eastern Front and took part in the campaigns in Ukraine. Hans Kreysing, who had quarrelled with Dietl, was promoted to full general and awarded both the Oak Leaf and the Sword of the Knight's Cross. He ended the war as commander of the 8th Army in Hungary and later settled down as proprietor of the Villa Ilse holiday hotel on the North Frisian island of Nordeneye. He died in 1969 at the age of 79.

Many of the other staunch Nazis in Dietl's corps later made further careers in other positions within the Führer's apparatus of power. The best known and most controversial of them, Ferdinand Schörner, followed Dietl as corps commander and was sent to the Eastern Front in the autumn of 1943. A year later, he was appointed head of the army's Nazi ideological office, becoming a field marshal in 1945 and Hitler's last Chief of the General Staff.

Schörner was a brutal and ruthless commander. Upon his return to West Germany from Soviet captivity in 1955, he was put on trial and sentenced to a further four and a half years' imprisonment. He remained in prison until 1963 and died ten years later.

Schörner was followed as head of the Nazi ideological office by Ritter von Hengl, who was promoted to full general and commander of Hitler's last Alpine fortress in Bavaria, where he surrendered to the Americans. He died suddenly during a mountain trip in the winter of 1952, at the age of 54.

Himmler's friend, Colonel Georg Hofmeister, was seriously wounded in the summer of 1942 and taken back to Germany where, as a major general, he became Berlin's last city commandant.

Mathias Kräutler stayed on in the northern sector and tried in the closing phase of the war to turn the fjords of Northern Norway into Nazi Germany's last bastion beyond the Alps. This effort failed. Major General Kräutler was arrested by the British, but released in 1947. He died in 1968, after he and another ardent Nazi, Karl Springenschmidt, had published the book *Es war ein Edelweiss*, about the mountain soldiers' battles at the Litza.

The two holders of the Nazi party's Blood Order, who had been alongside Dietl during Hitler's failed Beer Hall Putsch in 1923, Chief of Staff Karl Maximilian von Le Suire and his operations officer Eduard Zorn, also became major generals.

While serving as commander of the 189th Infantry Division, Zorn was killed in battle with American and French troops in the Colmar Pocket in Alsace in the winter of 1945, aged 43. He was promoted posthumously to major general and awarded the Knight's Cross with Oak Leaves.

Le Suire became a full general and was appointed head of the 49th Mountain Corps. The corps lost 77 men in a battle with Greek guerrillas in the autumn of 1943. Le Suire ordered a brutal revenge. In a tragedy known in Greek military history as 'The Massacre in Kalavryta', two villages were annihilated and 1,200 civilians murdered. Le Suire was taken prisoner by the Russians in the spring of 1945 and died in a prison camp near Leningrad nine years later, without having been brought to trial for his war crimes in Greece. The Greeks have not forgotten the atrocity. Le Suire's barbaric actions were a topic of discussion as recently as 2008, during the negotiations about German aid to Greece during the financial crisis.

Lieutenant General Noel Mason-MacFarlane returned to Great Britain in the autumn of 1941 when the shaky wartime alliance had been consolidated. He later served as Governor of Gibraltar and as head of the Allied Control Commission in Italy. He was elected to parliament as a Labour candidate after the war, but resigned because of poor health soon after. He died in 1953.

RAF 151 Wing left north-west Russia in October 1941 after providing valuable air support in the fighting at the Litza. Wing Commander Ramsbottom-Isherwood and three others were awarded the Order of Lenin for their contribution to the war in Russia, the only personnel from the Western Alliance to receive this honour. The New Zealander died while working as a jet plane test pilot in 1950, just 45 years old.

Geoffrey Sladen and Howard Bone both became captains and received the Distinguished Service Order for their brilliant operations against the German convoys on the Finnmark coast in August and September 1941.

Golovko had great respect for the two submariners and he gave Sladen the reindeer Pollyanna as a parting gift when *Trident* and *Tigris* left Polarnoje in November 1941. 'Pollyanna saw Sladen as a mother figure, and headed for the hatch whenever the signal to surface sounded,' a crew member recalled after the war. 'She wanted fresh air and wouldn't let anyone else near, apart from the skipper.' After arriving in Britain the reindeer was donated to London Zoo as a gift to the British from the Russian people.

General Valentin Frolov and Rear Admiral Arsenij Golovko both continued their careers in the Red Army after the war. They were both awarded the Order of Lenin four times, in addition to many other distinctions. Frolov, who died in 1961, finished his career as commander of Archangel Military District. Golovko became vice commander of the Soviet Navy and died the following year. His wife, the famous actress Kira Golovko of Moscow Art Theatre, was acclaimed by the Russian President on her 94th birthday in 2013 and is currently (2017) still alive at the age of 98.

The three regimental commanders in the 52nd Division – Khariton Khudalov, Nikolaj Shpilev and Fedor Korotkov – all became generals. Khudalov led the division, by then known as the 10th Guard Division, to Kirkenes in the autumn of 1944. Korotkov occupied the Danish island of Bornholm at the head of the 131st Rifle Corps and led the Russian Military Mission to Denmark.

Many people consider the three battalion commanders in the key 58th Regiment to be the best and most persistently determined tacticians on the Russian side. The commander of the 1. Battalion, Captain Andrej Sharov, was

45 years old and finished his career as colonel and second in command of the 101st Guards Division. His colleague in 2/58, Major Nikolai Soldatov, was a year older and was wounded three times. He was promoted to colonel and appointed second in command of the 117th Guards Division, which fought in Ukraine towards the end of the war. Lieutenant Vasilij Grinev, who led 3/58, was seriously wounded in the fighting at the Litza at the end of July. He recovered, but fell in Karelia in the spring of 1942 as a battalion commander in the 32nd Brigade.

'I can still see them, these three remarkable front-line commanders,' Vesjeserskij wrote in his memoirs. 'They were regularly cut off from HQ and surrounded, but they never gave up. They organised counter-attacks and drove the enemy back, time after time. Soldatov was strongly built, broad-shouldered and calm, with a gentle face, totally fearless and apparently invulnerable to hails of bullets. Grinev was tall and elegant, ice-cool and with a quick brain. Finally there was Sharov, full of passion and always in a hurry but never losing his head. They were friends and stuck together, but they never boasted of their achievements. They didn't need to. With officers such as these, we couldn't lose!'

In the trenches and hollows among the rocks on Fisher Neck the Red Guards continued to dream of peace. They had repulsed the brutal German attack and withstood Stuka bomber attacks and artillery bombardments. The battlefield now lay covered in snow, and the north wind whipped across the landscape.

'The snowstorm is sweeping over our position,' Lieutenant Alexander Gorjatsjik wrote in his diary in October. 'It's freezing cold, and we don't have any paraffin for the stove. I'm looking at the picture of little Svetlana, but I'd much rather be holding the real, living little girl in my arms. Rain, wind, snow. The days run into each other. Happily, it's a while since we last were on Height 122. We'll never forget that height! It's flying weather. The Germans are bombing Oserki and Mustatunturi. Other planes are going on to Murmansk. I have no doubt that we'll win in the end. The big question is: When? I feel depressed. The party committee asked why I hadn't learned the history of the Communist Party. Well, in peacetime there was always time, but now? If only the days could pass! I want to live, live and live!'[6]

The victory he was dreaming of would come, but it would take four years and cost millions of lives.

Lieutenant Gorjatsjik didn't survive to enjoy the peace. He was killed on Height 122 on Fisher Neck on 29 December 1941. He was just 21 years old.

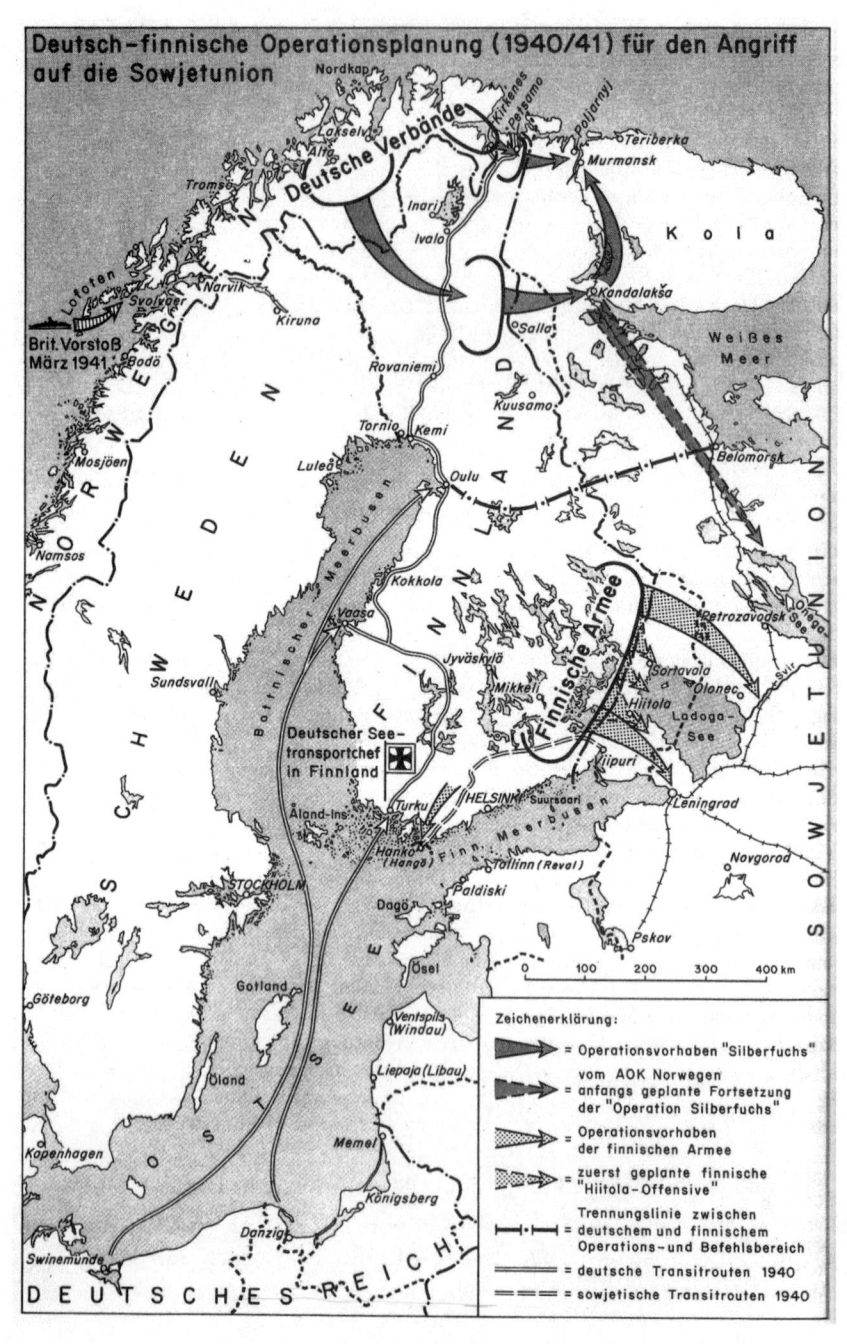

(Deutsche Verlags-Anstalt GmbH, Stuttgart 1983)

APPENDIX I

Wasted Opportunities – Lost Campaign

The German Offensive on the Litza Front in Strategic Perspective

General (ret) Sverre Diesen, former Chief of Defence of Norway

The fighting on the Litza front in north-west Russia in 1941 is a little known part of the history of World War II. In many ways, these operations form a sequel to the German campaign in Norway in 1940 – particularly to the fighting for the strategically important town of Narvik from April to June of that year. From this campaign we recall many of the German units, strategic appreciations, and key personalities. One man in particular stands out, the acclaimed German hero of Narvik, General der Gebirgstruppen[1] Eduard Dietl, who with his skeleton mountain division had conquered Narvik and now was to lead the German assault towards Murmansk at this extreme northern end of the Eastern Front.

With his previous four books about the war in Norway, Alf R. Jacobsen has established himself as one of the foremost writers of this particular genre, combining in-depth research into new source material with great storytelling ability. This makes his books compelling reading for readers with a general interest as well as for serious students of military history. The narrative contains numerous examples of strategic-level assessments as well as of operational- and tactical-level planning and conduct of operations. Furthermore, because of the logistic restrictions imposed on operations in this barren arctic theatre, almost completely devoid of infrastructure and human habitations, most operations were relatively small-scale engagements involving battalions and regiments, where small unit tactics and leadership often became decisive. This makes the campaign a particularly relevant subject for closer examination by officers who train to survive and operate under similar conditions.

Besides the technical and tactical features, the detailed accounts of the desperate fighting for hills and ridges on the desolate and empty tundra is also a useful reminder of what war in the final analysis is really about. These are stories, which, in their stark realism, remind us of the grim facts behind the laconic symbols on the operations maps.

The Strategic Interests

From Hitler's perspective, there was a strategic as well as ideological reason for the attack on the Soviet Union. First of all, a quick victory in the east would deprive Britain of the last hope of German defeat, and should consequently leave Churchill no option but to sue for peace. Secondly, the final contest for world domination with the Bolshevik giant was almost an inevitable historical and ideological necessity for Nazi Germany. This could only be achieved by a massive offensive along the entire width of the European continent, from the Baltic to the Black Sea, aiming at the destruction of the Soviet forces and the occupation of European Russia.

The arctic north-west Russia, where the Soviet Union bordered on Finland, was initially not considered by the Germans for a part in this titanic clash of civilisations, at least not in any offensive capacity. On the contrary, both Hitler and the military planners in the Oberkommando des Heeres – The Army High Command – regarded this as an area in which Germany's interests were essentially defensive, linked to the protection of the crucially important mineral resources. This applied equally to the Swedish iron ore from the mines in the Kiruna – Gällivarre area and the Finnish nickel mines in the Petsamo corridor retained by Finland after the Winter War 1939–40. Hitler also feared that a resumption of hostilities between Finland and the Soviet Union would lead to a Soviet conquest of the rest of Finland, and consequently create a threat to German sea control in the Baltic.

A particular note should be made of the fact that command of the ice-free port of Murmansk and the railway line from there to the interior of Russia – later to become decisive for the Allied arctic convoys with equipment and supplies for the Red Army – was not an issue at all during the initial planning of the campaign. This is logical as long the Germans were totally convinced that the Soviet Union would be quickly defeated, bound to collapse long before it could be saved by Allied support arriving via Murmansk.

After the German attack on Norway, however, there was yet another eventuality haunting Hitler, necessitating a defensive posture in the Arctic: The fear of a British landing in Norway, a country which for rather unexplicable reasons he insisted on seeing as of the utmost strategic importance – *das Schicksalsgebiet dieses Krieges* – the most fateful theatre of this war. From the British perspective, a landing in Norway was scarcely a rational idea at all, apart from the fact that it would have been totally beyond their resources anyway, at a time when they had to rebuild their forces almost from scratch only a few months after the evacuation from the continent.

Nor had the German planners any real reason to fear a Soviet offensive in the high north. To Stalin, this was also an area of primarily defensive importance, as the gateway to the Soviet Union for an invasion by the Western powers such as happened in 1918. However, he also understood the area's geopolitical significance as the only opening towards the Atlantic for the Soviet Navy, uninhibited by the narrow straits that restricted the exit for the Baltic and Black Sea fleets from their home ports. This is confirmed by his instructions to Admiral Golovko in July 1940. Lastly, he retained his fundamental scepticism towards the Finns – a feeling which was reinforced when they, after their defeat in the Winter War, turned to their historical ally Germany for assistance in rebuilding their armed forces.

The Winter War had cost Finland 10 per cent of its territory with 10 per cent of its population driven from their homes to be resettled elsewhere behind the country's new borders. The Finns therefore had an understandable ambition to retrieve the lost territories on the Karelian isthmus and north of Lake Ladoga. In addition to this, there existed in Finland a nationalistic movement working for the unification of all Finns and descendants of Finns living in neighbouring countries within a greater Finland. This was the so-called Lappo movement, which before the war had a substantial following in Finland.

As it became apparent that war between Germany and the Soviet Union was imminent, many Finnish politicians therefore saw that a Soviet defeat would enable Finland to restore the borders from 1939, and perhaps create a zone under Finnish control beyond that as a buffer against their historical enemy. To promote this ambition by joining Germany in a war against the Soviets was perceived by many as a long term investment in Finnish security. The end result, however, was a national tragedy, not just because of the loss of life and ultimate secession of swathes of Finnish territory, but because the peace terms gave the Russians a say in Finnish foreign policy which lasted right up to the fall of the Soviet Union in 1991.

For Britain, the possibility of a German defeat seemed to depend on the United States entering the war, in the same way that had been decisive in 1917. But failing that, it is a British strategic instinct going back hundreds of years always to maintain the balance of power in Europe by forging an alliance with the second strongest power on the continent. Historically, the combined strength of a superior British navy and the ground forces of its continental ally would be sufficient to keep the strongest power in check. With the situation during the grim winter of 1940–41 only the Soviet Union could fill such a role, despite Churchill's opinion of Stalin and his henchmen as a completely heinous regime.

Consequently, Hitler was right in assuming that a Soviet defeat would be felt as yet another serious setback in Britain. However, he miscalculated on two accounts. Firstly, he underestimated the persistence of the old warhorse Churchill, who was not going to negotiate with Nazi Germany under any circumstances. Secondly, even without Churchill at the helm, such a reaction could only be expected in the event of a rapid Soviet collapse and a resounding German victory. Should the war in the east drag on, the effect might well be the opposite. And the British were not as convinced as Hitler about the inevitability of a speedy Soviet defeat. In spite of the German triumphs in the opening phases of the offensive, the attack on the Soviet Union therefore came as a tremendous uplift during the difficult summer weeks of 1941. This was at a time when Britain was still alone and the rout of the Italians in North Africa had been reversed by the arrival of General Erwin Rommel and his Africa Corps now advancing on Egypt and the vital oil fields in the Middle East.

If we look at the strategic assessments of the actors in conjunction as they presented themselves at this time, an interesting point presents itself. In most conflicts, the powers involved will be capable of estimating the interests and intentions of their adversaries correctly on the basis of political, economic, geographical, military and other factors which cannot be kept secret. But in this case, the Germans wrongly assumed that the Soviet Union might attack Finland and Sweden to stop the flow of mineral resources to Germany, while Britain might attempt another invasion of Norway. Stalin, on the other hand, completely disregarded the possibility of a German attack on the Soviet Union right up until it materialised, implicitly trusting the Molotov-Ribbentrop pact of August 1939. Instead, he feared another attempt by the Western powers to land in the Archangel area like they did during the civil war following the 1917 Bolshevik revolution. In Britain the political and military leadership persisted in their belief that the Molotov–Ribbentrop pact would hold, even when the codebreakers at Bletchley Park informed them that the indications of a German attack in the east were overwhelming. The most remarkable thing about these assessments, in other words, is that none of the great powers involved actually judged the intentions of their adversaries accurately. This is why many of the initial plans and dispositions of forces may seem rather inconsistent with subsequent events as the campaign unfolded.

Plans and preparations

The German Plans

The German planning for the campaign in the Arctic was hampered by two factors from the outset – the splitting of responsibility for the planning between two separate headquarters and the persistent wavering between radically different courses of action as planning progressed. The preparations for the offensive on this front were more affected by the chaos prevailing at the top of the German military hierarchy than any other part of *Unternehmen Barbarossa*, the offensive on the Eastern Front. For General Nicolaus von Falkenhorst and the staff of Arméeoberkommando Norwegen – Army Command Norway – the problem was that in their capacity as the HQ responsible for the occupation of Norway they came under the direction of the German joint armed forces command – Oberkommando der Wehrmacht, OKW. However, as the planning staff responsible for one of many sectors of the *Barbarossa* offensive, they came under the direction of the headquarters exercising supreme command of that operation, which was the Army High Command – Oberkommando des Heeres, OKH. As these two tasks strongly affected each other, this violated the sound military principle of unity of command. It was this principle Napoleon referred to with his famous dictum that an army is better served by one bad general than two excellent ones. It was only after the Allied raid on Lofoten in March 1941 – a raid which reinforced Hitler's fear of a major Allied landing in Norway – that Army Command Norway came under OKW also with regard to the operations against the Soviet Union. This was probably a better solution than the original, but at the same time hardly ideal, as it complicated a properly coordinated planning process for the entire eastern front. Nor was OKW as competent as OKH when it came to campaign planning, which would have serious repercussions in the final phase of the planning.

At the same time, it is worth noting that there was no joint German-Finnish command of operations in Finland, besides a certain coordination of command arrangements on the boundary between German and Finnish forces. This was in spite of the German offer to Marshal Mannerheim of command of all German forces in Finland. Mannerheim declined, however, giving as his reason that this would be too great a responsibility, whereas in actual fact this was probably another manifestation of the Finnish desire to keep a certain distance to their German partners.

Taking into account Hitler's fear of a British landing in Norway, his concerns about a Soviet offensive in North Scandinavia and the German requirement for the strongest possible concentration of effort on the central front against the Soviet Union, a defensive posture in the north with Finland remaining out of the war made a lot of sense. Furthermore, in the first operational sketch for Operation *Barbarossa* produced by OKH in September of 1940 there was no German line of operations towards Leningrad, therefore no active Finnish participation and consequently no offensive effort from occupied Norway at all. A concurrent study at OKW, however, recommended three instead of two lines of operation on the continent, one of which was directed at Leningrad.

When Hitler's Directive No 21, the *Barbarossa* directive, came out in December 1940, it therefore included an attack from Finnish territory – not as originally suggested by OKW with its main effort in the south-east, but with a line of operation towards the White Sea from the central and northern part of Finland. The operational idea was based on two attack wedges, with one army corps on the Petsamo – Murmansk axis and one army corps on the Rovaniemi–Salla–Kandalaksha axis.[2] The purpose of this, paradoxically, was to cut the Murmansk railway in order to prevent supplies and reinforcements flowing not from but to the Murmansk region from the interior of Russia – not the other way around, as would later prove vital. Hitler in particular feared that the Murmansk railway line could be used in a Soviet attack on Finland and Northern Sweden, possibly also against Kirkenes, the small Norwegian town on the border with Finland. Consequently, it became vital to reach the White Sea at Kandalaksha to cut this line. Only later, when this had been achieved, would offensive operations towards Leningrad on both sides of Lake Ladoga be resumed in support of the northern line of operations on the continent.

The implication of the *Barbarossa* directive, in other words, was that OKH had to detach two army corps in an offensive towards north-west Russia, an area where Germany only had a defensive strategic interest and where a quick German victory on the central front would no doubt cause a Soviet collapse anyway. These two corps would have to be formed by divisions from the occupation forces in Norway, tasked with the defence of that country against an expected British invasion, which meant that only the smallest possible number of divisions could be detached. Thus, the Germans were already about to sacrifice the course of action which would have been most consistent with their own strategic priorities as well as the overall concept of operations and resource requirements for the *Barbarossa* offensive.

On the basis of OKW's planning guidance, General von Falkenhorst and the staff at Army Command Norway developed the more detailed study *Unternehmen Silberfuchs* (*Silver Fox*) – dealing with the two-pronged assault towards Murmansk and Kandalaksha. General Dietl's Gebirgskorps Norwegen – Mountain Corps Norway – consisting of the 2nd (Major General Ernst Schlemmer) and 3rd (Lieutenant General Hans Kreysing) Mountain Divisions would attack from Petsamo towards Murmansk. The main effort, however, would be on the Kandalaksha axis, which was given to General of Infantry Hans Feige's XXXVI Corps,[3] consisting of two infantry divisions from the occupation forces in Norway, with an additional SS brigade-size formation, the SS Kampfgruppe Nord (SS Combat Group North) – as well as support and logistic units. Feige also got the III Finnish Corps under General Hjalmar Siilasvuo,[4] consisting of the 3rd and 6th Finnish divisions, under command, to screen his right flank during the advance on Kandalaksha.

Army Command Norway therefore laid plans for a two-pronged pincer movement with the right wing as the main effort, XXXVI Corps advancing towards the White Sea and the Murmansk railway at Kandalaksha. From there, the corps would swing north, advance on Murmansk and with Dietl's corps coming from Petsamo close the ring around the Russian 14th Army on the Kola Peninsula. German intelligence estimated the Russian strength in this area to be two divisions, with the 14th Rifle Division[5] in the north and the 52nd Rifle Division further south, around the city of Monchegorsk in the central part of Kola. The Finnish corps would secure the right flank of XXXVI Corps, advancing on Ukhta and from there towards Kemi on the White Sea. Only when this had been achieved would the offensive towards Leningrad on both sides of Lake Ladoga be initiated in accordance with the *Barbarossa* directive, coordinated with Finnish operations in Karelia. Looking at the total number of divisions engaged on both sides we see that there is a slight German superiority in numbers. But the German planners were already falling into the trap of underestimating the limitations imposed by the terrain and the lack of sufficient infrastructure to sustain the advance and resupply of forces of this magnitude.

With the *Silberfuchs* study began a period of several months where various alternative plans bounced back and forth between Army Command Norway and the HQs in Germany, first OKH and later, after the Lofoten raid, OKW. The German allocation of forces was first significantly reduced before being increased again, while a change of *Schwerpunkt* – the main effort – from the Kandalaksha to the Murmansk axis was considered in case of a Swedish refusal to let the two divisions destined for XXXVI Corps transit from central Norway by rail through Sweden. At the same time, however, it was reiterated that Army Command Norway's first priority was the defence of Norway, with the attack on the Soviet Union as a secondary effort. Such uncertainty was not the best foundation for a successful offensive and violated another tenet of operational planning – the need for a clear and unambiguous statement of the commander's intent.

However, it is worth noting that Army Command Norway as early as the end of February 1941 warned against shifting the main effort to the Murmansk axis, pointing out the conditions in this part of the theatre of operations with respect to the climate as well as the absence of infrastructure – particularly the lack of an east-west road with the capacity to serve as a main supply route for a corps level formation. Here we can register the first acknowledgement of what was to be the core problem of the entire Murmansk operation throughout – that even the minimum force required to break through the Soviet defences and advance on Murmansk was bigger than anything which could be logistically sustained on the roadless tundra. The feasibility of the operation, in other words, was limited by logistic rather than operational constraints.

As the date set for the attack on the Soviet Union approached, however, the many staff appreciations with their different alternatives had to be consolidated in a firm operations order from Army Command Norway to its two subordinate army corps. This eventually happened in mid-April, but at a time when the scepticism in the HQ about the viability of the operation was at its highest. This order, therefore, only tasked the Mountain Corps with securing Petsamo with a reinforced division, but otherwise remain on the defensive and only plan for a possible later advance on Murmansk. This part of the operation was code-named *Platinfuchs* (*Platinum Fox*). The attack on the southern axis towards Kandalaksha – code-named *Polarfuchs* (*Polar Fox*) – would still constitute the main effort, but XXXVI Corps was now reduced to just one division initially. This would be transported by sea from Norway, with another division transferred by rail via Sweden if the Swedish government acceded to this after the opening of the offensive against the Soviet Union. The course of action once Kandalaksha had been taken was left open, to be decided in due course depending on the situation.

Had this order remained in effect, no campaign would probably have ensued in the high north at all, and certainly no attack towards Murmansk. But at this stage, chance intervened as is often the case in war, when General Dietl was briefed about the order and the mission of the Mountain Corps. As an old Nazi sympathiser and friend of the Fuehrer he was in Berlin on 21 April to congratulate Hitler on his birthday, and used the opportunity to raise the question of the operation in the far north. Dietl was one of Hitler's absolute favourite generals, not just because he was an *alter Kämpfer* – an old comrade in arms – but also because he had snatched victory from the jaws of almost certain defeat at Narvik the year before. Nazi propaganda had elevated him to almost the same levels as Erwin Rommel, 'the desert fox', who at this moment was chasing the British out of Libya. Dietl and Rommel also had another trait in common which endeared them to Hitler. None of them came from the Prussian military aristocracy that dominated the top echelon of the German officer corps, whom Hitler with his social inferiority complex distrusted and almost detested. Dietl was a Bavarian whereas Rommel was from Württemberg, and both of them had a middle class background.

In his conversation with Hitler on 21 April, Dietl apparently agreed on principle with von Falkenhorst and Army Command Norway that Murmansk should not be the objective of the attack on the northern axis. In the first place it would be a very tough nut to crack, and furthermore it might not be necessary. As soon as Kandalaksha fell to the southern pincer, Murmansk would be isolated and the strategic objective achieved. Dietl emphasised Army Command Norway's concerns about the terrain and made it clear that the planners in Berlin underestimated the difficulties even a limited operation would face. As long as the Mountain Corps was tasked with the defence of all of Norway north of the Ofoten Fjord as well as securing the mines at Petsamo, they would be spread over a distance of 1,200 km, which in practical terms made it an impossible mission.

Hitler listened attentively to his old comrade and eventually instructed OKW to revise the plan for the offensive. But here we arrive at one of the most baffling questions of the confusing tangle of alternative plans and courses of action confounding the preparations for the campaign. Exactly what advice did Dietl mean to give Hitler with his assessment of the operation, and what conclusions did Hitler draw from the discussion? That the attack towards Murmansk was unfeasible and should be abandoned in favour of the Kandalaksha offensive? Or that the attack on Murmansk could succeed, provided the Mountain Corps was given sufficient resources? There is much to suggest that Dietl, with his colourful description of the tundra as a desolate moonscape, 'untouched since the Creation', meant the former – also based on the logic that the same strategic objective could be achieved much simpler by prioritising the southern axis towards Kandalaksha, where conditions were after all more favourable. Not only was there an adequate east–west road, but from Salla there was a railway line which via Alakurtti joined the Murmansk railway at Kandalaksha. A revision in line with this interpretation of Dietl's suggestion would have meant the cancellation of the attack by the Mountain Corps towards Murmansk in favour of a reinforced offensive on the Kandalaksha axis.

Instead, the end result became a compromise between the original, extremely ambitious *Silberfuchs* study and Army Command Norway's more modest operations order. If we look for an explanation for this, there seems to be only two possibilities. Dietl may have meant that the attack towards Murmansk was feasible, if adequate resources were given to the Mountain Corps, and Hitler understood him correctly. Or Dietl may have suggested that the Murmansk operation should be shelved because of the adverse conditions, but Hitler misinterpreted him as saying that more forces must be allocated to the northern axis if the attack were to succeed.

Whatever the explanation, OKW's revised plan turned Army Command Norway's operation order on its head. On the northern axis, both mountain divisions were committed to the attack, whereas XXXVI Corps got the SS brigade back, as well as – although conditionally – a Finnish division. This division, however, was taken from the corps assigned to protect the German right flank, and therefore represented no net increase in the forces in the southern part of the theatre. Air and naval support was also extremely limited. Sea control could not be wrested from the Soviets until the naval bases along the Kola Fjord were taken, and consequently the Mountain Corps could not be resupplied by sea as they moved forward. As for air support, only 60 of Fliegerführer Norwegens (Commander German Air Forces Norway's) 260 operational aircraft were assigned to the entire operation, with two axes of advance 350 km apart. But now – contravening all the intermediate appraisals – the ambition of the first *Silberfuchs* study was retained; the Mountain Corps to take Murmansk and XXXVI Corps to take Kandalaksha, followed by the turn north and the destruction of the Soviet 14th Army in a huge encircling movement. This in spite of the fact that the extra forces allocated to the operation did not meet the requirement of troops to task in the *Silberfuchs* study – even that a requirement which under the circumstances must be considered marginal.

OKW's final plan for the attack on the Soviet Union from Finland thus in many ways became an incoherent and illogical compromise between different considerations and requirements, particularly for the *Platinfuchs* or northern wing of the offensive. Developing operational compromises which represent elements of several different strategic courses of action – and consequently are not compatible – is a well-known trap in military history. They quite often lead to operational plans and decisions that are not consistent with strategic objectives, resource constraints or other preconditions, and lead to disaster. This was also destined to happen here.

The Soviet plans

The disposition of forces on the Soviet side initially reflected Stalin's fear of a landing by the Western powers in the White Sea region, as happened in 1918 when they intervened on the side of 'the whites' in the civil war against 'the reds'. So convinced was he about German intentions to stick to the non-aggression pact of 1939 that this did not change after the German invasion of Norway, not even when the German build-up of forces in Norway's northernmost county of Finnmark started in earnest. The Soviet 14th Army was therefore deployed more with a view to defence of the Kola Peninsula against an attack from the sea, with the 14th Division forward along the coast from the Finnish border and eastwards, and the 52nd Division in the area around the town of Monchegorsk about 120 km inland in the central part of Kola. This was a sound deployment given its reason – but in light of the actual circumstances it meant exposing the entire Soviet left flank to a German attack from Petsamo.

Nor did Stalin become more apprehensive when the British started to feed him intelligence clearly indicating that a massive German attack on the Soviet Union was imminent. Instead, he chose to see the British intelligence as disinformation, providing confirmation of his own paranoid notions that the British would try to feed him false information in order to create a conflict between Germany and the Soviet Union, relieving the pressure on themselves and at the same time disguising their own aggressive intentions. This is a useful reminder that the personality cult set up by absolute rulers, emphasising their near god-like abilities, carries the risk that they gradually start believing it themselves. Not least the purges of the greater part of the Soviet military elite in 1937–38 had silenced all criticism of the dictator from the officer corps. However, as previously mentioned, Stalin was aware of the significance of Murmansk as a geopolitical window open to the west. This was a realisation which would prove critical when the war broke out.

German Forward Movement to the Start Line

For the Mountain Corps, the first phase of the attack on the Soviet Union did not involve the actual crossing of the Finnish-Russian border, only the occupation of the Petsamo area with the nickel mines – an operation code-named *Unternehmen Renntier* (Operation Reindeer). The forming-up along the Norwegian–Finnish border of two mountain divisions with supporting corps troops in the days before 22 June, crammed together along the few and barely adequate roads in the Pasvik valley was a superb feat of German organisation, command and control. It would only be surpassed three years later when what had by then become the 20th Mountain Army withdrew through the same area in one of the most demanding fighting retreats in military history, from Northern Finland to the Lyngen line in Northern Norway in the late autumn of 1944 – a *katabasis* worthy of comparison with anything from Xenophon's march to the sea with his 10,000 hoplites in the 5th century BC to the Chosin Reservoir campaign in Korea in 1950.

There is a striking difference between the preparations on the German side and those taking place on the other side of the Russian border during the final days before *Barbarossa-Tag* – Barbarossa Day – Sunday 22 June. The Soviet commanders had to perform a delicate balancing act, watching with growing apprehension the German build-up under their very noses on the Norwegian side in the eastern part of Finnmark but at the same time fearful of infuriating Stalin by taking defensive measures which he would consider 'provocations'. Still, two decisions were made which would have a decisive impact on the campaign. One was the order of the commanding general of 14th Army, General Valerian Frolov, as early as the beginning of April to start the construction of a line of concrete bunkers along the north–south ridge between the Titovka river and the Finnish border, at right angles to the designated front line of the 14th Division. The other was the decision by the commander of Leningrad Military District, General Markian Popov, to regroup the 52nd Division on the night of 21 June.

In spite of the fact that the bunker line was not nearly finished when the Germans crossed the Russian border on 29 June, a week after the opening of the offensive on the continent, they ran into much tougher resistance than they would otherwise had done, in an extremely rocky terrain where more improvised fox-holes and slit trenches could not be dug easily with entrenching tools after the actual fighting had started. Even more important was the decision to bring forward the 52nd Division from Monchegorsk, to reinforce the 14th Division in the bunker line on the Titovka on the eve of the opening of the offensive. This meant that the front of the 14th Army was altered from north to west, to face the attack at the latest possible moment. But on top of that, the late decision should turn out to be the very salvation of the Soviet defence, since the main part of the division was too late to reach the Titovka in time for the attack. Had the order been given before and the division been in place, the defensive position there could have been extended and made more solid – but at the price of having no depth at all. If the Germans had managed to break through this line, the road to Murmansk would have been open. Instead, the 52nd Division now had to form a hasty defence along the Litza river, thereby presenting the Germans with the problem of having to penetrate two successive lines of defence 15–20 km apart, where all supplies would have to be hauled by horses or manpower from the first to the second line.

Another factor which contributed to the same result was the delay between the German entry into Finland to secure the Petsamo area, and the crossing of the Russian border a week later. This gave the Russians a week's respite which they used to their advantage, making up for weeks and months of delay at Stalin's behest. One of the battalion commanders in the German 137th Mountain Regiment, Major Mathias Kräutler, should later call this week *die versäumten sieben Tage* – the wasted seven days – which tilted the scales against the Germans' favour.

The Attacks

Opening attacks on 29 June

The plan of attack called for Mountain Corps Norway to attack with its two divisions, the 2nd and 3rd Mountain Divisions, in line, take the partly fortified ridge on the far side of the border and cross the Titovka river. At this stage, a singular weakness in the German order of battle which would make itself felt almost immediately should be noted. The Mountain Corps consisted of only two divisions as opposed to the normal three or four divisions in other corps formations, whereas each division had only two instead of the normal three regiments as their subordinate combat units. This meant that the Mountain Corps had only four regiments in total with which to engage the enemy, instead of the nine regiments normally organic to other corps. This did not just affect the overall combat strength of the corps negatively. Having three subordinate combat or manoeuvre units at each level is standard military organisational practice, enabling the commanders at every level to engage with two units while retaining one in reserve to respond to the development of the battle. In defence to counter-attack and retrieve a lost position, in attack to reinforce and exploit success. With only two such subordinate units, both Dietl as corps commander and his two divisional commanders, Kreysing and Schlemmer, would be seriously constrained in terms of their ability to deal with the unexpected.

Still, the opening phase of the attack, with the assault on the Russian bunker line and the crossing of the Titovka, stands out as a textbook example of basic infantry tactics.

Particularly 137th Mountain Regiment (Colonel Ritter von Hengl), the regiment on the right of the 2nd Mountain Division, gave a powerful demonstration of how an operation like this should be conducted by letting one of its three battalions (II/137) attack frontally and tie down the Russian defenders. The other two battalions (I and III/137) executed a turning movement to roll up the defenders from the flank. This is a tactical solution which is so standardised in the tactical manuals of all armies that it is almost a stereotype, and as such entirely predictable. However, when properly executed it is a simple, well exercised and therefore effective tactical pattern.

While the battalion which had seen the lion's share of the combat in the first phase by attacking the Russian bunker line was reorganised and resupplied, the two flanking battalions repeated the pattern in the following crossing of the Titovka. One battalion engaged the Russians frontally, where the primitive road crossed the river on a bridge, while the other crossed further upstream to attack the defenders in the back. This demonstrated the value of having three tactical subunits at every level of command. The regiment could conduct a two-phase offensive operation and still retain a measure of flexibility also in the second phase. The lack of this ability at division and corps level, however, resulted in the attack bogging down more quickly than it might otherwise have done. Following the crossing of the Titovka, almost a week passed before the Rybachy peninsula isthmus was secured – an operation requiring two instead of one battalion as estimated – and the village at the estuary of the Litza river had been taken.

Nor can there be any doubt that the Germans paid dearly for the deficiencies of their intelligence preparations. Not only had they underestimated the strength and tenacity of the defenders, with the presence of the 52nd Division behind the Litza river and the resolve with which the Russian soldiers were fighting. Furthermore, in spite of the celebrated German thoroughness, they had seriously underestimated the difficulties of sustaining offensive operations in the roadless arctic tundra. The clearest indication of this is that the 3rd Mountain Division received a completely revised order from corps HQ only 11 hours into the attack across the Titovka. And already that same afternoon, on the first day of the operation, after a discussion with the corps operations officer, Dietl cancelled the entire original plan of attack. Instead, we can read in the corps' war diary a short, concise order whereby both divisions are ordered to concentrate on the far side of the bridge over the Titovka and retain a bridgehead on the eastern bank until a road of reasonable sufficiency to the rear could be established.

That a plan of operations cannot be carried out as anticipated is in itself no sensation – in fact quite the opposite. Particularly German officers were raised in the spirit of the great Chief of the German General Staff in the 1860s, Helmuth von Moltke's famous dictum that no plan survives the first contact with the enemy. That company or battalion commanders have to revise their plans in a matter of hours after the start of an operation is therefore routine. But when the same thing happens at corps level, less than a day into an operation, it suggests that the plan was not entirely realistic in the first place. The amount of robustness necessary for an army corps plan involving tens of thousands of troops to survive at least 24 hours is normally to be expected, with the lower levels of command dealing with the unforeseen within that sort of timeframe. Now Dietl had to give up an attack with both divisions in line, and concentrate on a smaller front.

However, much as this is a clear indication of the weakness of the initial German plan, once it happened it is also an illuminating example of the flexibility of the German command system. The entry in the war diary is a striking example of how the commander's intent can be communicated to subordinate units, not just in terms of what he wants them to do, but also why. The order is short and yet complete, leaving commanders of divisions and other subordinate units great latitude when it comes to the actual use of their forces, while remaining within the framework of the corps commander's overall operations design. Dietl's mission statement runs as follows: *Das Gebirgskorps sammelt mit der Masse der 2. Und 3. GebDiv im Raum Titovkabrücke – Höhe 228 und halt diesen Brückenkopf bis zur Herstellung der rückwärtigen Strassenanschlusses.* In just two lines are encapsulated an entirely new plan involving the retasking of more than fifty thousand troops, based on a revised appraisal of the situation, but allowing lower levels of command the necessary freedom of action to deal with the details. This is a style of command in which the Germans excelled, and which they themselves called *Auftragstaktik* – mission tactics – which remains an ideal to this day, laid down in the manuals of all NATO armed forces. In NATO parlance this kind of instruction is called a fragmentary order, or 'frago' for short. But the historical origin of this principle is the sort of order Dietl was giving an excellent example of here.

Could the initial attack have been more successful if Dietl had had a third division at his disposal, or even if the divisional commanders had had a third regiment? This is in many ways the core question when analysing Operation *Platinfuchs*. The answer is not in any way obvious, precisely because the logistic constraints presented by the terrain and the lack of adequate roads set the limits for what could be achieved tactically. The dilemma, in other words, was that the force required to break Russian resistance was bigger than what could be sustained with the organic supply units of the Mountain Corps. However, if more troops were assigned to carry provisions forward, then implicitly the corps' combat power became too weak to break through. We will therefore come back to how the Germans might have utilised a bigger force in the summing-up of the campaign.

Thus Dietl's reservations in his conversation with Hitler on 21 April proved justified. But it is worth noting that even Dietl was surprised by the severity of the problems, since his own plan had to be abandoned within 24 hours of the opening of the attack.

First Attack on the Litza Line

After consolidating the position between the Titovka and Litza rivers, the Germans planned the first attack on the Litza river line for 6 July. Again the problem of tactical vs logistical considerations cropped up in the discussion between Dietl and General Schlemmer of the 2nd Mountain Division about whether to go for a narrow envelopment of the Russian position behind the bridge over the Litza, or a wider turning movement. Schlemmer feared massive casualties if the outflanking movement became too limited, whereas Dietl was afraid that a wider, more sweeping movement could not be sustained logistically and consequently would fail to break through. Which solution would prove the better of the two would thus depend on how the ratio between German offensive power and Russian defensive resilience would develop in the two alternatives.

Not surprisingly, Dietls assessment prevailed, but as Schlemmer had feared, the attack was met by fierce resistance. The 2nd Mountain Division only managed to get one battalion across the river and the 3rd Division only two in a very shallow bridgehead on the eastern bank. Simultaneously, the Russians demonstrated the advantage of controlling the sea flank by landing two battalions in the Litza bay, to which the Germans had to respond immediately by detaching one of the attack battalions and sending it to contain the Russian landing. Dominating the waters outside the Kola Peninsula therefore allowed the Russians to extend the German front line by another 70 km, from the Norwegian-Finnish border to the mouth of the Litza.

Stiff resistance east of the river, the landings in Litza bay and more flanking attacks by the Russian forces across the isthmus of the Rybachy peninsula, well to the rear of the German front, led to the attack being suspended on 8 July, with the forces in the bridgeheads being pulled back to the west bank. Furthermore, Hitler intervened and demanded that yet another battalion and three artillery batteries should be detached for securing Petsamo against a British landing – a totally baseless concern on his part. With two battalions guarding the Rybachy peninsula isthmus and one committed against the landing in Litza bay, this meant that four of Dietl's total of 12 battalions plus a significant part of his artillery had been detached for defensive tasks. His offensive hitting power, marginal even at full strength, had been reduced by a third.

Dietl now demanded reinforcement by at least another mountain regiment before offensive operations could be resumed. Even this was scarcely sufficient, bearing in mind that one regiment would not even compensate for the four battalions already drained from the main force and the losses sustained during the first two weeks of the campaign. Nothing of what had happened so far, in fact, seemed to disprove his first assessment – that an offensive from Petsamo towards Murmansk was bound to fail. A more consistent request would have been to argue that the attack towards Murmansk be abandoned altogether in favour of a concentration of effort on the Kandalaksha axis.

Instead OKW chose to persist with the Murmansk attack, falling in with Dietl's request and ordering von Falkenhorst to transfer forces from XXXVI Corps to the Mountain Corps – in other words weakening the intended main effort in order to reinforce a part of the front where resistance had proved to be tougher than expected. This is what in military jargon is called 'reinforcing failure', which may safely be called a serious violation of the fundamentals of tactics. At this stage, the offensive on the southern axis had barely begun, after being launched on 1 July, but the Germans and the Finns would enjoy much greater progress here than on the northern axis. Arguably, this confirms that OKW should have stuck to the plan and kept the main effort in the south.

Second Attack on the Litza Line

The second attempt to break the Litza line was launched on 13 July, this time with the *Schwerpunkt* on the left flank of the Mountain Corps, in the 2nd Mountain Division's sector. This division would now attack across the Litza in a south-easterly direction towards a cluster of small lakes approximately 10 km east of the river. From there, the division would turn south and take the defending forces in front of 3rd Mountain Division in flank.

With the defences on the east bank broken, both divisions would turn east and attack towards Murmansk on both sides of the road.

This attack enjoyed greater progress initially than the first. By evening on the first day, the 2nd Division had a considerable part of its forces across and up to 3 km from the river. But during 14 and 15 July, resistance stiffened, carefully coordinated with new sea landings and break-out attempts from the Rybachy peninsula. On 16 July, Dietl concluded that the threat from the sea against 2nd Mountain Division's left flank and rear must be eliminated before another attempt could be made.

Even when the Germans were forced on the defensive, trying to hold on to a foothold on the eastern side of the river, logistics came to decide the issue. The situation kept deteriorating as more units had to be committed to defend the bridgehead and could not be used to carry supplies forward. On 18 July, 2nd Mountain Division was pulled back to an even smaller bridgehead on the east bank, while 3rd Mountain Division gave up its precarious hold on the eastern side altogether. Thus the second attempt at breaking the Litza line ended with nothing more to show for it than an extremely shallow bridgehead on the far side of the river, a gain not in any way commensurate with the cost in blood. As early as 17 July, Dietl informed Army Command Norway that further attempts at breaching the line of the river would have to be abandoned, the bridgehead reduced even further and the troops relieved by this withdrawal redeployed to wipe out the Soviet force clinging to the bridgehead in Litza bay like a thorn in the German side. Subsequent operations towards Murmansk would then require not just a fresh regiment, but an entire division.

We have now come to 17 July, when the offensive on the Kandalaksha axis had gained considerable ground. XXXVI Corps took Salla on the 7th, while the Finnish Corps had penetrated to a depth of 65 km on the axis towards Ukhta. A reasonable suggestion from Dietl at this stage therefore would have been for Army Command Norway to stand on the defensive in the north while reinforcing XXXVI Corps in the south, rather than asking for another division to be committed on the Murmansk axis.

On 21 July, a meeting was held between von Falkenhorst, his chief of staff, Colonel Erich Buschenhagen and Dietl, the three officers agreeing that two courses of action were possible. Either to withdraw to Finland and go into winter quarters there or renew the attack and take Murmansk. To stay on the Litza through the winter and resume the offensive in the spring was not considered possible, as long as the Russian threat from the sea flank remained and the Mountain Corps could not be supplied by boat from Kirkenes. Both problems would require that the Russians were denied access to the waters off the Kola coast, which in its turn required German control of the naval bases in the Murmansk area, or at least control of the outlet from the Murmansk Fjord at Polarnoje.

But instead of abiding by their own initial judgment and what was by now rather overwhelming supporting evidence, Army Command Norway continued to throw more troops and resources into the Murmansk operation – an attack, it should be remembered, they considered neither feasible nor necessary only a few months before. On 23 July, Dietl was informed that he would receive another two battalions transferred from Norway and was ordered to resume the offensive. Dietl replied on the 24th, pointing out that his mountain regiments were exhausted and well below strength. With only two battalions as reinforcement there was nothing he could do, other than getting rid of the tenuous Russian beachhead in the Litza bay. A renewed attack towards Murmansk was out of the question.

Now, however, the consistency of German operational planning seemed to break down altogether, as OKW suggested to Army Command Norway that the offensive on the Kandalaksha axis should be curtailed and some of XXXVI Corps' formations transferred to Mountain Corps Norway. Army Command Norway duly objected to this, *but giving as their reason that Dietl could take Murmansk if a fresh Mountain Division was assigned to the Mountain Corps.*[6] Both HQs, in other words, discarded their own original judgment and supported another effort in the north, but disagreed about what number of forces this would require and where they should be taken from. Yet again the higher German command seemed in total disarray, with little understanding of the conditions prevailing in the theatre of operations.

Not surprisingly, however, Hitler accepted the OKW assessment and decided on 30 July that 6th Mountain Division should be transferred from Greece to Norway, where it was expected to be ready in the second half of September.[6] In addition another two regiments were added to the order of battle of the Mountain Corps, 388th Infantry Regiment and 9th SS Infantry Regiment both being transferred from the occupying forces in Norway. Thus an operation designated as a secondary axis of attack was allowed to develop gradually into a major effort, sucking in troops and resources, but without being able to force a decision. Resources which, if committed from the very beginning and on the axis of attack offering the greatest possibility of success, might have achieved a breakthrough were wasted in a piecemeal fashion, where the force ratio was never solidly in favour of the Germans. Moreover, this happened at a time when the offensive on the southern axis, the designated axis of main effort, was going well and therefore should have had priority on resources and reinforcements.

Third and Final Attack on the Litza Line

The third and final attack on the Litza line was both the strongest and the most meticulously planned attempt to break through to Murmansk. Considering the German experience with the first two attacks, it is therefore surprising that they continued to make a number of the same mistakes, since this time they were not planning under the same sort of pressure.

Von Falkenhorst wanted to break through the Litza defences even before the arrival of the 6th Mountain Division, using the new division to exploit the breakthrough as it arrived and reach Murmansk before the onset of winter. It is admittedly another tenet of tactics that in order to develop a successful attack into a decisive victory, a retreating enemy must be pursued and denied the opportunity to conduct an orderly withdrawal. This is normally the task of a fresh and uncommitted reserve, a *corps de chasse*, which must be launched at the precisely right moment, just as the enemy's defensive position is breaking. But to set in motion an attack before this reserve has even arrived in the theatre of operations, relying on it to turn up just in time to be hurled into battle, is an extremely hazardous and questionable undertaking. This was proved to be right also in this case, as HMS *Trident*'s sinking of several ships off the Norwegian coast on 30 August demonstrated to the Germans that the planned transport of the 6th Mountain Division by sea to Kirkenes was indeed highly dangerous.

In spite of this, Army Command Norway ordered Dietl to continue attacking towards Murmansk after breaking through on the Litza, even if at that time 6th Mountain Division had not arrived – an operation Dietl now doubted would be possible, even if reinforced by a completely fresh division. These uncertainties did not diminish when D-day for the next attempt was set as late as 8 September, with winter only a few weeks away at this latitude, normally in the beginning of October. Army Command Norway's plan consequently incurred two serious risks, launching the attack without having the necessary forces in theatre to break through to Murmansk, and seeing that should the attempt fail the oncoming winter would not permit them to make another attempt once the 6th Division did arrive. If that happened, the only course of action open to the Mountain Corps would be a retreat back to Finland, as von Falkenhorst and Dietl were in agreement that staying at the Litza for the winter was not an option.

The final afterthought about the German dispositions is that Dietl reported to OKW as early as 5 September – three days before the attack – that even if Murmansk was taken, XXXVI Corps taking Kandalaksha and gaining control of the railway line from there to Murmansk was still mandatory for sustaining the Mountain Corps in Murmansk throughout the winter. The position there could not be held based on a logistical shoestring stretching back across the tundra with its one, inadequate road to Petsamo. This is actually an absolutely crucial point, as long as controlling Murmansk was not a precondition for taking Kandalaksha, whereas the opposite was. This proves that both Dietl's and Army Command Norway's initial assessment was right – that the *Schwerpunkt* of the offensive should have stayed with XXXVI Corps and not with Mountain Corps Norway. But the question still remains – if this was Dietl's opinion as late as 5 September, why was the attack launched in the first place, when all losses and sacrifices on the Litza would be for naught as long as Kandalaksha was still in Soviet hands? And how could Army Command Norway waste thousands of soldiers on an operation which not only required Kandalaksha to fall first, but also – if and when Kandalaksha fell – would be completely redundant anyway, since the strategic objective of the whole campaign would then be achieved?

When the attack was launched on 8 September, it had considerable progress for the first couple of days. The concept of operations this time was that both mountain divisions should attack on either side of the bridge over the Litza in a rather wide double envelopment, before turning inwards towards the Murmansk road as it passed a narrow strip of land between the two lakes Knyrk and Traun. Controlling this defile with the adjacent Hill 322 would close the ring around the Soviet 52nd Division. According to the original idea, while the two mountain divisions completed the annihilation of those parts of the Soviet division that did not escape before the pincer movement was complete, the newly arrived 6th Mountain Division would pursue the remnants eastwards and take Murmansk. However, with the third division not available, the whole undertaking was hanging in the balance.

On 10 September the advance was grinding to a halt under pressure from repeated Russian counter-attacks, and even with renewed efforts by the 2nd Mountain Division on 12 September and the 3rd two days later, the two prongs of the German attack never came closer than 5 km apart. Winter now made its first call, the weather turning atrocious with rain, sleet and wind. On 14 September, six days into the operation, the attack culminated, followed by two days of aggressive German patrolling to disrupt Soviet preparations for a counter-offensive. Furthermore, new sinkings of German shipping by British submarines off the Norwegian coast on 12 and 13 September had led to the final cancellation of 6th

Mountain Division's deployment by ship to Kirkenes, the division being re-routed via the Baltic, finally arriving in the theatre in the second half of October. The combination of the same logistical problems as during the first two attacks, the lack of a strong reserve, fierce resistance and the coming of winter had put paid to the third and final German attempt to storm the Litza defensive position and take Murmansk in 1941.

On 18 September Dietl halted all offensive operations in Mountain Corps Norway. 21 September his order was approved by Army Command Norway and on 23 September by OKW and Hitler himself. At this point, German intelligence had identified a third Soviet division in 14th Army's order of battle, the so-called Polarnoje Division which proved that the Russians were also now scraping the bottom of the manpower barrel, since this division consisted of slave labour released from the gulag camps in the White Sea region. It may also seem that Army Command Norway had finally realised that committing more troops to the Litza front only led to the logistical problems increasing more rapidly than the combat power, since they proposed that the 6th Mountain Division should be deployed to the sector in central Finland after the termination of the Murmansk offensive. This was rejected by Hitler, however, who in a conference with von Falkenhorst in Berlin as early as 15 September had decided that the division should relieve the 2nd and 3rd Divisions in place on the Litza and hold this line throughout the winter, renewing the offensive the coming spring – in other words the option that both Dietl and von Falkenhorst considered an impossible compromise.

Conclusions

Closing assessment of Operation Platinfuchs

Considering what it achieved and at what cost, Operation *Platinfuchs* must be rated as an ignominius German failure – the first on the Eastern Front. Mountain Corps Norway only succeeded in advancing 27 of the 90 km between Petsamo and Murmansk at a price of 10,300 casualties. The strategic objective of the operation was to prevent a Soviet attack to gain control of the mineral resources in Northern Scandinavia, something the Russians never even contemplated and which might probably have been achieved more easily and at a lower cost by prioritising Operation *Polarfuchs*, the other wing of the attack from Northern Finland.

To sum up, the five most important reasons why the offensive failed are probably these:

- Hitler's strange obsession with the need to defend Norway and the mineral resources in Scandinavia against a British invasion meant that the forces made available to the offensive were understrength with regard to both the overall force, the number of sub-units at corps and division level in the Mountain Corps and in terms of the balance between tooth and tail – between combat troops and logistic support on the Mountain Corps' axis of advance.
- In spite of the fact that the OKW, Army Command Norway and General Dietl himself held the opinion that the *Schwerpunkt* of the offensive should be on the axis Rovaniemi–Salla–Kandalaksha, they let the supporting effort – the attack towards

Murmansk – gravitate into the main effort. Not unlike the fateful French attack on Chateau Hougoumont at Waterloo, the *Platinfuchs* attack was allowed to suck in a steady stream of reinforcements – forces that, had they been concentrated in time and space, could have forced a decision, but instead were wasted for no good reason. On 18 September, the day when Dietl halted all offensive operations on the Litza, XXXVI Corps had its leading elements on the Verman river, barely 10 km from the Murmansk railway line south of Kandalaksha. This had been achieved in spite of the fact that the corps repeatedly had had units taken away and transferred to the Murmansk attack. It is therefore highly likely that the Germans, by adhering to their original concept, would have managed to take Kandalaksha and cut off the Murmansk railway before the beginning of winter.

- The German intelligence preparation of the campaign failed to appraise the commanders of the full extent of the rigours presented by the terrain, the climate and the lack of infrastructure on the axis of advance of the Mountain Corps, nor did they assess the order of battle of the defending 14th Army accurately.
- German intelligence also seriously underestimated the morale and tenacity of the Russian soldiers, probably based on their poor performance during the Winter War, missing that important steps had been taken to correct the weaknesses during the year that had passed. Presumably, the average Soviet soldier was also prepared to sacrifice more in the defence of Mother Russia than he had been invading a strange country under gruelling winter conditions. Particularly the 52nd Rifle Division fought heroically, taking advantage of the possibilities offered by the terrain, while the Army command shrewdly used their position on the Rybachy peninsula and their control of the sea flank to disrupt and dislocate successive German attempts to break through on the Litza.
- The seven-day delay of the opening of the offensive in the north compared to the rest of *Barbarossa* proved critical, because it enabled the movement of the 52nd Division from central Kola to the line of the Litza – but not beyond – saving the situation for the Russians after the mauling of the 14th Division in the bunker line and on the Titovka.

The third attempt, however, came closest, which poses the question: would a sufficiently early arrival of the 6th Mountain Division have made a difference? In other words, at what time could that division have arrived at the earliest, and would that have been in time to effect a breakthrough and an advance to Murmansk before the onset of winter?

It was the British naval operations in the beginning of September which convinced the Germans that the sea route from Tromsø to Kirkenes was too exposed to risk the transport of the division by ship, prompting the decision to re-route it via the Baltic. If we assume that the British operations had not taken place, or that the Germans had persisted with their plan and succeeded, the 6th Mountain Division might have been in place and forming up behind its sister divisions as corps reserve around 20 September at the earliest. Even so, in other words, D-day must have been postponed by another two weeks, getting dangerously close to the first winter storms. Furthermore, for the operation to succeed, the two leading divisions must have managed to close the ring around the 52nd Division to prevent it from retreating to fight another day, leaving the 6th Mountain Division free to advance unhindered in the direction of Murmansk.

And finally, the Germans would have had to crack the logistics nut bedevilling the whole campaign, with incoming reinforcements adding more to the problem than to the solution by gobbling up more supplies than could be brought forward. It is difficult to see how this could have been achieved without providing more labour units whose task was exclusively to carry provisions forward, in order to avoid the siphoning off of combat troops for such tasks. But even so, the problem would have been exacerbated as the divisions moved forward towards Murmansk, the lines of communication becoming more extensive with every mile, requiring more and more labour to shift the same amount of supplies. The overall conclusion, therefore, must be that not even the quickest possible arrival of the 6th Mountain Division could have turned this campaign around in favour of the Germans.

If for argument's sake we continue to make assumptions about what might have happened, the next question is obviously whether the Germans, had they taken Murmansk that autumn, could have held the naval bases and the port for the next year or so. Two things seem to contravene that. First of all, Dietl was probably right when he pointed out that Murmansk could not be held unless Kandalaksha was also taken and the Mountain Corps could be supplied via the Rovaniemi–Salla–Kandalaksha–Murmansk railway connection. On top of that, for reasons of strategy and the way the greater war in the east was developing, the significance of Murmansk would have changed immeasurably over the coming months. In the wake of the many Soviet defeats during 1941 and the opening months of 1942, the opening of a lifeline from the Western powers to the Soviet Union with arms and materiel for the Red Army became a matter of the highest strategic importance. This meant that had Murmansk fallen in the autumn of 1941, forces on a totally different scale would have had to be committed by the Soviets to retake the town. With their control of the waters of the Barents Sea they could have transferred forces from the interior of Russia to any point along the coast of the Kola Peninsula to retake either Murmansk, Kandalaksha or both. In so doing they would have had to face many of the same problems as the Germans had to grapple with, but these were problems the Russians showed themselves capable of overcoming during later offensives in Karelia in 1944. Combined with attacks from the south along the railway line this would have put the German position on the Murmansk Fjord under pressure that it did not have sufficient forces to resist.

The Resilience of the Red Army

The German underestimation of the Red Army's resilience and fighting power is perhaps the most understandable of their misconceptions, considering both its performance during the Winter War and Stalin's purges in the years immediately before the war. In the dictator's mass liquidations of anyone who might conceivably represent a political opposition, it became the military elite's turn in 1937. Three of the five marshals were murdered, among them Stalin's former rival and one of the most brilliant military theorists of the Soviet Union, Mikhail Tukhatsjevskij. Thirteen of 15 commanders of field armies, 50 of 57 corps commanders and 154 of 186 division commanders – 90 percent of the entire officer corps above the level of regimental commanders, all of them exterminated in a frenzy of senseless killings. The implication of this was obviously that a number of key position in the Soviet military by the time the war broke out were held by inexperienced or downright incompetent officers who were also completely demoralised by the purges. In addition, the system of having political commissars with the same rank and authority as the commander of all units at every level effectively meant that the fear of the secret police, the NKVD – and behind that demotion, prison or execution – permeated the entire military organisation from marshal down to the humblest private. Not surprisingly, therefore, many Soviet units during the opening phases of *Barbarossa* had little stomach for fighting and simply disintegrated in front of the German steamroller. However, there are also numerous examples – not only the 52nd Rifle Division – of Red Army units and formations fighting with a zeal bordering on fanaticism. The explanation for that is probably a mixed one, ranging from genuine patriotism to soldiers being brainwashed by the propaganda fed to them by the commissars. And in the final analysis, it was of course a simple choice. If you stand and fight you still have a chance, run away and the ignominious death of a deserter is certain. Facing this plight, many chose to surrender, and the Germans took millions of prisoners of war during the first months.

There is, however, another explanation that should be considered when we are dealing with a country like Russia. That soldiers in the West had thrown down their weapons and refused to fight for a political system like that of the Soviet Union stems from the fact that our thinking have been shaped by living in liberal democracies. But Russian soldiers and to a great extent the average Russian had never known any other kind of system than autocracy and repression of one kind or another. Many Russian soldiers probably fought to the death simply because the alternative did not occur to him; so thoroughly was obedience to the authorities and Mother Russia drummed into him by a culture centuries old, dating from long before the Bolsheviks came to power.

Another implication of the purges, paradoxically, was of course that it also created opportunities for young, aspiring and talented officers who might otherwise, like in most military hierarchies, have had to wait for years while more senior but less gifted officers blocked their path up the chain of command. Stalin's murderous excesses, in their own perverse way, therefore worked as a trigger for the process which all wars initiate in the armies they involve – the consistent selection and promotion of the more capable over the less capable, regardless of age and status.

Implications for Norway

The German attack on the Soviet Union provoked the first steps on the road to what would eventually become the alliance between the big three – the Soviet Union, Great Britain and the United States. Stalin's request that Britain should immediately open another front to relieve the pressure on the faltering Red Army is interesting, not least because he insisted that the most suitable place for this would be Northern Norway. Later on, the Soviet demand for a second front would concentrate on the continent, but initially Stalin's focus was on the Arctic. To the extent that something like that had been within the realm of the possible for the British at the time, the suggestion also has a lot going for it. The limited German forces located there had made this a far more feasible proposition than going back to the continent, attempting to land in France or the Low Countries. Furthermore, there was no flaw in Stalin's logic, since Hitler's obsession with exactly this kind of scenario meant that any idea of a German attack on the Soviet Union from Finland would have gone out

The infamous commissary system contributed strongly to this failure by ensuring tight political control over the internal affairs of the military. A commissar had to authorise all important orders in units of battalion size or above. The commissars were selected mainly on their background and on their loyalty to the Communist Party, and they were seldom qualified in military matters. Some confined themselves to political indoctrination and moral encouragement, but many interfered in military affairs. Within the military units, members of the party's youth organisation, Komsomol, were also requested to hold meetings where officers were criticised and condemned. This led to respect being lost, and in many instances discipline broke down. After the catastrophe in Finland measures were taken to reduce the power of the commissars, but these were inadequate and too late.

Organisation

In 1941, the Red Army was the world's biggest in number of soldiers, but it was full of contradictions. When war broke out many Soviet soldiers fought courageously, but they were seldom capable of carrying out coordinated operations. They had to choose between fleeing, surrendering or fighting to the last man. Recklessness and fearlessness were induced in many instances by large quantities of vodka – which had highest priority in the logistics chain – and by the NKVD (forerunner among other things of the KGB) which stood behind the lines and made short shrift of deserters.

When war broke out, there were about 5.3 million Soviet citizens under arms. The recruits from the villages were often easy to satisfy; they managed with little and lived for long periods on salted fish, dried meat and cold-cooked grain. Most of them were Russian, Belorussian or Ukrainian. Very few were from the Asiatic or Caucasian minorities, even though these comprised almost 25 per cent of the population. Within the first five months of the war, the Red Army lost about five million men. This total comprised one million dead and the rest taken prisoner, of whom many died in captivity. Altogether, this amounted to 60 per cent of the total troop losses during the four years of the war.[4] Very large quantities of material were also lost in the same period. The army lost 20,000 armoured vehicles, six times more than the Germans themselves had when they attacked on 22 June 1941. Starting in the summer and continuing until December, the Red Army called up reservists and established 400 new divisions. Despite this mobilisation the forces had been reduced to 80 divisions by the end of the year.

After the great losses in the last half of 1941 the holes in the ranks were filled with volunteers from older age groups and personnel transferred from other branches of the service. In addition, more soldiers were recruited from the non-Slav minorities. Women also filled increasing roles in anti-aircraft defence and in the air force and were recruited as tank crew and snipers, though they seldom found a way into conventional infantry units. The gap between Soviet soldiers and their German counterparts in training and tactical knowledge was clearly apparent at company and platoon level, but as part of the plan there was a new generation of officers on the way up. In Soviet propaganda, loyalty to the party was replaced by patriotism as the most important motivation.

APPENDIX II

The Red Army 1941

The World's Biggest Army – Full of Contradictions

Frode Lindgjerdet

The Soviet Five Year Plans of the inter-war years had a single main aim: to prepare the world's only communist state for the confrontation with capitalism which according to Marxist-Leninist doctrine must inevitably come, sooner or later. Emphasis was put on heavy industry, and especially arms production. In 1941 the Soviet Union had more planes and tanks than the rest of the world put together and was also well equipped with artillery and other weapons. So how did Nazi Germany dare to attack a giant who was armed to the teeth?

Myths about the inferiority of the Slav race obviously played a part, but there was also practical experience behind the decision to invade the Soviet Union. Soviet forces in the Far East under the leadership of General Georgij Zjukov had defeated the Japanese at Khalkin Gol in 1939, but these engagements attracted little attention in Europe. Instead, the Germans had studied the Soviet forces which entered Poland in 1939 and then how they struggled against little Finland in the Winter War. Hitler therefore doubted the Red Army's capacity to carry out modern, mechanised operations.[1]

The problems the Germans had observed were mainly a result of Stalin's purges and political oppression. During the Moscow Trials the Red Army had lost its greatest thinkers, not least Marshal Mikhail Tukhatsjevskij, who was the leading proponent of a *blitzkrieg* doctrine not unlike what the Germans themselves would come to use against the Soviet Union under Operation *Barbarossa*.[2] The military leaders who survived the Moscow Trials were mediocre, and in addition any ideas resembling what Tukhatsjevskij had stood for were considered counter-revolutionary and therefore dangerous. Promotion depended on loyalties and connections rather than on ability. The lack of experienced officers was precarious, and there were too many incompetent sycophants in command of units. Fear, incompetence and indecision spread down through the ranks[3] and explain much of the inability to act which was to cost an enormous number of Soviet lives during the Winter War and the first year of the Great Patriotic War.

to the Allies. But what about the post-war period – how important has this region been for the Soviet Union, and later for the Russian Federation?

Russian strategy has historically been heavily influenced by their proclivity for geopolitical thinking – the tradition whereby geographical factors take precedence when it comes to deciding strategic interests. In this paradigm, strategic interests can be derived almost directly from looking at the map; the location of states in relation to each other, to the oceans and the lines of communication between the continents. This implies a certain continuity and permanence in strategic perspectives. This was also the case during the Cold War, when the geopolitical importance of the area was significantly enhanced by events in a totally different part of the world – the Cuban crisis in October 1962.

That crisis culminated when the Soviet Union had to withdraw their missiles from Cuba in the face of American naval superiority in the Atlantic. This led to a massive build-up of the Soviet navy under the supervision of Admiral Sergej Gorshkov, aiming at making the Soviet Union a global naval power on par with the United States and ensuring that it would never be subjected to that sort of humiliation again. The Northern Fleet, based on the Kola Peninsula around Murmansk therefore grew in size and capability, not just in terms of conventional ships and planes, but also with a growing fleet of nuclear submarines armed with intercontinental ballistic missiles. This has made the somewhat remote and apparently insignificant theatre of operations from the Litza campaign one of the strategically most important areas for modern Russia. Not only is it the home port of the most powerful fleet in the Russian navy and the base for their nuclear retaliation capability. It is also the region where the trajectory of intercontinental missiles and strategic bombers from North America enter Russian airspace, and thus a focal point for Russian early-warning and air-defence capabilities. By the same token, as pointed out by Stalin to Admiral Golovko in 1940, this is also the area over which Russia's own strategic bombers have to fly in order to reach the Western hemisphere. Add to that the fact that the White Sea is an important proving ground for new air- and seaborne Russian weapon systems, and we have the explanation why this region is the center of attention for a lot of intelligence-related activity by the United States and other Western powers. On top of its military consequence comes the growing economic importance of the region, with the huge reserves of oil and natural gas that are effectively bankrolling most of Russian government spending, not least on its military.

The question most frequently asked by defence planners in the Scandinavian countries is what this implies for the countries on Russia's rim in the high north. How far are the Russians prepared to go when it comes to using their military capabilities to secure their interests in the Arctic? To a certain extent, Russia's strategic posture is also a consequence of the monstrous human and material losses suffered during World War II, which convinced Russian leaders about the necessity of a strategic buffer zone between Russia and a perceived threat from the Western world. An absolute certainty in that respect is that they will never again risk having to fight for their very survival against an invader on the banks of the Litza river.

of the window immediately. However, since a major landing anywhere on the European mainland was totally out of the question, Britain had to consider other options. Arming and supplying the Soviets of course also carried the risk that it might be a case of too little too late, and that the Germans might win anyway, in which case Britain risked having their own weapons and equipment turned against them. Their solution, not surprisingly, was therefore in keeping with centuries of British strategic thinking – to use their superior navy and their control of the sea to influence the situation in theatres where they could not or would not become involved on the ground. Initially, the support for the Soviets was a typically 'Churchillian' operation, with operational realism being sacrificed in the interest of political symbolism – not unlike his vexations of General Mackesy at Narvik the year before to launch premature attacks on the town. Insufficient planning, training and intelligence resulted in a naval raid which achieved nothing and failed to impress Stalin and the Russians. Even highly symbolic military operations, in other words, cannot be disconnected completely from their actual military results.

Gradually, however, the impact of British naval operations began to make themselves felt, among other things forcing the Germans to abandon ferrying troops and supplies along the coast from Tromsø to Kirkenes. Most significant from the Norwegian point of view was the decision to evacuate Spitsbergen and demolish the coal mines. Norwegian foreign minister in exile Trygve Lie clearly realised that this was a situation laden with both risks and opportunities when he was briefed by Eden about the Anglo-Russian plan. On the risk side he noted that if the Russians, with British support, were allowed to garrison Spitsbergen as a strongpoint on the sea lines of communication to north-west Russia, bringing Spitsbergen back under Norwegian sovereignty after the war might become difficult. On the other hand, precisely this gave the Norwegian government considerable leverage in terms of forcing the Soviets to recognise the Norwegian government in exile and resume diplomatic relations. In that way, Norway would become a fully fledged ally, not just of Britain but also of the Soviet Union.

Thus Lie, later to become the first secretary general of the United Nations, understood that if Norway and Norwegian interests should not lose out in a war that the Allies would almost certainly win, it had to become a credible and fully committed ally. Only by securing a seat at the table could a Norwegian government feel reasonably confident of coming out of the post-war settlement with no ill effects. Otherwise, Norway risked another Kiel treaty of 1814 in miniature – with the great powers using Norwegian interests to balance the greater strategic and geopolitical score card. This required a different attitude to the pedantic protestations that Admiral Vian met from the Norwegian governor and the chief executive of the Store Norske coal mining company in Longyearbyen, clearly indicating that they had no idea of what was at stake. Viewed in this perspective, Trygve Lie was one of the first Norwegian politicians who realised that Norway had to turn its back on a pacifist tradition of neutrality and become a partner and an ally – which Norway has remained to this day.

Russian Strategic Interests in the Arctic

We have seen that Stalin was aware of the strategic significance of the Arctic, and as soon as the war started the high North became a theatre of operations of the utmost importance

Seventy-five per cent of the Soviet divisions in 1941 were 'rifle divisions' made up of three regiments, 14,483 men in all. Only a few were mechanised. On paper, divisions each had an anti-tank battalion, an anti-aircraft battalion and just 16 light tanks. On the other hand, they were set up with two artillery regiments. However, after the outbreak of war the divisions shrunk to 10,859 men and the divisional artillery was also severely reduced. Some units were also given so-called 'Guard status.' These were units which had distinguished themselves in battle and thereby earned higher wages and higher priority in the allocation of clothing and other equipment.

The Red Army also had 33 mechanised rifle divisions. Two of these were independent, but the rest were earmarked as follow-up infantry behind the tanks. They were mostly however only mechanised in name; the personnel mostly sat on the tanks on the approach to the field of battle. The Soviet Union was the only great power which didn't develop an armoured personnel carrier during the war years. After the war, German officers claimed that the lack of these was one of the Soviet infantry's greatest tactical weaknesses.[5]

The Soviet Union also maintained several mounted cavalry units. The large areas available for pasture, the vast, trackless expanses of land and the lack of mechanisation may partly explain why at the end of 1941 they had as many as 82 cavalry divisions of 3,000 men, but the cavalry also had an almost mystic status among the circle around Stalin, who had fought together on horseback during the civil war in the 1920s. The place of the Cossacks in traditional Russian culture also had an effect. Moreover, horses were usually more robust than many vehicles in the cold Russian winter.

At the outbreak of war the Soviets had a formidable fleet of tanks, with as many as 28,000 tanks and armoured vehicles divided into 29 mechanised corps. Each corps consisted of two tank divisions and a motorised rifle division, but these numbers must be interpreted with reservation. Quantity was what mattered in the Five Year Plans, and even though the design of the T-26 and BT 5/7 were on a level with contemporary German models, quality of production was often poor.

Another consequence of this system was an acute shortage of spare parts. When it was a matter of choosing between living or succumbing to Stalin's terror programmes, the recording of absurdly great production quotas was more important than achieving quality. As a result, about 44 per cent of the Soviet tanks were inoperative on 22 June 1941.

The quality of the tanks varied, from the mediocre T-26 to the fast BT 5/7 with poor armour and weapons and the T-34, considered by many to be the best tank of the Second World War. The T-34 had a 76.2 mm gun, sloping armour plating and broad tracks to ensure good performance over the terrain. However, at the end of 1941 these and the heavier KV model were only just beginning to reach the front in significant numbers and they had not yet been cured of their teething troubles.

By December the Soviet Union had lost most of its tanks and was left with only about 2,000 in the whole of their European territory. The tank units were also afflicted with the same problems of limited tactical skill and inadequate training as the infantry. The crews were sent to the front with only basic proficiency, and the Germans observed that Soviet units often drove along exposed ridges and followed very predictable routes which were technically easy but tactically very unwise.

Military planes were mainly used in support of the ground forces. This was because of experiences in the Spanish Civil War, which had shown that strategic bombing had little effect on the enemy's fighting strength. The Soviets also had their own air defence system – with anti-aircraft guns, fighter planes and so on – to protect the biggest cities and industrial centres against air attack.

The Soviet Navy was less important and lay idle at its bases for much of the war, though the crews were often retrained for infantry duties when need was greatest, for example at Leningrad.

The artillery, which Stalin called his 'war god', enjoyed high priority and prestige. At the beginning of the war the artillery was organised in divisions, but it gradually came to be divided into free-standing artillery reserves allocated to army and front commanders and deployed for the larger offensive operations.

Uniform

Especially in 1941, but also throughout the war years, standardisation of uniforms was inconsistent. Of necessity, items of civilian clothing were often worn. Supplies of Canadian and American uniforms also reached the Red Army in the convoys coming through Persia, Murmansk and Vladivostok. The regulations gave very little guidance on uniform. At the beginning of the war, Soviet private soldiers generally wore a brown khaki field uniform, known as *zaschitny tsvet*, made of cotton in summer and wool in winter. In winter they were also issued with a grey-brown cape. Headgear varied, but in 1941 consisted mainly of a cap in summer and a hat with ear-muffs in winter. Steel helmets only came into normal use later in the war. The shirt (*gymnastiorka*) resembled the shirt often worn by Russian peasants, and the trousers (*sharovari*) looked like old-fashioned riding breeches. Only reconnaissance scouts, snipers and a few other specialists wore camouflage uniforms. Men and NCOs were issued with low shoes and puttees, or with high boots (*sapogi*) made of leather or sealskin. The officers were given long, black leather boots. The rucksack was not unlike the Norwegian Bergans *ludviksekk*, except that the top flap had only one closing strap. A personal canteen set was carried in the belt, under the rucksack. Following the Winter War, padded trousers (*vatnie sharovari*) and jackets (*telogreika*) were introduced for winter use. Sheepskin jackets and coats were issued to officers. Felt boots and sealskin overalls could sometimes be used in the far North.

In theory, a rifleman was supposed to carry on his belt four clips with a total of 20 bullets, plus a reserve of 30 bullets. There were also bandoliers with room for 14 clips of five bullets each and a pocket for grenades. However, very few soldiers were issued with this full range of equipment, including other items such as tent canvas or field spades. Many soldiers were sent to face enemy fire with a pouch of only 20 bullets. Gas masks were issued, but seldom carried by the troops.

Speed and economy of production determined the nature of Soviet equipment. In the course of the war, Soviet factories produced 18.3 million rifles and sub-machine guns, with sub-machine guns making up 34 per cent of the total. There were two reasons for this. Such weapons were cheap to produce, and the ammunition they used required less brass and less powder than standard rifle bullets. Also, the production process was simplified. In comparison with the equivalent German MP38/40 sub-machine guns which were beautifully crafted, the Russians used cheaper material where possible and cut down on finishing touches.[6] Sub-machine guns were also easier for untrained soldiers to handle.

The Soviet Union did have an exceptional rifle in the 7.62 mm Mosin-Nagant, but learning to use a rifle accurately took time. The most important sub-machine gun, the 7.62 mm PPSh1914G was a formidable weapon in the hands of a Soviet soldier, delivering 900 shots per minute. In normal rifle units the sub-machine gun was the platoon sergeant's weapon, but otherwise the NKVD units and the motorised rifle units who followed the tanks had priority in the allocation of these weapons. The PPSh was very reliable, and German soldiers also used them whenever they could get their hands on them.

Across the range from small arms to tanks, the Soviet arms industry applied simple measures to increase productivity. Because of this, the weapons had few moving parts that could wear out or cause misfiring. Not all the ideas were equally successful, however. Out-dated models often continued in production just for want of anything better. Among others, the Simonov PTRS1941 anti-tank rifle was the last of its type in the world to be produced (comparable to the British BoysAT rifle and the German Panzerbüchse PzB39). This weapon was only capable of penetrating 1.2 inch steel plate, and was of little effect even against the tanks the Germans were using in 1941. Under perfect conditions with a direct hit at 90° to the target it could penetrate the armour on the front of the first Panzer 38(t) models (30 mm front armour), but it had little to offer against, for example, the Panzer III, which had 80 mm front armour. As the armour of German tanks improved throughout the war, Soviet infantrymen increasingly had to use mines and grenades. Another Soviet weapon with limited success was the Degatjarjov DP1928 light machine gun. Many of these were produced, and they had a firing rate of 500–600 shots per minute. However, the drum magazine was difficult to load and soon broke down. The loading and firing mechanisms could also be damaged if the barrel became too hot.

In 1941 the Soviet version of the Maxim machine gun was still standard issue in the Red Army. It was reliable, but heavy to carry. Unlike the western versions, the Soviet model was mounted on a wheeled gun-carriage with a shield.

The Red Army's 76.2 mm field gun was one of the best in its class and was used in large numbers throughout the war. The carriage was built to facilitate transport through the terrain, pulled by horses if necessary. It could be used both as a field gun and as an anti-tank gun, and could fire a 7 kg high-explosive shell almost 15 km, or break through 90 mm steel at a range of 550 metres. Another artillery weapon that became legendary during World War II was the Katyusha rocket launcher. The rockets in use in 1941 were generally of 82 mm calibre. The rocket launcher took a long time to load in comparison with traditional artillery, but could on the other hand deliver heavy fire in a short time, before being pulled back quickly to avoid enemy counter-fire.

A Russian Rifle Division's Establishment in 1941

	April	*July*	*December*
Soldiers	14,483	10,8590 – is this right?	11,626
Horses	3,000	2,500	2,400
Lorries	558	203	248
Rifles	10,240	8,341	8,565
Sub-machine guns	1,204	171	281
Liught-machine guns	392	162	251
Machine guns	166	108	108
Anti-aircraft machine guns	33	27	12
Anti-tank rifles	0	0	89
45 mm anti-tank guns	54	18	30
37 mm anti-aircraft guns	12	10	6
76 mm field guns	34	28	28
122 mm howitzers	32	8	8
152 mm howitzers	12	0	0
Mortars	150	78	162

Source: Zaloga 2001

The figures in the table give the numbers each division should have according to the war production plan, but hardly any divisions achieved the full complement.

Notes

Prologue

1   The development of the fishing industry in Northern Norway during the war is described in my book *Forlis*, pp. 108 f, plus the criminal trial of Johannes Overå in the National Treason Archive in the National Archive in Oslo. The plans are also discussed in my books *Fra brent jord til Klondyke* and *Nikkel, jern og blod*, p 125 f. The description of Trondheim is taken from the newspaper *Adresseavisen* for the week 12–17 August 19421, found on microfilm in the National Library, Oslo.
2   See Pohlman's typewritten reminiscences, *Norwegen 1940* (*Norway 1940*), pp. 11 f. in the author's possession, and Falkenhorst's various documents in Nachlass Falkenhorst N/300 in the German military archive in Freiburg, hereafter referred to as BAMA. On the conflicts between Falkenhorst and Dietl, see also Kaltenegger, *Krieg am Eismeer. Gebirgsjäger im Kampf um Narvik, Murmansk und die Murmanbahn*; Feurstein, *Irrwege der Pflicht*; Rüf, *Gebirgsjäger vor Murmansk*; the Mountain Corps Norway War Diary (*Kriegstagebuch*), hereafter referred to as KTB; and the war diaries of Norway Army Command in RH-19 and RW-39, BAMA, Freiburg.
3   Falkenhorst is the German for falcon's lair.
4   Dietl had joined the NSDAP, the predecessor of the Nazi party, in 1919 as member no. 24. That was *before* Hitler and his camp follower Ernst Röhm, the leader of the *Sturmabteilung* (the Nazi Storm Battalion), became members. See Kaltenegger's biography of Dietl, now available in two volumes, *Die Symbolfigur der Deutschen Gebirgstruppe 1890–1933* and *Der Held von Narvik*. See also *General Dietl. Das Lieben eines Soldaten* by his adjutant, Colonel Kurt Herrmann and his widow, Gerda-Luise Dietl.
5   The preliminaries to *Barbarossa* are described in several books. My presentation is built on Chris Bellamy's *Absolute War*, which was published in 2008 and therefore incorporates much of the very latest research, and the German standard work from 1983, *Das Deutsche Reich und der Zweite Weltkrieg*, volume 4: *Der Angriff auf die Sowetunion*, pp. 13 f. The quotation from the conversation with Jodl is from the disputed David Irving's *Hitler's War*, pp. 321 f., which draws on sources which otherwise have been little used. The War Diary of Wehrmacht Supreme Command (OKW; *Oberkommando*

der Wehrmacht) is presented in full text in The Internet Archive: www.archive.org/stream/kriegstagebuchde01jacorich.txt.
6   See Warlimont, *Im Hauptquartier der deutschen Wehrmacht 1939–1945*, pp. 126 f.
7   Von Leeb's diary, p. 251 f. The diary can be found on the otherwise bizarre website www.trialreview.info.
8   The meeting is described by Dietl's adjutant Herrmann in Dietl and Herrmann, *General Dietl. Das Leben eines Soldaten*, pp. 210 f.
9   See Hinsley and Stripp, *Codebreakers. The Inside Story of Bletchley Park*, pp. 2 f. There are many good books about the work of the codebreakers and its importance in determining the outcome of the war. I particularly recommend Hinsley, *British Intelligence in the Second World War*, volumes I and II, Hugh Sebag-Montefiore, *Enigma. The Battle for the Code* (revised edition 2011) and David Kahn, *Seizing the Enigma*. The first of these is the first book to discuss the importance of Enigma for the campaigns along the Finnmark coast in the summer of 1941.
10 See Copeland's biography of Turing, *Turing: Pioneer of the Information Age*. pp. 60 f.
11 For a simple account of the history of the Kola Peninsula and Murmansk, see Wikipedia. My presentation is based on material I have received from military historian Miroslav Morozov in Moscow, plus the important material found in the German War Archives in BAMA, especially RH 28-2 which contains the 2nd Mountain Division's war diary with enclosures and intelligence analyses, and RH-24-19-151 and 152 which contain interrogations from 1941 of about 500 Russian prisoners of war. This source is unique and must obviously be interpreted with utmost caution. I use the interrogation reports primarily to provide insights which I can then check against other sources.
12 Neutral Sweden had in 1916 been forced by Germany and the Central Powers to close the access to the Baltic Sea by mine belts in the Øre Sound. Supplies bought by the Tsar's regime in the West therefore had to be shipped through the Barents Sea to the new Murmansk port.
13 See Golovko, *Zwischen Spitzbergen und Tiksibucht*, pp 6 f. and Morten Jentoft's fine books on Kola, for example *De som dro østover: Kola-nordmennenes historie*. Golovko's memoirs were published by the East German Military Publishing House in 1986, and like all other war literature from the post-war period have a strong Stalinist bias and heroic tendency. A new and more reliable way of writing history did not prevail until several years later.

Chapter 1

1   Quoted from Copeland, *Turing: Pioneer of the Information Age*, p. 66 f. Some of the previously highly classified reports on events at Bletchley Park can be found on the website www.alanturing.net.
2   The telegram can be found in Defe 3/1, National Archives, London, hereafter referred to as NA.
3   See *Der Angriff auf die Sowjetunion*, pp. 202 f. and for the operations in the North, *Die Einbeziehung Skandinaviens in die Planung Barbarossa*, pp. 365 f. See also Bellamy, *Absolute War*, pp. 118 f.

4   Nachlass Falkenhorst N/300, BAMA. Regarding Buschenhagen, see Pohlman, *Norwegen 1940*, p. 13. The author wishes to point out that the exact dates of the various meetings are rather unclear. What is clear, however, is that the top brass in Army Headquarters Norway were informed about *Barbarossa* at the beginning of December 1940.
5   Op. cit., Nachlass Falkenhorst.
6   See 'Studie über Operationsabsicht Silberfuchs' with attachment dated 27 January 1941, in the archive of Army HQ Norway, RW 39-6, BAMA. All subsequent quotations are from the same source.
7   See 'Kampanweisung für die Verteidigung Norwegen' of 26 March and 'Weisung an der Wehrmachtsbefehlshaber Norwegen über sein Aufgabe im Fall Barbarossa' of 7 April 1941, RW 39-6, BAMA. The first of these documents is the one with the exclamation marks in the margin.
8   The High Command of the Wehrmacht (Oberkommando der Wehrmacht, OKW) was a joint headquarters supposed to coordinate the operations of all services. In actual fact it served as Hitler's personal military HQ.
9   Dietl is quoted in Springenschmid/Kraütler, *Es war ein Eelweiss*, pp. 134 f. The subsequent meeting between Dietl and Hitler took place in April, but there is still some doubt about the exact date. Hitler ordered Dietl to report to Berlin immediately after he had taken command of the Arctic theatre of war in March, but he himself went to Vienna on 24 March, where he was surprised by the news of the coup in Yugoslavia three days later. The Balkan campaign followed immediately, and from 10 to 28 April Hitler stayed on his HQ train *Amerika*. Hess and Herrmann from the Norwegian Mountain Corps date the meeting around 'the middle of April,' while SS-Obersturmbannführer Paul Schmidt says 21 April – the same day as Foreign Minister Ribbentrop came to visit the very busy Führer. The smooth-tongued anti-Semitic Schmidt (1911–97) was Ribbentrop's Chief Press Officer and was very probably there. Under the pseudonym Paul Carrell, Schmidt had a very successful career as a journalist and author. Among other things, he worked for the Axel Springer publishing company, and his book about Operation *Barbarossa* sold in millions throughout the world. He was investigated in the 1960s for murder and for his part in the Holocaust, but he was never condemned. His description of the meeting between Dietl and Hitler is the only one in existence and can be found in the book *Unternehmen Barbarossa. Der Marsch gegen Russland*, p. 364 f.
10 The main source is Professor Gabriel Gorodetsky's eminent study *Grand Delusion. Stalin and the German Invasion of Russia*. See also Konstantin Pleshakov's *Stalin's Folly* and David Murphy's *What Stalin Knew*, plus Bellamy, *Absolute War*, pp. 136 f.
11 Quoted from Gilbert, *Finest Hour*, pp. 1050 f. See also Gorodetsky's analysis in *Grand Delusion*, pp. 155 f.
12 The transport operations are described in Captain Vilhelm Hess's note 'Welche Ereignisse kann der Sommer bringen?' in the archives of the Norway Mountain Corps, RH 28-2-116, BAMA. The note later formed the basis of his book *Eismeerfront 1941*, published in 1956.
13 Quoted from the book *In Eis und Tundra*, pp. 66 f.
14 Quoted from Larsen's memoirs *Jeg var Sovjet-spion*, pp. 19 f. See also my book *Rød august: Den virkelige historien om partisanenes skjebne*. Fisherman Alfred Mathisen's war

effort continued until October 1941, when he was arrested by the Germans following the unsuccessful Soviet raid on the Varanger Peninsula. He was mishandled in prison and shot in the summer of 1942, only 34 years old. See *Rød august*, pp. 57 f.

15 The NKVD (later KGB, now FSB) has not released the archives with information on the truth about the Larsen brothers, Alfred Mathisen and his network in the period from the autumn of 1940 to the outbreak of war on 22 June 1941. However, my researcher Morozov has found intelligence reports in the archives of Leningrad Military District with information (repeated as an excerpt in the quotation) which in my opinion must have come from the network.

16 Golovko, *Zwischen Spitzbergen und Tiksibucht*, p. 15.

Chapter 2

1 The collection of essays *Barbarossa; the Axis and the Allies* edited by David Dilks and John Ericsson is an invaluable aid to understanding the developments during the weeks immediately before the outbreak of war. See Hinsley's study *British Intelligence and Barbarossa*, pp. 43 f. and *Grand Delusion*, p. 275.
2 Hinsley, *British Intelligence in the Second World War*, p. 68.
3 The result of the negotiations can be found can be found in the archives of AOK Norwegen, RW 39-6, BAMA.
4 See 'Kampfbericht 2. Gebirgsdivision', RH 28-2-116, BAMA.
5 See reports of the Mountain Artillery, RH 41-730 and RH 41-759, BAMA.
6 See Dietl and Herrmann, *General Dietl. Das Lieben eines Soldaten*, p. 215.
7 See McKay, *The Secret Listeners*, pp. 67 f. The telegram can be found in Defe 3/2, NA, London.
8 See McKay and Beckman, *Swedish Signal Intelligence 1900–1945*, pp. 130 f.
9 Hinsley, *British Intelligence in the Second World War*, p. 70.
10 See Maisky, *Memoirs of a Soviet Ambassador*, p. 149 and *Grand Delusion*, pp. 302 f.
11 On the arrival of the British Military Mission, see Gorodetsky's study 'An Alliance of Sorts' in *Barbarossa: The Axis and the Allies*, pp. 101 f.

Chapter 3

1 Quoted from Springenschmid, *Die Männer von Narvik*, pp. 142 f. The key document for the description of the events of the campaign in this and subsequent chapters is 'Kriegstagebuch Russland 1' for Mountain Corps Norway (hereafter referred to as KTB Dietl), which records hour by hour the developments in the field and the discussions between the corps, the 2nd and 3rd Mountain Divisions and Norway Army HQ in Rovaniemi, RH 24-19/11, BAMA. There are also the following attachments and reports for the 2nd Mountain Division: Gefechtsbericht 29.6–18.9.1941, RH 28-2-19; various attachments in RH 28-2-16; the report 'Kampf gegen Russland' from the 137th Regiment in RH 28 – 110; the reports from Vilhelm Hess in RH 28-2-166 plus Berichte 1C in RH 28-2-117. For the 3rd Mountain Division, see particularly: Attachment to KTB for the period 19.6 to 31.12.1941 in RH 28-3/8, 9 and 10.

He sources for the 111th and 112th Mountain Artillery Regiments can be found in RH 41-517, 730 and 759.
2. Hess's personal report summer 1941 in RH28-2-116, BAMA.
3. Admiral Kuznetzov's memoirs, *On the Eve of the War*, are published in English translation on the website www.admiral.centro.ru.
4. Golovko, *Zwischen Spitzbergen und Tiksibucht*, pp. 20 f, plus additional information from Morozov.
5. See Gilbert, *Finest Hour*, pp. 1119 f. and Colville, *The Fringes of Power*, pp. 350 f.
6. See Butler, *Mason-Mac*, pp. 130 f.
7. Hess, 'Welche Ereignisse kann der Sommer bringen?', and KTB Dietl.
8. Golovko, *Zwischen Spitzbergen und Tiksibucht*, p. 31, plus information from the archives from Leningrad Military District and the 14th Army, Moscow; political commissar Shabunin's memoirs; and the POW interrogation of Lieutenants Paul Abramoff and Paul Savtsjenko in RH 24-19-151 and 152, BAMA.
9. Gorjatsjik's diary was confiscated and translated from Russian into German, and can be found in RH 28-2-117, BAMA.

Chapter 4

1. KTB Dietl, and documents listed in note 1, Chapter 3. On Hengl, see Kaltenegger's study *General der Gebirgstruppe Georg Ritter von Hengl*, plus his service record in Personalakten 6/189, BAMA.
2. The office was called *Nationalsozialistischen Führungsstab des Heeres* and was the Nazi party's watch-dog in the German army. It was established on 1 February 1944 with the controversial later Field Marshal Ferdinand Schörner as its first head, aiming at educating the soldiers of the Third Reich in the true spirit of Nazism. Schörner was replaced by Von Hengl in May 1944.
3. The hills and stony outcrops in this Arctic wilderness were mostly nameless, which explains why the Germans marked them with numbers on the maps, the numbers giving their height in metres above sea level.
4. Rüf, *Gebirgsjäger vor Murmansk*, pp. 24 f., plus Hess, 'Welche Ereignisse kann der Sommer bringen?' and *Der Kampf gegen Russland* in RH 28-2-110, BAMA.
5. See Butler, *Mason-Mac*, p. 51.
6. Gorodetsky, 'An Alliance of Sorts', pp. 103 f. The military mission's war diary with detailed inserts about all the meetings can be found in WO 178/25, NA, London.
7. Vesjeserskij's memoirs translated in an extract from Morozov. See also Golovko, *Zwischen Spitzbergen und Tiksibucht*, p. 24.
8. See note 15, Chapter 1. Otto Larsen (1922–55) later fought as a partisan behind the Litza Front in the summer of 1941. A year later he was landed on Sørøya in West Finnmark as a radio agent, but the radio equipment failed and the group made their way to Sweden. When he returned to the Soviet Union after the war he was arrested and condemned to ten years imprisonment, unjustly accused of spying. He was released in 1953, but died two years later from injuries he had sustained in the gulag.

9   A copy of the letter is found on the Russian website www.blockhouse.ru, plus a lot of other information about Zhurba.
10 Rüf, *Gebirgsjäger vor Murmansk*, p. 26, plus Hess, 'Welche Ereignisse kann der Sommer bringen?', and KTB Dietl.
11 The *Blutorden* was a silver medal given by Hitler to his old fighting political comrades from the early days of the Nazi party, and especially to those who had marched with him through the streets of Munich during his failed coup d'etat on 9 November 1923. It was the highest honour a party member could achieve, only matched by the party's Golden Badge.
12 Zorn's report is found in RH 28-2-117. His support of the Brownshirts ever since the days of fighting in Munich in the early 1920s is documented in his military record, Pers 6/2091, BAMA.
13 Müller's comments in POW interrogations, RH 24-19-151, BAMA.
14 Website blockhaus.ru, plus Abramoff's interrogation and I formation from Morotzov.
15 Rüf, *Gebirgsjäger vor Murmansk*; Hess, 'Welche Ereignisse kann der Sommer bringen?', and Springenschmid, *Die Männer von Narvik*.
16 Khudalov, *Am Rande des Kontinents*, pp. 12 f.
17 Rüf, *Gebirgsjäger vor Murmansk*, p. 27.
18 Meeting and Mason-Mac's commentary from the war diary, WO 178/25 and Butler, *Mason-Mac*, p. 136.
19 See Kharlamov's memoirs, *Difficult Mission*, p. 29. According to the admiral, what raised the most interest was that Mason-Mac arrived in Moscow wearing short trousers. That was before it was explained to the Russians that shorts were part of the general's summer uniform.
20 POW interrogation of Abramoff, op. cit. In addition, the remains of the major general's body was discovered in 1976 and buried in the graveyard in Murmansk. His disappearance and death are still topics of debate in Russia.

Chapter 5

1 Rhode's account is found in RH 28-2-116, BAMA.
2 Rüf, *Gebirgsjäger vor Murmansk*, pp. 36 f.
3 The Knight's Cross of the Iron Cross worn around the neck on a silk ribbon. *A sore throat* was German army slang for officers who desperately wanted the recognition conferred by a Knight's Cross.
4 Golovko, *Zwischen Spitzbergen und Tiksibucht*, pp. 32 f., plus information from Morozov.
5 Gorjatsjik's diary, RH 28-2-117, BAMA.
6 In his report, Rohde quoted Hitler's infamous Commissar Orders as justification. He was not reprimanded, but on the contrary was promoted a few months later. The mountain troops took photographs of the execution, some of which are reproduced in this book.
7 Mahon's report is found on the website www.alanturing.net.
8 Quoted from Hinsley, *British Intelligence in the Second World War*, p. 470 f.

9   The deciphered telegram can be found in Defe 3/23, NA, London.
10 See Gorodetsky, 'An Alliance of Sorts', pp. 103 f. and ADM 1/11158, NA, London.
11 KTB Dietl, op. cit.
12 Rüf, *Gebirgsjäger vor Murmansk*, pp. 47 f.
13 See Simon Sebag-Montefiore, *Stalin. The Court of the Red Tsar*, and Bellamy, *Absolute War*.

Chapter 6

1   Order of the day to the troops 5 July, KTB Dietl.
2   The discussion is taken from KTB Dietl. Information about Le Suire is from his service record, Pers 6/254 and Nachlass Le Suire N600, BAMA.
3   Khudalov, *Am Rande des Kontinents*, p. 20.
4   Zorn's analysis in RH 28-2-117, BAMA.
5   See Golikov's memoirs, *On a Military Mission to Great Britain and USA*, p. 29 f.
6   Kharlamov's work on the same topic, *Difficult Mission*, p. 33.
7   The first battle at the Litza is described in detail in KTB Dietl and also by Hess, Rüf and Springenschmid.
8   The arrival and the meeting are described in detail in KTB Dietl. Schmundt (1896–1944) was the Führer's roving trouble-shooter and emissary. He had come north mainly to investigate why SS-kampfgruppe Nord had broken up and fled during the attack on the Salla Front. Schmundt later became head of the Wehrmacht Personnel Department and was the only person to die of injuries sustained during the bomb attack on Hitler in July 1944. See the article on Schmundt in German Wikipedia.
9   To relieve Falkenhorst and Dietl for *Barbarossa* and the new commitments in Northern Finland, the defence of Norway was split into two parts: one for Southern Norway commanded by the former leader of the 2nd Mountain Division, Lieutenant Valentin Feurstein; and the other for Northern Norway commanded by Lieutenant General Emmerich von Nagy. Feurstein was appointed in March, but Nagy didn't take up his post until 1 July, so that Dietl to his annoyance still had responsibility for the northern part of Norway until after the invasion had begun.
10 See Kharlamov, *Difficult Mission*, pp. 35 f and Gorodetsky's comments in 'An Alliance of Sorts', p. 112.
11 Khudalov, *Am Rande des Kontinents*, pp. 22 f., plus information from Morotzov.
12 Cripps's letter in FO 371/29561, NA, plus Gorodetsky, 'An Alliance of Sorts'.
13 Churchill's letter in Gilbert, *Finest Hour*, p. 1133.
14 The note is in WO 193/666, NA, London.
15 About the mood of crisis, see Rüf, *Gebirgsjäger vor Murmansk*, pp. 64, 68. All quotations and dialogue in the following section are from KTB Dietl with attachments.
16 See Beaumont, *Comrades in Arms*, pp. 34 f.
17 Exchange of notes between Churchill and Pound, found in ADM 199/1934, NA, London.

Chapter 7

1. Springenschmid, *Die Männer von Narvik*, pp. 211 f.
2. Rüf, *Gebirgsjäger vor Murmansk*, pp. 76 f., plus KTB Dietl and KTB 2nd and 3rd Mountain Divisions.
3. Khudalov, *Am Rande des Kontinents*, pp. 3 f., plus infor from Morozov.
4. Vian, *Action This Day*, pp. 62 f. See also *Naval Review*, No. 2 from April 1981.
5. Golovko, *Zwischen Spitzbergen und Tiksibucht*, pp. 76 f.
6. The forming-up position of an attack is the position close to the objective where the attacking units deploy from the approach march to the formation of attack, before crossing the start line at the designated hour (H-hour).
7. Khudalov, *Am Rande des Kontinents*, p. 40, plus information from POW interrogation, op. cit.
8. Rüf, *Gebirgsjäger vor Murmansk*, pp. 86 f. Vielwerth was one of many officers who fell in the Litza Valley a few weeks later.
9. Rüf, *Gebirgsjäger vor Murmansk*, pp. 79 f., plus POW interrogation, op. cit.

Chapter 8

1. See Gilbert, *Finest Hour*, p. 1138, plus Gorodetsky, 'An Alliance of Sorts', pp. 112 f.
2. Wake-Walker's report in ADM 199/447, NA, London.
3. Birch's report to Denning is found in Defe 3/22, NA. About the problems in summer 1941, see also Sebag-Montefiore, *Enigma*, pp. 166f.
4. KTB Dietl with daily weather reports; Khudalov, *Am Rande des Kontinents*, pp. 42 f; plus POW interrogations and Morozov.
5. Rüf, *Gebirgsjäger vor Murmansk*, pp. 104 f.
6. Golikov, *On a Military Mission to Great Britain and USA*, pp. 42 f. See also FO 371/29488, NA, London.
7. See Steen, *Norges sjøkrig*, volume 7, pp. 172 f., plus Riste, *London-regjeringen*, volume 1, pp. 134 f. See also FO 371/29432 and WO 193/666, NA, London.
8. Vian, *Action This Day*.
9. See Irving, *Hitler's War*, pp. 411 f., plus *Angriff auf Sowjetunion* and Bellamy, *Absolute War*.
10. Nake (1888–1947) was put on the sick list and returned home to Austria, where he gradually rose through the ranks to Lieutenant General and served as commander of various reserve divisions in France and elsewhere. Hofmeister was seriously wounded on the Litza Front in the summer of 1942 and spent many months in hospital in Munich. His wife was a close friend of Heinrich Himmler's wife, Margrete, who had been abandoned by the SS leader in favour of his younger secretary. See Magda Himmler's diary on www.ffp.co.uk.
11. All descriptions of the action against Kirkenes and Petsamo are from ADM 199/447, plus KTB Admiral Polarküste and KTB MRS *Bali*, which naval warfare expert Erling Skjold has kindly made available to me.

Chapter 9

1. See Gilbert, *Finest Hour*, pp. 1144 f.
2. See Captain Bevan's war diary for SNO Polarnoje, ADM 199/1106, NA, London.
3. KTB Dietl, op. cit.
4. Khudalov, *Am Rande des Kontinents*, pp. 58 f.
5. The mountain artillery's report is found in RH41-759, BAMA. See also POW interrogation op. cit.
6. Rüf, *Gebirgsjäger vor Murmansk*, pp. 118 f.
7. See Steen, *Norges sjøkrig*, volume 7, pp. 183 f., plus Vian, *Action This Day*.
8. The troop movements are described in 'Tätigkeitsbericht 1A' for September 1941 for Abschnittsstab Nord-Norwegen/70. AK, roll 2699 in NHM's collection of German microfilm.
9. Wake-Walker's report, ADM 199/447.
10. The telegrams can be found in Defe 3/25, NA, London.
11. Khudalov, *Am Rande des Kontinents*, p. 59.
12. This was the name given to a military camp in Murmansk with barracks to accommodate several thousand men. POW interrogations op. cit.

Chapter 10

1. Sladen's log-book in ADM199/1106. See also website www.lintonsview.blogspot.com.es/2009/12/captain-geoffrey-mainwaring.html.
2. Telegram in Defe 3/26, NA.
3. See 'Tätigkeitsbericht Abschnittsstab Nord-Norwegen,' plus KTB Admiral Polarküste and the war diaries of the escort ships, in the hands of the author.
4. KTB Dietl and Admiral Polarküste.
5. The letter is reproduced in Steen, *Norges sjøkrig*, volume 7.
6. The debate can be found in ADM 106/1995A, NA.
7. Vian, *Action This Day*, plus ADM 199/72, NA.
8. Coward spent three weeks on board the cruiser, wearing an unmistakeable silk smoking jacket and carrying a long cigarette holder. The voyage appears to have inspired the film *In Which We Serve*, premiered in 1942. Several other literati were on board the Dervish Convoy on the voyage to Russia, including the Polish-English artist Feliks Topolski, the American journalist Wallace Carroll, the British Charlotte Haldane from *The Daily Sketch* and the Polish writer and diplomat Xavieri Pruszynski, who all were to describe the developing new alliance.
9. Steen, *Norges sjøkrig*, volume 7, and Vian, *Action This Day*, plus WO 106/1986. See also Brazier, *XD Operations*, pp. 11 f. and Report no. 74 from Canadian Military HQ, in the hands of the author.
10. Vian, *Action This Day*, p. 72, plus ADM 199/72. From Wake-Walker's report on the Dervish Convoy it is apparent that he happened to hear of Denning's signals when he met Vian's fleet in the Barents Sea on 27 August. 'It is astonishing that only one of the

182 • MIRACLE AT THE LITZA

fleets in the area has had access to this type of information,' he noted in his report before throwing himself into a race about who would attack the German shipping first. On the night of 2/3 September he sent several bombers toward the coast from the carrier HMS *Victorious*. Six of them observed three vessels east of Honningsvåg, but as they had been ordered, they broke off the attack when they were discovered and the opportunity of surprise was lost. The three ships may have been Norwegian.

11 See the British battle reports in ADM 199/447 and 'Bericht über die Gefecht der Bremse 7.9.1941' in KTB Admiral Polarküste, in the hands of the author.

Chapter 11

1 See sources listed in note 1, Chapter 3.
2 Khudalov, *Am Rande des Kontinents*, p. 62 and POW interrogations op. cit.
3 Ura-Guba consisted of a cluster of decrepit wooden houses in a side arm of the Motovskij Fjord. The phrase 'seaside resort' is used ironically, referring to an old sauna which the soldiers could make use of in the few, short rest periods that were permitted. POW interrogations op. cit.
4 The report of the conversation is in ADM 199/106. See also Golikov, *On a Military Mission to Great Britain and USA*, p. 114 regarding the purchases in the United States and the shipping plans.
5 See KTB Dietl and 388th Regiment, plus Daser's service record in Pers 6/509, BAMA.
6 Panin replaced Frolov on 23 August 1941 when he was posted to the Karelian Front.
7 The former Leningrad Military District was divided in two on 23 August. Frolov became head of the new Karelia Military District, with responsibility for the 14th Army, the Northern Fleet and the 7th Army further south. The new commander of the 14th Army was Major General Roman Panov, who took up his post in late August/early September. Two German prisoners told the Russians that a fresh attack was imminent, information that as late as 5 September prompted the decision to establish the new Polarnoje Division. The first units were sent to the front in great haste on 11 September, but the main force only arrived a week later. Moreover, the Russians had already on 8 September found a copy of Dietl's plan of attack among the possessions of an officer in the 388th Regiment. This made it possible to launch the counter-attack on the North Front in time.
8 The bike had belonged to a German despatch rider who had taken a wrong turn and been captured on 11 July at Fisher Neck. He had with him the order for the big attack on 13 July, with the result that Dietl had to change the plan at the last minute.
9 The extract from Shabunin's memoirs was provided to me by Morozov. See also Savtjenko's comprehensive explanation in POW interrogations, RH 24-19-151, BAMA.
10 Rüf, *Gebirgsjäger vor Murmansk*, p. 141.
11 See Kaltenegger, *Schörner: Feldmarschall der letzten Stunde*, pp. 184 f., plus Rüf, *Gebirgsjäger vor Murmansk*.

Epilogue

1. All the figures are from KTB Dietl with attachments, plus information from Morozov about Soviet losses.
2. The telegram can be found in Defe 3/27, NA.
3. Report of the conversation in Bevan's diary, ADM 199/1106, NA.
4. Nachlass Falkenhorst, N300, BAMA.
5. The exchange of letters between Dietl and Jodl is reproduced in Dietl and Herrmann, *General Dietl*, pp. 231 f. The subsequent information about his closest officers is taken from the service records and various military websites, such as www.lexikon-der-wermacht.de, www.feldgrau.com and others.
6. Gorjatsjik's diary, RH 28-2-117, BAMA.

Appendix I

1. German for General of Mountain Troops, no equivalent British or American rank, sandwiched between Lieutenant General and full General
2. An army corps was a formation consisting of 3–4 divisions with supporting units of artillery, engineers, logistic units etc of around 50,000 men. In German army organisation two or more corps would normally form a field army (*Armée*), with two or more such armies forming an army group (*Arméegruppe*). At the level below corps, the division was the usual formation in most countries' ground forces, this was a formation of approximately 10,000 men consisting of units from all arms and services of the ground forces – infantry, cavalry or armoured troops, artillery etc.
3. German army corps were normally numbered with Roman numerals
4. General Hjalmar Siilasvuo was one of Finland's outstanding generals, and had made his name during the Winter War in the fierce battles around the village of Suomissalmi in December 1939, when, despite being vastly outnumbered, his small Finnish force annihilated two Soviet divisions.
5. A rifle division was standard Russian nomenclature for a non-motorised infantry division, see also Annex 2
6. The 6th Mountain Division was commanded by Major General Ferdinand Schörner, an arch-Nazi and later convicted war criminal going by the nickname *Blutiger Ferdinand* – Bloody Ferdinand – because of his well-known brutality.

Appendix II

1. Steven J. Zaloga, *The Red Army of the Great Patriotic War 1941–45* (Oxford, Osprey 2001), p. 3.
2. Richard Simpkin, *Deep Battle, The Brainchild of Marshal Tuchachevsky* (New York, Brassey's 1988).
3. Andrei Kokoshin, *Soviet Strategy Thought 1917–1991* (Cambridge MA, MIT Press 1998), p. 18.
4. Zaloga, *The Red Army of the Great Patriotic War*, p. 5.
5. Zaloga, *The Red Army of the Great Patriotic War*, p. 12.
6. John Shaw (tr. By Isak Rogde), *Sovjetunion slår til* (Oslo, Gyldebdal 1981), pp. 96–105.

Bibliography

Barnett, Corelli: *Engage the Enemy more Closely*. London 1990.
Beaumont, Joan: *Comrades in Arms. British Aid to Russia 1941–1945*. London 1980.
Bekker, Cajus: *Verdammte See. Ein Kriegstagebuch der Deutschen Marine*. Oldenburg 1971.
Bellamy, Chris: *Absolute War*. London 2008.
Below, Nicolaus von: *At Hitler's Side. The Memoirs of Hitler's Luftwaffe Adjutant 1937–1945*. Barnsley 2010.
Boehm, Hermann: *Norge mellom England og Tyskland*. Oslo 1957.
Bonatz, Heinz: *Seekrieg im Äther*. Herford 1981.
Boog, Horst m.fl: *Das Deutsche Reich und der Zweite Welkrieg*. Volume 4, Stuttgart 1983.
Brazier, Clifford: *XD Operations. Secret British Missions Denying Oil to the Nazis*. Barnsley 2004.
Butler, Ewan: *Mason-Mac*. London 1972.
Carell, Paul: *Unternehmen Barbarossa. Der Marsch nach Russland*. Berlin 1972.
Churchill, Winston: *Den annen verdenskrig*. Volumes 1 and 2. Oslo 1951.
Claasen, Adam: *Hitler's Northern War. The Luftwaffe's Ill-Fated Campaign 1940–45*. Lawrence 2001.
Colville, John: *The Fringes of Power. Downing Street Diaries 1939–1945*. London 1985.
Copeland, Jack: *Turing. Pioneer of the Information Age*. Oxford 2012.
Corrigan, Gordon: *Blood, Sweat and Arrogance and the Myths of Churchill's War*. London 2006.
Danchev, Alex and Todman, Daniel: *Field Marshal Lord Alanbrooke: War Diaries 1939–1945*. London 2002.
Derry, T. K.: *The Campaign in Norway*. London 1952.
Dietl, Gerda-Luise and Herrmann, Kurt: *General Dietl. Das Leben eines Soldaten*. München 1951.
Dilks, David: *The Diaries of Sir Alexander Cadogan 1938–1945*. New York 1972.
Dilks, David and Ericksson, John: *Barbarossa. The Axis and the Allies*. Edinburgh 1998.
Erickson, John: *The Road to Stalingrad. Stalin's War with Germany*. London 1975.
Ericson, Lars m.fl: *Beredskap i väst. Sveriges militära beredskap och västgrensen 1940–1945*. Stockholm 1991.

Feurstein, Valentin: *Irrwege der Pflicht*. München 1963.
Fjærli, Eystein: *Krigens Svalbard*. Oslo 1979.
Fullilove, Michael: *Rendezvous with Destiny*. New York 2013.
Fritz, Martin: *German Steel and Swedish Iron Ore*. Göteborg 1974.
Fröhlich, Elke: *Die Tagebücher von Joseph Goebbels, sämtliche Fragmente. 1. januar – 8. juli 1940*. Volume 4. Stuttgart 1997.
Fure, Odd-Bjørn: *Mellomkrigstid*. Oslo 1996.
Furre, Berge: *Norsk historie 1905–1940*. Oslo 1971.
Gilbert, Martin: *Finest Hour. Winston S. Churchill 1939–1941*. London 1983.
Golikov, F. I.: *On a Military Mission to Great Britain and the USA*. Moskva 1987.
Golovko, Arseni: *Zwischen Spitzbergen und Tiksibucht*. Berlin 1986.
Gorodetsky, Gabriel: *Grand Delusion. Stalin and the German Invasion of Russia*. London 1999.
Gorodetsky, Gabriel: *Stafford Cripps in Moscow 1940–1942. Diaries and Papers*. London 2007.
Haarr, Geirr H.: *The Battle for Norway*. Barnsley 2010.
Hafsten, Bjørn, Larstuvold, Ulf, Olsen, Bjørn and Stenersen, Sten: *Flyalarm – luftkrigen over Norge 1939–45*. Oslo 2005.
Haldane, Charlotte: *Truth Will Out*. London 1949.
Hambro, Johan: *C. J. Hambro – liv og drøm*. Oslo 1984.
Hartmann, Sverre: *Spillet om Norge*. Oslo 1958.
Harvey, John: *The Diplomatic Diaries of Oliver Harvey 1937–40*. London 1970.
Hastings, Max: *Finest Years. Churchill as Warlord 1940–45*. London 2009.
Hastings, Max: *All Hell Let Loose*. London 2011.
Heysing, Günther: *Propagandatruppen der Deutschen Kriegsmarine*. Hamburg 1964.
Hinsley, Harry: *British Intelligence in the Second World War*. London 1979–90.
Hinsley, Harry and Stripp, Alan: *Codebreakers. The Inside Story of Bletchley Park*. Oxford 2001.
Hubatsch, Walther: *Weserübung. Die Deutsche Besetzung von Dänemark und Norwegen 1940*. Göttingen 1960.
Irving, David: *Hitler und seine Feldherren*. Berlin 1975.
Isaksson, Anders: *Per Albin*. Stockholm 2002.
Ismay, Lord Hastings Lionel: *The Memoirs of Lord Ismay*. London 1960.
Jacobsen, Alf R.: *Svartkammeret*. Oslo 1987.
Jacobsen, Alf R.: *Scharnhorst*. Oslo 2001.
Jacobsen, Alf R.: *Forlis*. Oslo 2002.
Jacobsen, Alf R.: *Nikkel, jern og blod*. Oslo 2004.
Jacobsen, Alf R.: *Krysseren Blücher*. Oslo 2010.
Jacobsen, Alf R.: *Kongens nei*. Oslo 2011.
Jacobsen, Alf R.: *Angrep ved daggry*. Oslo 2012.
Jacobsen, Alf R.: *Bitter seier*. Oslo 2013.
Kahn, David: *Seizing the Enigma*. Barnsley 2012.
Kaltenegger, Roland: *General Dietl. Der Held von Narvik*. München 1990.
Kaltenegger, Roland: *General der Gebirgstruppe Georg Ritter von Hengl*. Würzburg 2012.
Kaltenegger, Roland: *Gebirgsartillerie auf allen Kriegsschauplätze*. München 1998.
Kaltenegger, Roland: *Krieg am Eismeer. Gebirgsjäger im Kampf um Narvik, Murmansk und die Murmanbahn*. Graz 1999.

Keegan, John: *Churchill's Generals*. London 1991.
Kennedy, John: *The Business of War*. London 1957.
Kharlamov, N.: *Difficult Mission*. Moskva 1983.
Khudalov, Khariton: *Am Rande des Kontinents*. Berlin 1983.
Klatt, Paul: *3. Gebirgs-Division 1939–1945*. Bad Nauheim 1958.
Koht, Halvdan: *For fred og fridom i krigstid 1939–1940*. Oslo 1957.
Kotze, Hildegard: *Heeresadjutant bei Hitler 1938–1943. Aufzeichnungen des Majors Engel*. Stuttgart 1974.
Kräutler, Mathias: *Es war ein Edelweiss*. Graz 1962.
Leasor, Hames: *War at the Top*. Kelly Bray 2001.
Liddell Hart, Basil: *The German Generals Talk*. London 1948.
Liddell Hart, B. H.: *History of the Second World War*. London 1970.
Linge, Heinz: *With Hitler to the End*. Barnsley 2009.
Lossberg, Bernhard von: *Im Wehrmachtführungsstab*. Hamburg 1950.
Lundberg, Lennart: *Krigsmalmens offer*. Danderyd 1993.
Lunde, Henrik: *Hitler's Pre-emptive War*. Newbury 2009.
Maisky, Ivan: *Memoirs of a Soviet Ambassador. The War 1939–43*. London 1967.
Mann, Chris and Jörgensen, Christer: *Hitler's Arctic War*. New York 2002.
McKay, C. G. and Beckman, Bengt: *Swedish Signal Intelligence 1900–1945*. London 2003.
McKay, Sinclair: *The Secret Listeners*. London 2012.
Megargee, Geoffrey: *Inside Hitler's High Command*. Lawrence 2000.
Meretskov, Kiril: *Im Dienste des Volkes*. Moskva 1968.
Milward, Alan S: *The Fascist Economy of Norway*. Oxford 1972.
Moran, Lord: *Churchill at War 1940–1945*. London 2002.
Murphy, David: *What Stalin Knew*. New Haven 2005.
Nevakivi, Jukka: *The Appeal that Was never Made. The Allies, Scandinavia and the Finnish Winter War 1939–1940*. London 1976.
Nicholson, Nigel: *The Harold Nicholson Diaries 1907–1964*. London 2005.
Olson, Lynne: *Citizens of London. The Americans who stood with Britain in its Darkest Finest Hour*. New York 2010.
Overy, Richard: *Russia's War 1941–1945*. London 1997.
Peck, John: *Dublin from Downing Street*. Dublin 1978.
Pleshakov, Konstantin: *Stalin's Folly*. New York 2005.
Pruszynski, Xavier: *Russian Year. The Notebook of an Amateur Diplomat*. London 1944.
Read, Anthony: *The Devil's Disciples*. London 2004.
Rhys-Jones, Graham: *Churchill and the Norway Campaign*. Barnsley 2008.
Rickman, Alfred: *Swedish Iron Ore*. London 1939.
Roberts, Andrew: *Masters and Commanders*. London 2008.
Rohwer, J. and Hümmelchen, G.: *Chronology of the War at Sea*. London 1974.
Roskill, Stephen: *The War at Sea*. London 1954.
Roskill, Stephen: *Churchill and the Admirals*. New York 1978.
Ross, Graham: *The Foreign Office and the Kremlin*. Cambridge 1984.
Rüf, Hans: *Gebirgsjäger vor Murmansk*. Innsbruck 1957.
Ruge, Friedrich: *Der Seekrieg 1939–45*. Stuttgart 1962.
Salewski, Michael: *Die deutsche Seekriegsleitung 1935–1945*. Frankfurt 1970–75.

Salmon, Patrick: *Scandinavia and the Great Powers 1890–1940*. Newcastle 1997.
Schroeder, Christa: *He was my Chief. The Memoirs of Hitler's Secretary*. Barnsley 2009.
Schwarz, Walter A.: *Generalmajor a. D. Alois Windisch. Ein Soldatenleben*. Vienna 1996.
Sebag-Montefiore, Hugh: *Enigma. The Battle for the Code*. London 2011.
Sebag-Montefiore, Simon: *Stalin. The Court of the Red Tsar*. London 2005.
Seraphim, Hans-Günther: *Das politische Tagebuch Alfred Rosenbergs*. Göttingen 1956.
Shakespeare, Geoffrey: *Let Candles Be Brought In*. London 1949.
Shirer, William: *The Rise and Fall of the Third Reich*. London 1960.
Shirer, William: *This is Berlin*. New York 1999.
Shirer, William: *Berlin Diary*, Baltimore 2002.
Showell, Jak P. Mallmann (ed.): *Führer Conferences on Naval Affairs, 1939–1946*. London 2005.
Showell, Jak P. Mallmann: *German Navy Handbook 1939–45*. Stroud 1999.
Skodvin, Magne (ed.): *Norge i krig*. Oslo 1984–87.
Smith, Bradley: *Sharing Secrets with Stalin*. Lawrence 1996.
Speer, Albert: *Inside the Third Reich*. London 1975.
Springenschmid, Karl: *Die Männer von Narvik*. Graz 1982.
Steen, Erik Anker: *Norges sjøkrig 1940–1945*. Volume IV. Oslo 1954.
Stein, Marcel: *Österreichs Generale im Deutschen Heer 1938–1945*. Bissendorf 2002.
Stevens, R. H. (ed.): *The Falkenhorst Trial*. London 1949.
Tooze, Adam: *The Wages of Destruction. The Making & Breaking of the Nazi Economy*. London 2007.
Topolski, Feliks: *Russia in War*. London 1942.
Trotter, William: *A Frozen Hell*. New York 1991.
Ueberschär, Gert: *Hitlers militärische Elite*. Darmstadt 1998.
Vian, Philip: *Action This Day*. London 1960.
Warlimont, Walter: *Im Hauptquartier der deutschen Wehrmacht 1939–1945*. Bonn 1964.
Week, Albert: *Russia's Life-Saver*. Plymouth 2004.
Weinberger, Andreas: *Das gelbe Edelweiss*. Berlin 1943.
Wiesbauer, Toni: *In Eis und Schnee*. Berg am See 1983.
Woodman, Richard: *Arctic Convoys*. London 1994.
Ziemcke, Earl: *The German Northern Theatre of Operations*. Washington 1959.

Index of People

Abramoff, Paul 34, 42, 46, 49
Alexander, Hugh 2, 57
Andrejev, Viktor 86

Barbolin, Vasilij 53–5
Baur, Hans 79–80
Bevan, Richard 100–1
Bichik, Varvara 57
Birch, Frank 90, 108
Boehm, Hermann 9
Bone, Howard 100, 113, 136, 142
Bovell, Henry Cecil 98
Brandl, Josef 71
Buschenhagen, Erich 4, 75, 92–3, 96–7, 101–2, 110, 121–3, 134,

Cadogan, Alexander 21–2
Canaris, Wilhelm 96
Chernov, Sergei 46
Churchill, Sir Winston 98, 100, 118–9, 137
Colville, John 31–2
Coward, Noel 119
Cripps, Sir Stafford 12, 33, 73, 81–2

Dalton, Hugh 39
Daser, Wilhelm 101, 130–1
Dekanozov, Vladimir 27

Denning, Norman 90, 108–9, 113–14, 121, 122, 137–8
Deutsch, Ernst 101, 129
Diesen, Henry 95
Dietl, Eduard 2, 4, 5, 10–11, 13, 18–21, 25–6, 33–4, 37, 42, 45, 49–51, 56, 59–69, 71–3, 75–6, 78–9, 80, 87, 90–3, 96–7, 99, 101–3, 105, 107, 109, 110–11, 115, 117, 121–2, 125, 127, 129, 130–6
Dill, Sir John 32–3, 39, 40, 48
Drück, Walter 42, 45, 49
Drygin, Junior Lieutenant 55
Dönitz, Karl 58

Eden, Anthony 21, 69, 93–4
Engel, Gerhard 11

Fløtten, Finn 14
Frolov, Valerian Aleksandrovitsj 109–10, 131, 142
Fullover, Michael 37
Fuschlberger, Wolfgang 37, 62, 63, 71–3, 75–6, 87

Godfrey, Arthur 105–6
Golikov, Filipp 66, 69–70, 93–4, 128
Golovko, Arsenij 16, 29–31, 33, 41, 52–3, 82–3, 99, 128, 138, 142

INDEX OF PEOPLE • 189

Golovko, Kira 142
Gorjatsjik, Alexander 35, 53, 56, 87, 133, 143
Govorov, Sergej 65, 81
Grinev, Vasilij 143
Gromov, Pjotr 65, 81
Guderian, Heinz 96
Göring, Hermann 10

Halder, Franz 5, 6–7, 9–10, 12, 95–7, 129
Halvari, Åge 15
Harnack, Arvid 12
Hess, Vilhelm 14, 25–6, 33, 44, 67, 70–1
Heusinger, Adolf 7
Himmler, Heinrich 80, 129, 141
Himmler, Marga 97
Hinsley, Harry 58
Hitler, Adolf 3–9, 10–13, 17–22, 25–6, 29, 31–5, 39, 63, 68–9, 76, 79–80, 88, 93, 95–7, 101–2, 110, 121–2, 127, 129, 133–41
Hofmeister, Georg 97, 126, 141

Jebsen, Dr 123
Jodl, Alfred 122, 139, 140

Kammel, Friedrich 37, 43
Kanarski, Andrej 128
Keitel, Wilhelm 9–10
Kharlamov, Nikolai 47, 61, 66–7, 69–70, 93
Khudalov, Khariton 46, 65–6, 71, 81, 83, 85, 91, 102, 104, 109, 127, 142
Kirejev, Lieutenant 87
Koht, Halvdan 94
Konrad, Rudolf 122
Korotkov, Fedor 46, 65, 67, 85, 127, 142
Krasilnikov, Daniel 34, 52, 86, 131–3
Kreysing, Hans 68, 72–3, 79, 101–2, 111, 130, 134, 136, 140
Krylov, Gleb 46, 49
Kräutler, Mathias 37, 45–6, 62, 65, 67, 70, 86, 127, 141
Kurjatsjev, Lieutenant 87

Kutsjerov, Stepan 30
Kuznetsov, Nikolai 28–30, 53, 81

Larsen, Olaf 41
Larsen, Otto 15, 41
Lenin, Vladimir 142
Lie, Trygve 94
List, Wilhelm 10
Loskutov, Ivan 132
Lukjanov, Ivan 85

Mahon, Patrick 57
Maisky, Ivan 21, 82, 93–4, 119–20
Mannerheim, Carl Gustav 18
Margesson, David 70
Marlow, Wolmer 106
Mason-MacFarlane, Noel 32, 39, 47, 142
Mathisen, Alfred 15, 41
Miles, Geoffrey 61
Molotov, Vjatjeslav 5, 34–5, 47–8, 61
Mussolini, Benito 10
Müller, Werner 44

Nake, Albin 50-1, 54, 56, 97
Nikishin, Nikolai 65–6, 71–2, 81, 131
Nikolajev, Aleksander 30
Nilsen, Andreas 20

Pashkovskij, Mikhail 52-3, 131-3
Paulus, Friedrich 5
Popov, Markian 29
Popov, Pietr 46, 49
Portal, Charles 46, 118
Pound, Dudley 70, 76–7, 89
Putin, Vladimir 108

Quisling, Vidkun 95, 106–7

Ramsbottom-Isherwood, Henry 128, 142
Rohde, Hans-Wolf 50–1, 54–6, 75
Roosevelt, Franklin D. 31, 76, 118, 137
Rutsjkin, Aleksej 15
Rüf, Hans 36, 43–4, 46, 50–1, 54, 59, 75, 78, 83, 85–6, 91, 105, 126, 129, 133

Savtsjenko, Paul 132
Schenk, Otto 117
Schlemmer, Ernst 26, 63, 67, 79, 87, 101, 129
Schmidt, Karl 10
Schmundt, Rudolf 68-9, 121, 140
Schpak, Lieutenant 85
Schultze-Hinrichs, Alfred 117
Schulze-Boysen, Harro 12, 27
Schörner, Ferdinand 97, 107, 134, 138–41
Shabunin, Pavel 131–2
Sharov, Andrej 142–3
Shpilev, Nikolaj I. 81, 142
Simonov, Konstantin
Sjarov, Captain 83
Skvirsky, Lev 46
Sladen, Geoffrey 100, 112–16, 142
Soldatov, Nikolai 71, 81, 102, 133, 143
Solovjov, Chief of Staff 81
Springenschmid, Karl 23, 78, 80, 85, 141
Stalin, Josef 4, 11, 13, 15–7, 21–2, 26–30, 39–42, 47, 60–1, 66–7, 72, 74, 88–9, 93–4, 96, 98, 105, 110, 118, 128, 132, 137, 139, 142
Stumpff, Hans-Jürgen 9, 60
Sverdrup, Einar 106, 120

Tamber, Ragnvald 95, 105, 107, 118, 120
Terboven, Josef 9
Timoshenko, Semjon 27–8
Torik, Nikolai 30
Tovey, John 90–119
Turing, Alan 1-2, 108

Vasiljev, Battalion Commander 57
Vesjeserskij, Georgij A. 41, 81, 102, 127, 131, 143
Vian, Philip 10, 77, 81–3, 88, 95, 105–7, 118–23, 138
Vielwerth, Johann 36, 42–3, 49, 62–3, 70, 85–6, 104–5
von Brauchitsch, Walther 5–6, 9–10, 95, 139
von Burstin, Alfred 46
von Falkenhorst, Nicolaus 4, 18, 37
von Hengl, Georg Ritter 36, 44–5, 47, 49, 62, 67, 78–80, 83, 85, 87, 104, 127, 129
von Le Suire, Karl Maximilian 63, 141
von Pranckh, Hans Freiherr 71
von Ribbentrop, Joachim 27
von Schulenberg, Werner 27

Wake-Walker, Frederic 89–91, 97, 107, 119, 121
Weiss, Wilhelm 62, 67, 71, 78–9, 127
Wells, Sumner 76
Wiesbauer, Toni 14
Windisch, Alois 79, 87, 127, 136

Zjukov, Georgij 13, 27–8
Zhurba, Alexander 33–4, 40, 42, 45–6, 49
Zorn, Eduard 43, 63, 65, 141

Made in the USA
Coppell, TX
24 June 2024